What Works for Women at Work

Four Patterns Working Women Need to Know

UPDATED EDITION

Joan C. Williams and Rachel Dempsey

FOREWORD BY ANNE-MARIE SLAUGHTER

 NEW YORK UNIVERSITY PRESS
New York

A New Girls' Network Book

NEW YORK UNIVERSITY PRESS
New York
www.nyupress.org

First published in paperback in 2018
© 2014 by Joan C. Williams and Rachel Dempsey
All rights reserved

Library of Congress Cataloging-in-Publication Data
Wiilliams, Joan, 1952–
What works for women at work : four patterns working women need to know /
Joan C. Williams, Rachel Dempsey ; [foreword by] Anne-Marie Slaughter.
p.   cm. Includes bibliographical references and index.
ISBN 978-1-4798-3545-4 (hardback)   ISBN 978-1-4798-1431-2 (paperback)
1. Women—Employment. 2. Women—Psychology. 3. Sex role in the work environment.   I. Dempsey, Rachel. II. Title.
HD6053.W477 2014
650.1'3082—dc23   2013029819

New York University Press books are printed on acid-free paper, and their binding materials are chosen for strength and durability. We strive to use environmentally responsible suppliers and materials to the greatest extent possible in publishing our books.

Manufactured in the United States of America

10 9 8 7 6 5 4 3 2 1

Also available as an ebook

Dedicated to the Wise Women, without whom we could not have written this book, in friendship and with gratitude:

Kara Baysinger

Alex Buck

Kirby Chown

Mary Cranston

Kathryn Burkett Dickson

Karen Edson

Joan Haratani

Alison Hooker

Susan Klooz

Catherine Lamboley

Roberta Liebenberg

Karen Lockwood

Mika Mayer

Michele Coleman Mayes

Laura McMahon

Sharon Meers

Leslie Morgan Steiner

Vernā Myers

Sandra Pierce

Marci Rubin

Carol Sabransky

Laura Stein

Phyllis Stewart Pires

Sally Thornton

The authors gratefully acknowledge the generous support of the National Science Foundation (NSF) ADVANCE PAID grant no. EHR 1106411, which funded the research reflected in chapter 11 of this work. Somewhat different versions of chapter 11 have been published as a report of the Center for WorkLife Law and as an article in the Harvard Journal of Law and Gender.

The women who were interviewed for this book represent a wide range of ages, ethnicities, and backgrounds. Joan C. Williams interviewed 67 women for The New Girls' Network. These women were roughly 40 to 60 years of age and at the top of their fields. They worked in business, medicine, academia, government, and the legal profession. Three ran their own businesses. Eleven identified themselves as women of color, specifically as black (or African American), Latina, and Asian (or Asian American). The interviews were conducted over the phone between June 2, 2010, and November 6, 2012.

For the National Science Foundation Project, 60 women-of-color scientists were interviewed by Erika V. Hall, a PhD candidate at the Kellogg School of Management at Northwestern University. The scientists interviewed represent a variety of scientific disciplines. Most of the women worked in academic settings. They are identified as black (or African American), Latina, and Asian (or Asian American). These women were roughly 30 to 60 years of age. The interviews were conducted over the phone between June 4, 2012, and October 5, 2012.

Contents

Foreword

ANNE-MARIE SLAUGHTER

Joan C. Williams and Rachel Dempsey, mother and daughter, have written a book that every working woman should read. It is also a book that every man who works with women should read. If women act on the prescriptions in these pages and men begin to understand the deep culturally embedded biases and assumptions that mean a book like this still needs to be written, the workplace will be a better place, the United States will be more competitive, and the intertwining of work and family life will be easier for all caregivers.

What Works for Women at Work is a project by The New Girls' Network, an all-star list of "Fortune 500 executives, entrepreneurs, bestselling writers, partners at major consulting firms, and rainmakers at some of the biggest law firms in the world" that Joan C. Williams, a law professor, put together. These women are not representative of the entire female American workforce, in either class or racial or ethnic terms, but they do include women of color, who face what Joan and Rachel call the "double jeopardy" of race and gender discrimination and have their own distinct tales to tell. Above all, these women are the face of female success.

Yet all these women, and frankly every woman I know who has ever worked in either a paid or volunteer capacity, recognize the four patterns of behavior that create the primary obstacles to women's advancement to leadership positions across every industry:

1. Prove-It-Again!
2. The Tightrope
3. The Maternal Wall
4. Tug of War

I am part of the first generation of women who were actually advantaged, at least in some circumstances, by our gender, thanks to the sacrifices and drive of the women a generation ahead of me —women like Joan C. Williams. By the time we entered the labor force in the late 1980s and early 1990s, university faculties, law firms, businesses, and government agencies were actively looking for women. The women they hired had to meet the same hiring criteria that men did, but if they were above the bar, they often had a leg up on their male colleagues, at least at the outset. In my own case, all-male law faculties were starting to look for women when I went on the law-teaching market in 1990; 20 years later, Hillary Clinton wanted to break the glass ceiling at the Policy Planning office, which was a "big think" job that no woman had ever even been considered for.

But even if overt gender discrimination has decreased dramatically, and women in the middle class are starting to outearn and rise higher than their mates, these four patterns ring so true, not for entering the workforce but during the ascent to leadership positions. We have all seen women held to higher standards of performance while male colleagues are given the benefit of the doubt for slipups and promoted on potential, the core of the "Prove-It-Again!" pattern. We have all seen women who are criticized for being too assertive when they act like men and too passive if they act like (traditional) women, which Joan and Rachel call "The Tightrope." Toward the end of my two years in government, when lots of jobs were turning over at the midpoint of the administration, I and other women I worked with tried to ensure that women candidates were considered for promotion. Over and over again, I would hear, "She's smart and has gotten a lot of things done, but she has sharp elbows." "Sharp elbows" is code for "she insisted on pushing her point or her position and won the day," behavior that in a man would be lauded.

Many of us live with the third pattern: "The Maternal Wall." Every time someone says, "Women today can do everything that men can do," the response should be, "Yes, absolutely, as long as they don't have children." Far too many women are still being asked to make significant trade-offs between their careers and their families, but when was the last time you or anyone else asked a man how he was going to manage his career once he had children?

The final pattern is the "Tug of War," in which women judge each other in ways that hurt our collective march forward. No one ever talks about daddy wars or dogfights (actually, we do talk about dogfights, but not pejoratively). Most of us can recall a situation in which another woman seemed more determined to shut us out of a largely all-male group than to help us in.

So as Joan and Rachel write, out of the 127 professional women they interviewed, only five said that they had not encountered these patterns, or not recently. We know that the evidence that Joan and Rachel have assembled from scores of scientific studies is true and present in our lives. But another part of us really doesn't *want* to focus on these patterns. We don't *want* to see our world full of male bias against us. We know, like, and respect most of the men we work with. We know that they don't actually *see* these patterns.

Indeed, the studies Joan and Rachel draw on show why so many men are blind: we are living and working in a world shaped by deeply, deeply embedded assumptions about gender roles. These assumptions are laid down from infancy onward and create a set of filters in our brains that condition our interpretation of virtually all human interaction. Only with cleverly designed experiments in the relatively new field of experimental social psychology are we able to tease them out.

The good news is that men can learn. Once in a meeting in Washington, D.C., I made a point that was generally ignored until a well-respected younger man made the same point, at which point everyone jumped on it. Joan and Rachel call this the "stolen idea" phenomenon; I have always heard it called the "butterfly syndrome," in which a woman makes a remark that stays on the table like a caterpillar until a man says the same thing and it becomes a butterfly. At any rate, I pulled aside the younger man who had picked up my thought after the meeting and told him that because he was already working for Hillary Clinton and over the course of his career he was going to work with many other women, it was important for him to understand what had just happened. I described the exchange in the meeting as I and the other women at the table had experienced it. He took it in, thought about it, and nodded. I phrased my advice in terms of something that would help him work more effectively with women over the course of his career, and he took it and learned from it in that spirit.

That is why every man who works with women, supports women, or parents girls should read this book. Men who get it can be enormously helpful by making other men aware of their biases and of course by promoting deserving women. I would never have succeeded in my career without strong male mentors dedicated to supporting strong women. More and more men are also now seeing the workplace through their wives' eyes as their wives encounter the four behavior patterns in this book.

Men should read this book to understand; women should read this book to act. Because the best thing about *What Works for Women at Work* is that it crystallizes these four patterns of behavior in order to advise all working women *what to do about them.* It is a practical "how-to" manual for women trying to figure out what concretely to do when they realize that something is wrong in their careers, that they are not advancing as fast as the men around them or have been turned down for a promotion they wanted, and either don't understand what is wrong or don't know what to do about it. Chapter after chapter offers specific, actionable suggestions drawn from women who have been there and succeeded. It's a book by and for Rachel as much as Joan.

The continual theme through all the valuable advice offered in this book is balance: balance between masculine and feminine, principle and pragmatism, niceness and authority, self-promotion and selflessness, and work and family. Balance should also be the watchword for all of us in reading this book. We know that its descriptions of bias against women, even in 2012, are true. But we will not succeed if we approach our lives angry and embittered. So we must balance awareness and activism with getting it done as professionally as we know how. This book will help us get there.

Preface

Joan's Story

This book started when I began reading a field of research that changed my life. That field, called experimental social psychology, led me to leave my job of 25 years and move my family 3,000 miles across the country. Only then did my career really take off and did I get rid of a heavy load of anger that was warping my personal as well as my professional life.

For years, I had been respected at work—but, to be honest, disliked. Now, I am the first to admit that I'm no Bill Clinton. Sometimes I speak up when I should keep quiet, and sometimes I keep quiet when I should speak up. If I believe in something, you'll hear about it, and if I think something is unfair, I'll say so. Not a shrinking violet. But I saw men around me who were less politically adept than I was—and they did just fine. I was a selfish prima donna. They were smart and quirky.

As I immersed myself in social psychology, I found this dynamic described with eerie precision. Reading the studies was such a "scales-from-eyes" experience that I saw my whole life in a different light—one that inspired me to start an organization called The Center for WorkLife Law, which I still direct today, and gave me the courage to move my family from Washington, D.C., where I was miserable, to San Francisco, which I adore. Moving was a big deal. My husband, a Washington lawyer, had to give up his executive director position at a major Washington think tank he had helped to build. My ninth-grade son, who had just entered a new school, had to start all over again in his sophomore year of high school. Rachel left for college the year we moved but felt torn away from her high school friends nonetheless.

Here's the insight that moved me: the workplace I left had a very specific role designated for white women like me. (Expectations were different for black women—itself an interesting pattern.) White women were expected to be helpful, to serve on a lot of committees, and to be supportive and deferential.

"Mike knows everything," one (brilliant) colleague once said to me, of her mentor, who was sitting right next to her at the time. Years later, when her reputation began to supersede his, she came to me for advice: Mike had begun to undercut her. Her prominence was interfering with her designated role as cheerleader and helpmeet, and she had come to understand why I was so unpopular.

Typically, I do not talk about my own experiences, because to do so carries with it the risk of being seen as a "whiner." But gender bias at work is something worth talking about. Sixty-eight percent of women believe that sex discrimination exists in the workplace, according to a 2010 study by Catalyst.[1] This includes 63 percent of architects and between two-thirds and three quarters of female lawyers.[2] Seventy-three percent of women professionals in Washington, D.C., felt that men have more opportunities than women do.[3]

This book is about when to take risks, and this is one I am willing to embrace.

After we moved to San Francisco, I began to wonder whether I was the only woman whose experience these studies described to a tee. After all, they typically are paper-and-pencil studies of college students performed in a university lab. Whether they describe what happens in real workplaces is controversial.[4]

To answer this question, I did something that had never been done. I consolidated hundreds of studies to identify, instead of an amorphous laundry list, the four crisp patterns that provide the framework for this book. I call these four patterns Prove-It-Again!, the Tightrope, the Maternal Wall, and the Tug of War, and each represents its own particular challenge for women as they navigate in the sea of office politics. Let me explain each in detail:

1. *Prove-It-Again!* is exactly what it sounds like: women have to prove themselves over and over again much more so than men in order to be seen as equally competent. Prove-It-Again! is *descriptive* bias that stems from assumptions about the typical woman.[5]

2. The *Tightrope* is *prescriptive bias*, which stems from assumptions about how women *should* behave. The Tightrope describes a double bind: women often find that if they behave in traditionally feminine ways, they exacerbate Prove-It-Again! problems; but if they behave in traditionally masculine ways, they are seen as lacking social skills.[6]

3. The *Maternal Wall* consists of both *descriptive bias*, in the form of strong negative competence and commitment assumptions triggered by motherhood, and *prescriptive bias* —disapproval on the grounds that mothers should be at home or working fewer hours. Women with children are routinely pushed to the margins of the professional world.

4. The *Tug of War* occurs as each woman tries to navigate her own path between assimilating into masculine traditions and resisting them. Women's different strategies divide them. Some women are tomboys, who just need access: all they want to do is to play the game as the boys play it. Other women want to preserve more of the traditions of femininity. Women's different strategies often pit them against each other, as do workplaces that communicate that there's room for only one woman. All of these pressures often lead women to judge each other on what's the right way to be a woman.

These patterns add up to the sobering truth that office politics are trickier for women than for men. "I think you have to have just emotional intelligence to be able to judge what situation needs what strategy," said a woman scientist.

Once I crystallized the four patterns, my first step was to create a game called Gender Bias Bingo, which can be found at www.genderbiasbingo.com. The game described the patterns and asked women scientists to document any experiences that seemed to fit. I received 400 e-mails in the first three days the site was up. What I learned was this: the experimental studies do appear to describe everyday workplace politics for many women.

I developed a lecture called "The Four Patterns of Gender Bias," and the response was electric. As soon as I started to describe the patterns, women's eyes got big, and they began to nod. When I gave the talk to 200-plus people at a reunion of Yale alumnae, I walked out of the auditorium to find one woman crying. "You just described my life." This was a common reaction.

But my lecture did not have the desired effect. It was supposed to empower women, but it just depressed them. Just giving a name to the experiences they found so frustrating wasn't enough; a common reaction was, "What's the use?" And then I realized the single most important truth this book offers: women need to be politically savvier than men in order to survive and thrive in their careers. Political savvy does not completely insulate you from gender bias, warns social psychologist Jennifer Berdahl. "As savvy as [women] may be, they may not be able to avoid bias and its devastating effects on their careers."[7] Fair enough. Savvy is not sufficient, but often it's necessary: more often for women than men, it is a threshold requirement.

One problem: I'm not major-league savvy. That's why I assembled about 20 of the wisest women I know to help me write the book. My initial plan was to meet only once, but we bonded and ended up meeting twice a year for two years. The group includes Fortune 500 executives, entrepreneurs, bestselling writers, partners at major consulting firms, and rainmakers at some of the biggest law firms in the world. These are the key members of The New Girls' Network. This book is theirs as much it is ours. I cannot thank them enough.

I had two goals. The first was to find out whether the experimental literature that had resonated so strongly with me resonated with other women, too. The second was to gather the strategies indubitably successful women had used to get where they are today. So I interviewed the key members of The New Girls' Network, as well as other women they recommended—basically, any savvy woman I could get my hands on. The interviews were simple. After describing the four patterns, I asked just two questions: (1) "Does any of that sound familiar?" and (2) "What strategies have you used, or seen others use, to ensure that these patterns did not derail your career?"

My next step was to address a nagging worry: how does the experience of gender bias differ by race? Relatively few experimental studies explore this, as compared with the hundreds of studies on "gender" alone (which tend to yield information about the experience of white women).[8] So I got a National Science Foundation (NSF) grant to study the experience of women of color, with the help of Erika Hall, a PhD candidate in management and organizations at Northwestern University. Erika conducted the NSF interviews. I am very grateful for her help and her insights. Of the initial 67 interviews of The New Girls' Network, 16 percent were women of color. But all of the NSF interviews were of women of color, making 56 percent of all interviewees women of color when both sets of interviews were combined.

These interviews confirmed that the experimental studies describe many women's experience of office politics. When I asked women whether anything in the four patterns sounded familiar, one said, "Every syllable." Another woman said, "Oh, God, you're in my head." Of the 127 women interviewed, only five—and not a single woman of color—said they had not encountered one or more of these patterns. Three of the five had founded their own businesses. Note that I do not have a random sample, so it's impossible to tell if these women's experiences match those of women in general. But it's clear this is news many women can use.

Another major message, rarely if ever noted, is that women experience bias of quite different types. Most women did not report all four types of bias: only 13 percent of white women did, and 10 percent of the women of color. Tightrope bias was most common. Nearly three-fourths (73 percent) of all women interviewed reported it. Next came Prove-It-Again!, reported by 68 percent of women. Maternal Wall came next, reported by 59 percent of mothers. Tug of War came in last—though it was still reported by a majority of women (55 percent). All of this highlights a social science finding that has received far too little attention: what works for women often is different from what works for men.[9]

Women of color were more likely to report each of the four patterns of bias than white women were. The biggest gap concerned Tug of War bias: 59 percent of women of color, but only 50 percent of white women, reported it. Next came the Tightrope, reported by 77 percent of women of color and 68 percent of white women. The Maternal Wall came third, reported by 63 percent of mothers of color and 56 percent of white mothers. Prove-It-Again! bias showed the smallest gap: 64 percent of white women reported it, as compared with 70 percent of women of color. Remember, though, that most of the women of color were scientists; we cannot tell to what extent these differences stem from race and to what extent they stem from science.

All this makes office politics more challenging for women than for men. Women have to prove themselves over and over again. They have to navigate a tightrope between being "too masculine" and "too feminine." Having children just compounds both those problems. And gender bias often ends up creating tricky and freighted relationships among women themselves. With all this going on for women but not for men, women have to be politically savvier than men in order to survive and thrive.

The final step in this process was to hire Rachel Dempsey to help me write the book, which offers savvy-in-a-bottle to help women navigate their careers. She was the obvious choice because I knew she would write a heartbreaking work of staggering genius. (She's my daughter.) I also chose Rachel because I wanted to coauthor this book with a much younger woman. Although I had been careful to include a broad range of ages in The New Girls' Network, everyone I interviewed was a highly successful career woman, so none were under 30. Including the voice of younger women was important because I was determined to preemptively strike back against a common dynamic that emerges when women try to give each other advice.

My hope is that this book will avoid the Tug of War that often emerges between different generations when they talk about careers. Reaching out across generations requires a lot of effort and some sacrifice. Women of a certain age (mine: I am 61) tend to have been more willing than younger women to assimilate into masculine traditions—otherwise, we would not have felt comfortable spending our lives in rooms filled with men. Younger women often feel differently. A woman professor clearly described this phenomenon: "I'm on kind of a backlash mission almost. I wear dresses, I bake cookies for my group meetings, I bring my child to class with me. I've just stuck it out there and said, 'I'm a woman, I'm someone's mother.' And you get the whole package. It is kind of a conscious choice on my part that I'm not going to compete as a boy because I'm not a boy."[10]

It's time for women to stop judging each other about what they believe to be the right way to be a woman. In workplaces still dominated by men, all women make compromises. If we begin to judge each other's compromises, the opportunity for women to help each other vanishes. *What Works for Women at Work* is designed to offer the kind of advice a good mentor offers her mentee. But good mentoring is reciprocal: this book is also designed around the premise that younger women offer insights to older women as well as vice versa.

While this book is designed to bridge generational divides, the intended audience is not only younger women. Another lesson we learned is that younger women tend to get more Prove-It-Again! bias, while older women often meet the Tightrope—the "what a bitch" pattern I encountered—as they get more accomplished and, as a result, more threatening. But the differences between younger and older women are easy to exaggerate. I found older women at the height of their careers who still felt they had to prove themselves constantly and younger women faulted for being too "outspoken" or for "having rough elbows."

So that's why I wrote this book.

After I moved to California, I found that my new workplace actually wanted me precisely because I had achieved some prominence. The atmosphere was just incredibly different. For the entire first year, I walked around amazed: I was no longer a bitch.

Your life may be very different from mine. Your personality may be very different. Your career may be very different. I don't know in which ways this book will help you. But, based on my interviews, it will.

Rachel's Story

My journey toward writing this book started when I was a kid. For years, all I understood of Joan's work was that it kept her away from me. Not that my mom wasn't (and isn't) an excellent mother: my brother and I have always come first. She was home at 5:30 every day she wasn't traveling (which she did quite a lot), stayed home with us when we were sick, came to our school plays, and even helped sew elaborate costumes. But I was more likely to remember the soccer games she missed for a business trip than the ones she came to with orange slices and Gatorade. It seemed to me the ultimate irony that my mother's life work of fighting for family-friendly policies and greater work-family balance took her away from her own family. And as a smart-ass 10-year-old with two lawyers for parents, I didn't hesitate to point that out.

In retrospect, I might have been noticing something else as well.

Even as a child, I saw how passionately my mother cared about her work, but I also saw for all that her work inspired her, drove her, and made her whole, she was unhappy at her job. "Love the work; hate the job" was how she put it. I heard bits and pieces about her experience without understanding much other than that the place she left me for didn't even seem like that much *fun*. That made it even harder for me to understand why she spent so much time there.

When I was a junior in high school, she decided to finally do something about her situation, accepting an offer for a visit at UC Hastings that seemed likely to turn into a job. Unfortunately, the semester she spent in San Francisco was, for me, a particularly rocky one in a generally rocky adolescence. I felt abandoned and got angry; she felt punished for pursuing her own happiness after a lifetime of putting it second (or third or fourth). We spent my senior year of high school on terms that could diplomatically be described as tense.

It wasn't until I went to college that my perspective began to shift. A few things happened at once: with distance, I started to see my mother as a person outside of myself. As I took on something resembling adult responsibility, I started to see how heroically she had juggled her responsibilities to make time for our family. And as she became noticeably happier in her new life in San Francisco, I began to understand the toll her former situation had taken on her and the extraordinary sacrifices that had kept her there so long.

At this point, I feel nothing but lucky to be Joan's daughter. But despite the strength of our relationship, the decision to write this book together might have been braver than either of us realized at the time. Around the time I quit my first postcollege job to back-pack around South America and write, Joan was beginning to think about writing the four patterns of gender bias into a book. She was looking for a journalist who could write accessibly and with humor about complicated topics.

"How am I ever going to find someone to help me write this thing?" she asked.

"What about me?" I answered.

I had been joking, but she took me seriously. Before leaving on my backpacking trip, I had gone through several rounds of interviews for a position in Google's legal department and was waiting to hear back from them. When Joan first proposed that I help her with the book, it was a backup plan.

I was in a tiny town in southern Bolivia where the Internet came and went when I realized that working with her was actually my first choice. I withdrew my name from consideration for the job at Google and committed to the project.

Joan would disagree, but it was crazy of her to offer me the job. I was 24 and almost entirely uncredentialed. I'd never written anything longer than my senior thesis. And if it didn't work out, she would have the New Girls to answer to.

It was also crazy of me to accept her offer. I turned down a prestigious and well-paid job to write a book that, at the time, we weren't even sure would be published. I ran the risk of the kind of gaping hole in my resume that this economy won't tolerate. And I had absolutely no idea how to write a book.

But, in the end, I felt that, as a young feminist, I had a valuable perspective to add to the New Girls' stories that Joan or any other writer she might hire would be likely to miss. I worry that the incredible progress made by feminists of earlier generations has made us complacent: things are better, and people are afraid to ruffle any feathers, so we're stalling out at good enough. This is in part because of the dynamic that develops when older feminists feel that young women are flip about hard-won battles and young feminists feel that older women are chasing after ghosts of sexism long dead. I hope together Joan and I have begun to bridge the generation gap. More importantly, I was incredibly grateful for the opportunity to be able to work alongside my mother. After decades of watching her struggle with these issues, they've become my issues, too.

The New Girls' Network meeting where we presented the first draft of the manuscript was one of the most frightening things I had ever done. The women in that room had entrusted me with their stories, and I wanted to tell them well. But as a young woman and Joan's daughter, I was well aware that I had better produce something excellent. Luckily, everyone has been tremendously supportive. I can't thank the New Girls enough for their faith in me and their commitment to the project.

I wrote this book for the most selfless reasons and the most selfish reasons. Through my mother, I've seen how difficult it can be to deal with the pressures professional women face, from the strain of work-family conflict to the constant slow grind of everyday sexism. If this book makes things a little bit easier for any working woman out there, I can feel that I've done my job. But my motives aren't entirely noble: these issues become more real for me every year. I write this book with an urgency that comes from knowing that it's my own future I'm describing and that the work we do now will determine how that future turns out.

I can't believe how lucky I am to have had a mother who taught me to take risks and fight for the things I believe in. I hope this book serves as a guide for other women to do the same.

Preface to the Paperback Edition

This book is now road tested. The Lean In videos based on it have been viewed well over half a million times, and I have heard from women from France to Iran to India who report the same patterns of bias as are described here. I'm always sad to hear it.

Sad but not surprised. Women all over the world are assumed to be less of a good fit for careers designed for, and dominated by, men. That explains why women in many countries find they have to "prove it again!" In many countries, too, a narrower range of behavior is still accepted from women professionals than from men. As we saw in the 2016 U.S. election, a man can be either a good man or a "real man," whereas a woman who is seen as unlikable triggers very intense and disqualifying dislike. That's the Tightrope, which also has proved remarkably resilient. So has the Maternal Wall, in the form of assumptions that working mothers aren't committed to their jobs—and that those who are committed are untrustworthy because, as mothers, they shouldn't be working in the first place. At far too many workplaces, too, aligning with men against other women remains a good move politically. So ambitious women still do it.

Since the book was published, I have helped develop the Workplace Experiences Survey, which has documented that the patterns of bias reported by the 127 women interviewed for this book are pervasive in today's workplaces. In a study of engineers (with over 3,000 survey respondents), 61 percent of women but only 35 percent of white men reported feeling that they had to prove themselves more than their colleagues; 49 percent of women but only 33 percent of men reported pushback for assertiveness; and 45 percent of mothers reported that their colleagues questioned their commitment after they had children, while only 20 percent of white men reported this. Some women engineers reported fraught relationships among the women at their companies, but far more reported that the real problem was the "boys' club"—many were the only women in their environments.

Also new is our Bias Climate Survey, online at www.biasinterrupters.org, which uses a validated scale to assess the bias climate you're reporting at your workplace. Go take it, and compare your experience with national averages.

The bias is still there, but there's progress, too: these patterns are beginning to be well known, so that when they occur, women think "there it is!" rather than "I knew this career thing wasn't going to work for me." Women are much more apt to locate the problem outside themselves than I was. For someone who came of age in the 1970s, I am sometimes sorry that my generation hasn't delivered more change, but I'm glad we've at least accomplished that.

The goal of this book was to give women a toolkit for navigating gender bias that remains clear-eyed about what's unfair but moves on to do something about it. It is truly irritating that women still need to be politically savvier than men to survive and thrive in the workplace, but "luckily this is not difficult," to quote Charlotte Whitton, former mayor of Ottawa.

Life goes on, and now Rachel, a recent college grad when we wrote this book, is a law school graduate and a full-fledged lawyer launching on a career of her own. Writing this book with her changed my life. I had long aspired to reach a larger, nonacademic audience and was a bit baffled that my books had largely failed to do so.

Until I read Rachel's manuscript for this book. Then I understood what I had been doing wrong and what I needed to do differently. As a result, we wrote this book, and it has been a great success. I continue to push myself to engage with a larger audience. I wrote an essay following the election of Donald Trump that has now been read by over 3.2 million people.[1]

This is just one thing my children have taught me, not by any means the most important one. As I look back, one of the things I feel most lucky about is that I have had both children and a career. For parents who are struggling, please know that the clouds part when your youngest child is four, and you get your life back when your youngest is twelve. That seems like a long time, but it really isn't—at least for someone who loves babies as much as I do. I feel lucky to have been born a woman. If I had been a man, I would have been a competent workaholic. Nothing more.

Rachel and I went back and forth a lot about how much to talk about the 2016 presidential election in this preface. Regardless of which candidate you supported, given how close the vote was, I think we can all agree that things may have turned out differently if Hillary Clinton had been a man. Even many who voted for Trump expressed disapproval of him,[2] but that discomfort with Trump had far fewer consequences than did the moral disapproval many felt of Clinton.

And yet, as someone who enjoys an imaginative challenge, I remain hopeful. On the one hand, we have a president who bragged about sexual assault ("Grab them by the . . ."). On the other hand, that boast almost cost him the election. Lena Dunham, Tina Fey, and Samantha Bee are three of the most influential performers alive, operating in spheres that had long remained unrelentingly male. Equality in politics would have been nice, for sure, but I remain confident it will come, as equal-access comedy changes our culture day by day.

I wrote this book during a black night of the soul when, after over 30 years of trying, I came to terms with the fact that I had failed to change mainstream organizations as much as I had hoped. After *What Works for Women at Work* was published, I pitched writing an article on it for the *Harvard Business Review*, but my wonderful editor there, Sarah Green, ultimately decided that her readership would be more interested in what organizations could do to level the playing field for women than what women could do for themselves. This spurred me to bestir myself out of my distress over women's lack of progress and invent what ultimately came to be called "Bias Interrupters."[3]

Bias Interrupters is a new approach to organizational change that responds to research that the standard ways we have attempted to increase diversity have failed.[4] Bias trainings, mentorship programs, and the like have produced remarkably little progress for women or people of color. The solution is to change the paradigm.

Businesses that are serious about solving their diversity problem at the top will do what businesses do about any problem they truly care about. They will use evidence to set metrics, and they will keep on trying until they achieve them. I call this model "evidence-based bias interrupters," which Sarah assures me is a name only someone from San Francisco could love—Bias Interrupters for short.

Using Bias Interrupters is a four-step process. First, the organization does a self-assessment to find out whether the long-documented patterns of bias are playing out and, if so, where: in hiring, performance evaluations, assignments, and so on. If women perceive bias, of course they may be wrong, so the next step is to establish an objective metric. If bias is found, for example, in assignments, then the organization should tweak its assignment process to interrupt the bias and then go back to its metric to see whether things have improved. If they have not, the next step is to ratchet up to a stronger Bias Interrupter until the problem is solved, going system by system.

In other words, the book that began when I had given up on changing organizations ultimately generated a new model of organizational change. The Center for WorkLife Law has generated a complete, open-sourced toolkit for interrupting racial and gender bias in hiring, assignments, performance evaluations, promotions, and compensation, available at www.biasinterrupters.org.

My amazing team at WorkLife Law—which has delivered three babies in the past year and not missed a beat—has also developed a new approach to bias training. It's designed to complement what's now the industry standard: the bias trainings based on the implicit association test (IAT). If you haven't taken the IAT, go check it out at www.projectimplicit.org. It is designed to provide an objective measure of unconscious bias. The trainings based on it are great at showing people that racial and gender bias are commonplace, even in people who believe themselves to be open-minded.

The limitation of IAT-based trainings is that they do not tell people how bias plays out in everyday workplace interactions or how to interrupt it. That's where my research comes in. The next step from *What Works for Women at Work*, with its concrete strategies women can use to interrupt bias, is my 90-minute "Bias Interrupters for Managers" workshop, which gives everyone—men as well as women—low-risk ways they can interrupt racial and gender bias without spending too much political capital. Often the best solution is not to call out the bias at all but rather to, in an evidence-based way, subtly interrupt it.

When I gave this workshop to all upper- and midlevel managers at one STEM (science, technology, engineering, and math) organization, six months later members of that organization reported higher levels of belonging, higher intent to stay, and lower levels of both racial and gender bias—including people who had never themselves taken the workshop. Even more dramatic, the gains among women and people of color did not come at the expense of white men, who also reported higher levels of belonging than before the workshop. My sense is that the training loosened the hold of a certain cowboy masculinity that was not only alienating many women and people of color but also marginalizing many white men.

All this began with *What Works for Women at Work*. WorkLife Law is now working with nearly a dozen employers to launch experiments to pilot Bias Interrupters and measure the results.

Yet my first love remains talking with other women, sharing strategies that my Wise Women shared with me about what works for women at work. It just doesn't get any better than that. For that reason, I also decided to write a workbook for *What Works for Women at Work* so readers could work through the many ideas we introduce in the book. One of the hallmarks of the original was its acknowledgment that gender bias plays out differently in every woman's life, depending on her personality and the culture of her workplace. The workbook provides concrete tools to help you analyze how bias is affecting you and to help you think through what strategies might feel comfortable, and work well, for you personally.

With Marina Multhaup, the second stunningly able coauthor I had the luck to find, I also incorporated into the workbook important material from WorkLife Law's annual Leadership Academy for Women. This new material does just what the original book did: it takes complex social science and boils it down into news-you-can-use. If I had understood more about the structure of social networks at the start of my career, I would have better understood how to build the networks I needed to succeed. If I had understood more about my own personality, I would have better understood how to network as an introvert for whom networking is effortful. All that, and more, is now at your fingertips in the workbook.

As I look back over the three years since the publication of *What Works for Women at Work*, I'm struck by how much writing it affected Rachel. But it affected me more. For someone who has been at this work for so long, sharing what I have learned from talking with women so much wiser than I has been more than comforting; it has been redemptive. I did not change the world as much as I'd hoped to, but I've made it a little bit easier for other women. That's enough for me.

Joan C. Williams

Leiden, The Netherlands

March 2017

Notes

1 Joan C. Williams, "What So Many People Don't Get about the US Working Class," *Harvard Business Review Online*, November 10, 2016, http://hbr.org.

2 Gary Langer, Gregory Holyk, Chad Kieweiet de Jonge, Julie Phelan, Geoff Feinberg, and Sofi Sinozich, "Huge Margin among Working-Class Whites Lifts Trump to a Stunning Election Upset," ABC News Online, November 9, 2016, http://abcnews.go.com.

3 Joan C. Williams, "Hacking Tech's Diversity Problem," *Harvard Business Review* 92, no. 10 (2014): 94–100.

4 Alexandra Kalev, Frank Dobbin, and Erin Kelly, "Best Practices or Best Guesses? Assessing the Efficacy of Corporate Affirmative Action and Diversity Policies," *American Sociological Review* 71, no. 8 (2006): 589–617.

1

Introduction: It's Not (Always) Your Fault

The test for whether or not you can hold a job should not be the arrangement of your chromosomes. — BELLA ABZUG

Jennifer is a consultant at a large management consulting firm. Since graduating from business school, Jennifer has worked hard, played by the rules, and thrived professionally. Things are going great for her: a few years ago, she was promoted to the prestigious position of director. Having achieved a measure of job security, she and her husband—a lawyer at a big law firm in town—decided to have a baby and got pregnant. She took off the full six months allowed at her company; her baby is now 11 months old.

Recently, though, Jennifer found out that her compensation is lower than her co-worker Mike's, even though he started after her and brings in less business to the firm. Jennifer, who has never really seen herself as different from the men she works with, realizes that she might have made a mistake in not asking for an increase in compensation earlier. She goes to her boss, Rick, to discuss the matter. To her surprise, instead of being supportive, he tells her he's heard some concerns from other people in her department but reassures her he has her best interests at heart: "You're a valuable part of the team. I know there were questions among the committee about whether your performance is sustainable, but

I'll be sure to bring up your contributions when we're deciding on compensation for next year."

Surprised by Rick's easy dismissal of her concerns, Jennifer goes to her mentor, Jane, for help. Jane, who does not have children, tells Jennifer there's not much she can do about it. "Once you have children," Jane says, "it gets harder and harder to balance everything. You just need to work extra hard to prove you're willing to do what it takes to stay in the game."

Jennifer leaves Jane's office feeling more unsure of herself than ever. She's starting to think there's more going on than meets the eye—but what can she do about it that won't make things worse?

As recently as a decade or so ago, gender discrimination was so obvious it was all but impossible to ignore. In 1982, Ann Hopkins was denied a promotion to partner at the accounting firm Price Waterhouse because, as male co-workers said, she needed to "walk more femininely, talk more femininely, dress more femininely, wear make-up, have her hair styled, and wear jewelry."[1] In 1997, Goldman Sachs financial analyst Cristina Chen-Oster was sexually assaulted by a co-worker after a business meeting that took place at a Manhattan strip club called Scores.[2] Sex discrimination cases this egregious are dwindling. Some holdouts certainly exist, but the age of the Boom Boom Room—of referring to female employees as "whores" and "playboy bunnies" and of holding meetings in men's clubs—is largely past.[3]

"Twenty years ago, it used to be visible to any woman," said a longtime consultant. "We were forced to wear a skirt. It was so overt. We were expected to get the coffee." Another woman, who started working in finance in the 1980s, remembered being made to go in the back door and up the back elevator to attend a meeting in a club that didn't admit women. As recently as 10 years ago, she said, she would regularly be the only woman at corporate golf tournaments. When she won, the prize was a men's shirt.

These days, litigation and changing cultural standards have eliminated many of the more blatant examples of sexism in the professional world. Unfortunately, that doesn't mean it's disappeared.

For this book, we interviewed over 125 women about their experiences with gender bias: women at the top of their fields in law, in business, in politics, in science; married and unmarried women; mothers and women without children; women in their 30s and women in their 70s.

"For the younger women who look at me and think, 'Why are you dredging up history?'" said one executive about her efforts to talk to young women about gender bias, "my response is, 'You know what? I hope you are so lucky that you make it through this life with no unfortunate encounters like those I've just described. But, in case you do, you should be able to identify them and understand what is occurring.'"

Which takes us back to Jennifer, who is facing bias of several distinct types. The bias she's facing may seem subtle, but it's having a huge effect on her career. In short succession, she ran into each of the basic patterns of bias:

Prove-It-Again!—Women are forced to prove their competence over and over, whereas men are given the benefit of the doubt. *Why didn't Rick acknowledge that Jennifer had more seniority and brought in more business than Mike?*

The Tightrope—Women risk being written off as "too feminine" when they're agreeable and "too masculine" when they're aggressive. *Did Rick think Jennifer was too assertive in asking about her compensation?*

The Maternal Wall—Women with children are routinely pushed to the margins of the professional world. *Is Rick worried that that Jennifer might have lost her commitment to work now that she has a child—or does he think she should?*

The Tug of War—All of the above pressures on women often lead them to judge each other on the right way to be a woman. *Are Jane's judgments shaped by her own choices?*

The conventional advice is that women's careers derail because they don't have enough ambition, because they don't ask, because they choose children over career—in other words, because they're not enough like men. This advice can hurt women's careers, because while women who *don't* ask get in trouble for failing to make it clear what they want, women who *do* ask get in trouble for failing to fulfill people's expectations about how a woman should act. Take Jennifer: she followed the advice that's out there and was left wondering where she went wrong. This book is for Jennifer and women like her.

The Stubborn Gap at the Top

In the past several years, there's been a renewal of interest in the gender gap: why it's still there and what to do about it. Women like Facebook COO Sheryl Sandberg and former Obama administration official Anne-Marie Slaughter have jump-started an important conversation by bringing attention to an issue that many people hoped would resolve itself: while women have made extraordinary strides in the professional world, something's going wrong at the top.[4]

The good news is, in many ways, women are doing better than ever. Women outnumber men in college by about 57 to 43 percent, and a 2010 study found that young, single women in urban areas actually earn median salaries about 8 percent higher than comparable men.[5] In an influential article (and later a book) called "The End of Men," journalist Hanna Rosin suggests the possibility that the "modern, postindustrial economy is simply more congenial to women than to men."[6]

The problem? As women get older, advance up the corporate ladder, and begin to have families, their advantage not only disappears, it turns into a striking handicap. As of 2011 only 3.6 percent of Fortune 500 CEOs were women—16 white women, 2 women of color, 17 men of color, and 465 white men.[7] That's one table of women in a restaurant packed with 27 tables of men. Professional women in other fields are in better shape, but not by much. In 2010, women made up 47 percent of first- and second-year law firm associates but only 15 percent of full-fledged partners in the United States, a number that has been fixed for the last 20 years.[8] In science and technology, the numbers are even worse: women constitute a mere 22 percent of software engineers and only 6 percent of chief executives at top technology companies.[9] We can talk about equality until we're blue in the face, but the numbers are pretty sobering.

So how does this happen? The answer is twofold. First, even if the disadvantages women now face in the workplace are small compared with disadvantages women faced a century (or even a decade) ago, relatively small problems have surprisingly large effects over time. Very small differences in how men and women are treated can lead to huge gaps in pay, promotions, and prestige, a phenomenon often called the *accumulation of disadvantage*. Psychologist Virginia Valian writes that "the well-meaning advice often given to women—not to make a mountain out of a molehill—is mistaken. That advice fails to recognize that mountains are molehills, piled one on top of the other."[10] She describes a meeting from the perspective of an outsider: John asks Monique to get the coffee, Rahul interrupts Cara. In those apparently inconsequential interactions, the outsider is left with a distinct impression of who is respected and powerful within the group: "people who were equal in my eyes when it began are [now] unequal."[11] Because small instances of bias like these are cumulative, women like Jennifer (from our original story) sometimes don't start to feel the effects of bias until they are already established in their careers.

"It's not until women have been around a long time that they start to say, 'Oh. Now I kind of get what you 50-year-olds have been talking about,'" said a consultant.

We're also just beginning to recognize some of the most powerful patterns of gender bias that kick in as women move up the ladder in their careers. New research shows that motherhood is the strongest trigger for bias: women with children are 79 percent less likely to be hired, only half as likely to be promoted, and earn a lot less money than women with identical resumes but without children.[12] The same results don't hold for fathers. In a country where 82 percent of women become mothers, that puts women at a huge disadvantage in the workplace relative to men.[13] Yet we talk a whole lot about women's *choices* surrounding motherhood and very little about the pressures driving them out of positions of leadership or the workplace in general. In order for things to change, we need to recognize and start to break down the Maternal Wall.

Another theme that's conspicuously missing from the way we talk about gender is that bias against women often translates into conflict among women. The resulting Tug of War has been taboo, silenced by the quest for sisterhood. Talking about conflict among women seems to confirm negative stereotypes about women as catty and petty. And we know instinctively that, as an underrepresented group in many industries, infighting isn't going to get us anywhere, so the impulse is to hush it up.

But the Tug of War exists, and denying it hasn't worked. When there's only room for a few women at the top, women will scramble to take those spots. And when women are conscious of being judged, some will be quick to jump on the other women they think are hurting their cause, whether it's because they feel those women are acting too much like men or because they're reinforcing stereotypes of femininity. When women receive the message that their hold on power is tenuous, they do what they feel is necessary to protect their futures.[14] Gender bias is built into office politics such that, as long as people pursue self-interest within that system, men will find it easier to get ahead than women. The problem is not a few rotten apples. It's the barrel.

Our basic message is simple: it's not your fault that the men at your company consistently progress up the career ladder more quickly than women do. It's not your fault that last year's review said you needed to speak up for yourself, and this year's review says you need to stop being so demanding. It's not your fault that you came back from maternity leave ready to dive back in, only to find yourself frozen out of major assignments. And it's not your fault that the woman you thought was your mentor has been arguing *against* the promotion you seek. Plenty of things may happen to you that *are* your fault, but gender bias isn't one of them.

UNDERSTANDING SUBTLE BIAS

Some bias—notably Maternal Wall bias—is both strong and blatant. But today, much bias is subtle.

Even subtle bias can have a strong effect. Inspired by research from Alice Eagly (coauthor of the excellent book *Through the Labyrinth: The Truth about How Women Become Leaders*), a group of scientists built a computer simulation of a fictional company with 500 employees at the bottom and only 10 at the very top. Each employee was assigned an evaluation score and promoted according to who had the highest score. The scientists gave the male employees in the simulation 1 percent higher scores, on average, to represent the effects of gender bias. After a relatively short time period, only about a third of the top positions —and a full 53 percent of the positions at the bottom—were held by women. When the bias variance was upped to 5 percent, only 29 percent of the positions at the top were held by women and 58 percent of the positions at the bottom.[a]

Why (*Almost*) *Everything Women Are Told about Work Is Wrong*

This isn't the first book to offer advice on how to change women's disadvantage in the professional world. There's a ton of business literature that offers a ton of advice: Ask for more money! Network more! Stop being such a bitch! Stop being such a doormat!

Most books focus on what women are doing wrong. But many of the obstacles women encounter stem from factors out of their control. A good example of well-meaning but misleading advice literature is *Nice Girls Don't Get the Corner Office*, published in 2004 and in many ways still the most influential book in the genre. *Nice Girls* takes the Man Up approach, telling women that we're all girls at heart and that when we're challenged, we tend to flee, "take a step back into girlhood and question our self-worth."[15] Similarly, the book *Women Don't Ask*, which made a splash when it was released in 2003, proposes that women's woes stem from their failure to ask for raises and promotions. Authors Linda Babcock and Sara Laschever point to the negotiation gap they identify between men and women and argue that women need to ask more if they want to get ahead.[16]

This advice is popular for a reason. Rather than pointing to the institutions, it tells women there's something easy they can change in themselves. It also reflects the popular assumption that all of women's problems stem from the fact that they're too girly. But women are expected to jump into compassionate roles inconsistent with what we expect from leaders. Women are expected to be nice, to be modest, to work collaboratively, and to be understanding. These are habits that don't fit with the established image of a leader.

The problem with books like *Nice Girls Don't Get the Corner Office* and *Women Don't Ask* is that they forget that not all women are Nice Girls. Women who are direct, are self-assured, and know their own worth encounter gender bias, too. As Babcock and Laschever themselves recognize, women face tight boundaries for what is considered acceptable female behavior, and "when women stray—or stride—across those boundaries they face penalties for violating society's expectations."[17]

If you've ever been called a bitch for sanctioning a subordinate who was out of line or suddenly become invisible to a man you've contradicted, this probably sounds familiar. Women often face backlash for "acting like men"—doing things like asking for a raise or raising their voices. In a chapter called "Scaring the Boys," Babcock and Laschever address what happens when women *do* ask: "Women may be perceived to be doing good work only as long as they are toiling away at less important jobs. Once they qualify for and start asking for more important, and therefore more 'masculine' jobs, their work may begin to be devalued and their 'personal style' may suddenly become a problem."[18]

So advice literature that assumes that all women are "too feminine" and just need to man up is misleading. (Note that here, and throughout the book, we use "masculine" and "feminine" to describe stereotypes about how men and women should behave—not to imply that men and women should or do conform to these categories.) So is another strain of women's leadership literature, the Taming the Shrew subgenre, which encourages women to soften their masculine traits. In *Taming Your Alpha Bitch*, published in 2012, authors Christy Whitman and Rebecca Grado teach women to become "femininely empowered": "By making the choice to abandon the fruitless quest for dominance and superiority, you gain the power to tune out the comparing, competing, fear-based mental chatter that keeps you from enjoying life experiences as they unfold."[19] Jean Hollands, author of *Same Game, Different Rules*, teaches women to cry in meetings, punctuate their speech with "ums" and stutters, and "wear softer-looking clothes."[20]

Again, this advice is useful to a relatively narrow band of women —those who tend to be so aggressive that it's unlikely that any level of softening would undermine their authority and effectiveness. For everyone else, it can be positively perilous.

Simple formulas are highly misleading, not only because different women face different problems but because different women can face different problems at different points in their careers. The truth is that women have to be politically savvier to survive and thrive in historically male careers.

Denial Doesn't Help: The Superstar Parry

Even as some women publicly address the issue of persistent gender inequality, other women insist that talking about discrimination is a dead end. When Carly Fiorina was appointed CEO at Hewlett-Packard, she famously said, "I hope that we are at the point that everyone has figured out that there is not a glass ceiling."[21] When asked to clarify, she backtracked—sort of: "The reason I wouldn't deal with gender when I became CEO of H.P. is that I believed in a

SHIFTING PERSPECTIVES

A lot of the career advice women receive assumes that the problems they're having in their careers are their own fault. How does our perspective change when we look for ways to fix the system rather than to fix the woman?

THE PROBLEM	FIX THE WOMAN	FIX THE SYSTEM
Women are still paid an average of about 80 cents to a man's dollar for comparable work.	Women don't ask for raises and promotions.	Women who ask for raises and promotions face backlash for being too assertive and self-promoting. Educate people about these biases and about fair ways of allocating "office housework."
The higher up you go on the corporate ladder, the fewer women there are. Women make up 51.4 percent of management and professional occupations but only 14 percent of Fortune 500 executive officers.	The ambition gap between men and women means women just aren't willing to make the sacrifices necessary to climb to the top.	Women burn out early because the effort of trying to prove their competence over and over ultimately proves exhausting. Adopt objective rubrics for measuring success that don't artificially disadvantage women.
When women have children, they are far more likely than men to drop out or leave the fast track.	Women "opt out" when they have children because they realize they have different priorities than men do.	Workplace ideals are designed around men married to homemakers. Create a variety of schedules and career tracks—for men as well as women.
Women are seen as a bad fit for jobs that require authority and power.	Women need to act more like men by being assertive, aggressive, and hard-charging at the expense of others.	Reflect more accurately the skills necessary to succeed, including emotional intelligence and other devalued but important skills traditionally associated with women.

meritocracy where gender isn't the issue," Fiorina said. "I wanted to play by the same rules. Look, I'm not an idiot. There are clearly things that are different for men and women in leadership. But I believe you have to be the change you seek."[22] Note that Fiorina said this while working in Silicon Valley, where fewer than 10 percent of company board seats are occupied by women and only 11 percent of venture-backed companies have a female CEO or founder.[23]

A common claim, in Silicon Valley and elsewhere, is that gender bias can't be a problem at [insert company name here] because the company is a meritocracy. But recent research shows that organizations that think of themselves as highly meritocratic tend to have *more* gender bias than organizations that do not. Emilio J. Castilla and Stephen Benard, in a study called "The Paradox of Meritocracy in Organizations," found that when an organization's core values state that raises and promotions are "based entirely on the performance of the employee," women were given smaller bonuses than men who received equivalent reviews.[24] Because meritocratic cultures perceive themselves as "unbiased and fair," people working within them worry less about how their actions will be perceived —and therefore succumb more easily to bias.[25]

There's nothing wrong with trying to be the change you want to see in the world. But when Gandhi proposed this, he didn't mean colonialism would disappear if Indians pretended British rule didn't exist—and we're pretty sure gender bias won't disappear simply because we deny its influence. Being the change you want to see in the world first requires an understanding of what needs changing. Ignoring the role bias plays in creating our reality is a good way to maintain the status quo.

No one would disagree that some of the most powerful people in the world are women: Angela Merkel; Sonia Gandhi, president of the Indian National Congress; Dilma Roussef, the president of Brazil; and Hillary Clinton, to name a notable few. These are, incidentally, the top four of the only *six* women in *Forbes*'s list of the 70 Most Powerful People of 2011.[26] But these are exceptional women with exceptional circumstances. Sonia Gandhi married into a political dynasty, and her husband was prime minister of India before his 1991 assassination.[27] Hillary Clinton's husband, of course, was president of the United States. Pointing to their pedigrees is not to denigrate or diminish their accomplishments. It's to say that holding such women up as proof that the glass ceiling has been shattered involves an astounding level of deliberate blindness.

For several decades now, superstar women have been held up as proof that women who don't make it to the top must not be trying hard enough. From Margaret Thatcher to Marissa Mayer, these women have more than held their own against men and achieved incredible professional success while simultaneously raising families and developing a highly visible public profile. If they can do it, why can't everyone?

Superstars are different from most women. Not everyone's father is Zbigniew Brzezinski. (That said, Mika Brzezinski's book *Knowing Your Value* is a good, eye-opening read: it's pretty shocking when even someone as successful and well-connected as Brzezinski, who is a cohost of MSNBC's *Morning Joe*, encountered open gender bias.)[28]

Superstars may actually get higher evaluations than equivalent men because women tend to get polarized evaluations: either very good or very bad. This occurs because in-groups (including men) tend to give polarized evaluations to out-groups (including women), whereas evaluations of one's own group tend to be more nuanced (some strengths, some weaknesses).[29] So superstars may well get great evaluations in environments in which women who are merely excellent get evaluations much, much lower than evaluations of comparable men.[30]

Superstars are different in more subtle ways as well. Two of the most successful women I interviewed, both of whom reached the top of large organizations, illustrate how superstars differ from the rest of us. Both had personal styles and aspirations that were a near-perfect fit for the organizations in which they had thrived. Perhaps because of this, both were more willing than many others Joan interviewed to put gender bias to one side and just go for the gold. One, when asked for her strategies to overcome the Prove-It-Again! problem, responded almost pityingly. "Well," she said, "I guess you have to prove it again."

Another New Girl had crusaded against male-only clubs early in her career. Then she stopped because she realized that it made her male colleagues uncomfortable. That didn't serve her purpose. In her view, the best way she could help women was to get to the top rung. So she did. She was the first woman to run a major international law firm, which, when she ran it, was probably one of the best places in the legal profession for women to work. Today she sits on corporate boards—and helps other women attain that role.

Many people aren't superstars for reasons that have nothing to do with raw talent. They just don't want the same things the superstars want. They are not as driven to succeed in conventional organizations because they want more work-life balance or are less willing to let go of outrage or are just plain quirkier: their goals and talents *don't* map perfectly onto those of conventional organizations. To quote Congresswoman Bella Abzug, "Our struggle today is not to have a female Einstein get appointed as an assistant professor. It is for a woman schlemiel to get as quickly promoted as a male schlemiel."[31]

Everyone's a Little Bit Sexist Sometimes

Attributing women's stalled advancement to gender bias can be a little hard to swallow these days. Years of hard work by several generations of feminists have ensured that it's no longer okay, legally or socially, to deny women opportunities because of their gender. We may like to think that the days of *Mad Men*–era boys' clubs are long gone. And after all, you may be thinking, "My husband or boyfriend or son isn't gender biased. My roommate isn't gender biased. George who works in the next cubicle isn't gender biased. *I'm* not gender biased."

Statistically, that's not true.

In 1998, a group of social scientists developed the Implicit Association Test (IAT) and with it a theory that has quietly changed the way we think about bias and discrimination.[32] The IAT measures the ease with which people associate certain photographs and words. In the classic test, white and black faces are paired with either positive or negative words. Subjects who respond more quickly when positive words are associated with white faces are described as showing an automatic preference for European Americans, while those who respond more quickly when positive words are associated with black faces are described as showing an automatic preference for African Americans.[33]

Results collected between 2000 and 2006 show that the vast majority of test takers display some level of automatic bias against African Americans—70 percent showed some automatic preference for white faces over black faces, while only 12 percent showed some preference for black faces over white faces.[34] A similar pattern holds true for bias associating men with science and women with the humanities: 72 percent of test takers showed some level of automatic association of male with science and female with liberal arts, while only 10 percent showed any level of association of male with liberal arts and female with science.[35]

What's really interesting about the IAT is that implicit bias shows very little correlation with explicit bias.[36] When people are asked directly about their biases, their responses tend not to reflect the patterns that show up on the implicit association test. A study coauthored by Anthony Greenwald, who invented the IAT, found that while the majority of white test takers claim to either be indifferent to race or to show a preference for black people over white people, their scores indicated a strong automatic preference for white people.[37]

The IAT reveals attitudes we didn't know we had. Confronting those attitudes may well make us uncomfortable, which is probably part of why people tend to convince themselves they are unbiased. A Stanford study, for example, showed that we tend to rate other people's actions as *more* influenced by bias than they actually are and our own actions as *less* influenced by bias.[38] When confronted by the suggestion that we may be biased, we generally turn to introspection and in good faith determine that we're being rational.[39] Alas, the IAT shows a more uncomfortable truth.

All this is to say that you're probably biased, as are the people around you. When we talk about biases, we're not necessarily talking about something ill intentioned or malicious. This is both good news and bad news. The good news is that it's not the case that everyone is out to get you. The majority of people you work with probably mean well, including the ones who treat you in ways you feel are unfair. The bad news is that it can be easy to dismiss this bias as innocent or impossible to reverse: if *everyone* has biases— and they don't even know it—then what the heck can we do about it?

This book proposes two different paths to overcoming bias, both of which are necessary if we're going to move past the challenges working women face. They're both premised on the basic fact that understanding gender bias can be powerful.

Path one is to educate yourself. If you understand the biases working against you, you can learn how to "hack" them—manipulate them to lessen their impact or even work them to your advantage. Path two is to educate others. As long as we ignore unconscious biases, they'll remain invisible. Only people who know their biases can rise above them.

Know the Rules, Then Break Them

The worst part of writing an advice book is having to give advice. We think there are certain things you need to know to understand what's going on in your career. We think it's not useful to ignore gender bias, and we think too much of the advice out there puts the blame squarely on women's shoulders without acknowledging that what works for a man may not work for a woman.

At the same time, we want to make it clear that there is no single answer to how to succeed as a woman in the professional world. In case this was somehow still ambiguous, both Rachel and Joan are women. But no woman is only a woman. We're both white. And middle class. And American. And straight. And able-bodied. All those things affect our outlook. This concept is known as intersectionality.[40]

BADASS WOMEN WHO BROKE THE RULES

Some women completely ignore some or all of the advice in this book and still get where they need to go. If you're more of a rule breaker yourself, here are some role models to get you started.

SOJOURNER TRUTH (1797–1883): An abolitionist and civil rights activist, Truth was a noted speaker who once, according to legend, flashed her breasts at a heckler who accused her of being a man. During the Civil War, she helped recruit black soldiers for the Union Army and afterward spent years lobbying the government for land grants for former slaves.[b]

GEORGE SAND (1804–1876): No Tightrope-walking for this French author: in addition to her novels, poems, and literary criticism, Sand was known for her gender bending and high-profile affairs. She smoked tobacco in public, which was taboo for women at the time, and wore pants because they were more comfortable and durable than dresses. Divorced young, she had a series of lovers including composer Frederic Chopin.[c]

HELEN GURLEY BROWN (1922–2012): Her bold book *Sex and the Single Girl* finally said out loud what everyone already knew: women have sex before marriage, *and they like it*. As the editor of *Cosmopolitan* magazine, Gurley Brown used the magazine as a platform to advocate for women's sexual revolution and shaped the modern-day media in the process.[d]

Remember: there's no right way to be a woman. This book is meant to serve as a guide to some of the biases that may affect how people react to you. The advice is geared toward counteracting that if you feel that's getting in your way. If something else works for you — get it, girl.

We spoke not only with women of color and white women. We also spoke with straight women and lesbians; women born in the United States and women from abroad; older women, younger women; women in business and law and politics and science and journalism. Bringing all of these experiences together is an ambitious undertaking, and we've done our best to include a diversity of voices without losing sight of the common themes that run through women's experiences.

We deal with race in two different ways. In all but one of the following 14 chapters, we include quotes from both women of color and white women without identifying the race of the women. We felt this was necessary to protect confidentiality, given the sensitive nature of the topics discussed. In chapter 11, we take a different approach and discuss the distinctive experiences of women of color.

The result of these 127 interviews isn't so much a road map as a "Choose Your Own Adventure." Chances are good that some parts of the book are going to speak to you more than others. Chances are also good that some parts will drive you nuts. That's okay. The debates that we had as a group during our New Girls' Network meetings have been impassioned and eye-opening, and we hope that debate continues moving forward.

As a result of our diversity, every New Girl breaks some rules and follows others, and it's up to you to decide on your own approach. What we're doing is teaching you the rules so you won't be caught off guard. If you decide to break them after that, you'll be doing it consciously. All we have to say about that is—go for it!

All New Girls internalize this approach in their own way. One woman who worked in marketing said she was careful to follow her office's conventions "to a tee" because she realized, "I'm a little bit of a minority here, and I need to make sure that the powers that be understand that I am a team player and I'm going to play it the way they say it has to be played." She got to work early and left late, adhered to memo-writing conventions and the published dress code, and generally tried not to break any "meaningless rules." At the same time, when she thought a particular policy was unfair, she didn't hesitate to challenge it—and her challenge actually carried extra weight, because she had already established that she wasn't the type to break a rule just for the sake of breaking it. Another woman, a vice president at a Fortune 500 company, said that when she was younger she used to try to blend in with the boys by reading the sports page and keeping quiet when controversial political issues came up. Over time, she learned that there were certain adaptations she just couldn't make if she wanted to stay true to herself. "I needed to be the same person at work and outside of work," she said. "It was too stressful to try to be two different people."

Every woman makes different sacrifices. The women we spoke with who had reached the top often said they let instances of gender bias pass. Their theory was that success is women's sweetest revenge, and making your point can interfere with your ability to achieve that success.

We know it's not fair that women should have to take on this extra burden. But as one New Girl's father told her at a young age, a lot of things in life just aren't fair. "I didn't want to hear it at the time, and it took me a number of years to figure out what he was trying to tell me," she says now. "You have to make a choice. And are you going to choose the principle over being effective? Sometimes that's the right choice, but not most of the time."

What Works for Women at Work arises from the tension between the principle of gender equality and the need for women to be effective leaders now. Our goal with this book is to help you balance matters of principle with effectiveness. You can make the adaptations necessary to be an effective leader without sacrificing your principles, no matter your style and personality. Whether you're a tomboy who always wins the office Super Bowl pool or a mother who wants to spend more time with her kids (or both), this book is designed to help you decide what rules you want to follow before you decide what rules you want to break, so that you can find the path to success that's best for you.

WHAT'S BEEN YOUR EXPERIENCE?

Rachel asked some of her law school classmates — all of whom have worked for one to five years between college and law school — whether they had experienced any of the four patterns yet. Here are some of their responses:

"My boss would call me into his office for an emotional debrief after meeting with the executive director, but never my colleagues. I also felt myself change a bit. I had spent college judging girls who 'played dumb,' . . . but I found myself doing it at work. I preferred to pipe up with a joke or a giggle than a substantive comment."

"I think particularly working in the context of criminal defense, I've attempted to balance between showing empathy and supporting my clients emotionally, while also not just appearing like a 'weak girl' or, worse, an object of desire instead of a resource/authority."

"Men can 'achieve' simply by befriending their male boss, forming a sort of 'buddy-buddy' type relationship, whereas women can't connect with their bosses in that way — either because gender dynamics don't allow it or because she would be seen as 'using her sexuality' to maintain that relationship (even if not actually doing the same things that a male associate were doing). The male bosses don't feel comfortable judging the females on any lines other than merit because they are afraid to be seen as this creepy older guy who is into his associate."

"I worry that the current discussion of work/family is perpetuating the idea that it's a 'women's issue' — something that women need to take into account when planning their lives but that men don't need to think about. That would seem to imply that the correct role for women is caretaker and anything else is a 'bonus,' whereas men can solely think about working and being the provider. I actually had an interesting talk with one of our classmates about this, where he was like, 'Why is that a women's issue? I want to have family-work balance as well! Why doesn't anyone care about that for dads?'"

"We're all snowflakes. We're so unique," an executive said. "You've got to pick and choose from everybody to make your own mosaic of who you are and what you want to be."

And yet for all our differences, there's one thing we all have in common: "The advantage of being a woman," said one New Girl, "is when they try to kick you in the balls, they always miss."

PART I

Prove-It-Again!

2

Spotting Prove-It-Again! Patterns

People might not get all they work for in this world, but they must certainly work for all they get.

— FREDERICK DOUGLASS

Imagine the typical professional. What are they wearing? A suit? A tie? Do they have long hair or short hair? How do they act? Are they independent or attuned to others? Dominant or sensitive? Assertive or retiring? When they get angry, do they yell or cry?

In other words, when you think of the typical professional, do you think of a man or a woman?

If you're like many Americans, your image of a successful professional is both male and masculine. Think Gordon Gekko and his anger, think Don Draper and his arrogance, think Mark Zuckerberg (real or fictional) and his notorious lack of people skills. All three are men, all three are leaders, and all three are severely lacking in characteristics we think of as feminine, whether that means gentleness or modesty or empathy.

The link between professional success and both maleness and masculinity has deep roots. When we look at CEOs, at law firm partners, or at engineers, we quite literally see men—because that's who are in those positions. And in part because we get used to seeing men there, jobs higher in prestige are generally typed masculine, and most of us unconsciously link men with the idea of a successful professional.[1]

As a result, women tend to be evaluated less favorably than men. In practical terms, this pattern works in two ways: One is that women receive fewer opportunities than men do in the first place. The other is that even when they are given the chance to try, women's work product may well be held to higher standards than men's.[2]

Just over two-thirds (68 percent) of the women interviewed for this book reported Prove-It-Again! bias. One might assume that Prove-It-Again! would be much more common among women of color, who often trigger negative competence assumptions based on race as well as gender. But we found that women of color were only 4 percentage points more likely than white women to report Prove-It-Again! problems. This was the smallest gap we found; the gap was larger with respect to each of the three other patterns of bias. (This issue is discussed further in chapter 11.)

The key principle underlying Prove-It-Again! bias is that information that supports preexisting stereotypes tends to be noticed

---

**PROFESSOR BEN BARRES, PROFESSOR OF
NEUROBIOLOGY AT STANFORD**

"I was born a woman. Thirteen years ago, at the age of 40, I decided to change my sex.

"By far, the biggest difference I have noticed is that people who do not know that I was a woman treat me with far more respect. I can even complete a whole sentence without being interrupted by a man. Some people even think that my research is better. Shortly after I changed sex, a faculty member was heard to say, 'Ben Barres gave a great seminar today, but then his work is much better than his sister's work.'

"And also, men tell me things that I don't think they would have told me when I was Barbara. A neurosurgeon at Stanford told me that he has never met a woman surgeon who is remotely as good as a man. Another told me he thinks women are like small children. Many have told me that they think gender stereotypes are generally true."[a]

WHY WOMEN HAVE TO PROVE-IT-AGAIN!

PATTERN 1: Men Are Judged on Their Potential; Women Are Judged on Their Achievements.

PATTERN 2: What's Important for a Given Job? Whatever the Male Candidate Has.

PATTERN 3: Men's Successes Are Attributed to Skill, While Women's Are Overlooked or Attributed to Luck. With Mistakes, It's Just the Opposite.

PATTERN 4: Objective Requirements Are Applied Strictly to Women but Leniently to Men.

PATTERN 5: Women Are "Gossiping"; Men Are "Talking about Business."

---

and remembered, while information that contradicts them tends to be overlooked and soon forgotten.[3] As a result, men have to prove their competence. Women have to prove it again—and again and again.[4]

Men Are Judged on Their Potential; Women Are Judged on Their Achievements

Popular wisdom holds that one of the best ways to negotiate a higher salary is to be willing to move to a new company. This is true for men, who the nonprofit Catalyst found earned nearly $14,000 more if they were at their second post-MBA job than if they were at their first post-MBA job.[5] No such advantage was found for women. Women who had worked at three or more companies since receiving their MBAs earned an average of $53,472 *less* than those who stayed at their first post-MBA employer.[6] This discrepancy arises because women, unlike men, are judged based on their achievement rather than their potential. While a younger man with good credentials but little experience may be seen as a hiring opportunity, a younger woman is more likely simply to be seen as inexperienced.

One consultant sees this pattern every year, when she and her colleagues are deciding whom to promote to partner at her firm. "You see in those discussions where men often are given the benefit of the doubt: 'This is such a strong senior manager; he's a great guy; he's really going to go places,'" she said. "And then you get to the discussion of some woman senior manager, and the discussion suddenly turns to, 'Well, we think she's talented, but she hasn't been given an opportunity to prove it yet. Maybe she needs another year.'"

Joan's favorite version of this phenomenon occurred when someone insisted that a man "had the whole package." Needless to say, some "packages" women just don't have.

A consultant said she fought the battle to be recognized for her potential "from day one" until she "became a rainmaker." "A man's okay if he's perceived to have the potential to bring in clients," she said. "I was not. I had a network bigger than any man, and it was not paying off, because of course it had to grow. And I was constantly told, 'You don't have the work. Yeah, you have the network, but you don't have the work.' Whereas a man could just take clients out to dinner or golfing, and even if he didn't have the work either, he was given credit for that."

Apart from being unfair, this double standard has serious repercussions for women trying to climb the corporate ladder: if a woman is kept off important projects because she hasn't proven herself yet on an important project, then she's never going to get the experience on important projects. What's more, it's so prevalent that women may internalize it: "I think that women need to be overly confident in something in order to self-promote," one New Girl observed. "The level of confidence they need to assert themselves in a particular role is much higher than a male equivalent. I

**WHAT TO SAY WHEN YOU'RE JUDGED ON
A STRICTER STANDARD THAN A MAN**

- Can you give an example of what I would need to do to get the same opportunity as Sam?

- I would like to understand how my performance is different from Nick's. Can you help?

- Thanks for the feedback on my performance. Can you tell me what I would need to do to get a raise as big as Joe's?

- Where do I stand in relation to my peers?

- I need this opportunity if I'm going to keep developing as a team member.[b]

---

see men volunteering all the time for things that they don't necessarily know that much about."

Because women seem less natural fits for high-stakes jobs as compared to men, often they are seen as more of a risk for a promotion or an appointment than a comparable man. We spoke with several women who said they were given a promotion but not the title or the increased salary that typically came with the new job. Often their supervisors have them "test out" the new position for months before they feel comfortable making the appointment official—or simply refuse to give them the title at all. Said one New Girl, "I think there was that, 'I'll take a chance on this guy, but I won't take a chance on this woman. I don't know what her experience is,' or 'I don't know if her experience is comparable.' There was this element of, 'Can this person be trusted?' I saw that much more pronounced with women than with men."

One woman, who works in sales and marketing at a major company, said she spent almost the entire nine months she was pregnant "basically on-the-job interviewing" for a managerial position that her superiors weren't sure she was ready to take. After several successful months, she approached her manager to ask why she hadn't yet gotten the title, as everything had been going well. He explained that, while she had been doing well under the current structure, the company had just hired someone new as her immediate supervisor, and it was he who would ultimately make the decision.

The New Girl eventually went on maternity leave not knowing whether she would get the title that matched her job. About a month before she was supposed to come back into the office, she finally got the call from her new boss telling her she had officially received the promotion. "I never understood what I did on maternity leave to demonstrate why I deserved that," she said dryly.

What's Important for a Given Job? Whatever the Male Candidate Has

In a study conducted at Princeton, researchers created a resume for two fictional candidates competing for a construction job.[7] One of the candidates was better educated; the other had more work experience relevant to the job. The researchers gave the resumes to study participants and asked them which candidate they would hire, varying the gender of the applicants such that in some cases participants were reviewing the resumes of a better-educated female and a more-experienced male and in other cases of a better-educated male and a more-experienced female.[8]

In a control group in which the gender of the applicants was left ambiguous, 48 percent of the study participants ranked education as more important than experience, and 76 percent of participants chose the better-educated candidate over the candidate with more work experience.[9] But when the gender was made explicit, a striking pattern emerged. When the better-educated candidate was male, this pattern held: 50 percent of participants said education was more important than work experience, and 75 percent chose a better-educated male over a female with more experience.[10] But when the genders were switched, only 22 percent of participants said they would choose a better-educated candidate over a candidate with more work experience, and only 43 percent of participants chose the better-educated female.[11] Study participants gave less weight to both education *and* work experience when a woman had them than when a man had them.

This pattern of bias is called *casuistry*, a technical term for what happens when people misapply general rules to justify a specific behavior or use specious reasoning to rationalize their behavior.[12] Casuistic bias is particularly pernicious because people think they're using objective criteria to make their decisions when in fact they're modifying the criteria used for judgment based on unconscious biases. In fact, some studies have shown that evaluators who shifted the criteria they used to make hiring decisions depending on the race or gender of an applicant actually rated themselves as *more* objective than those whose hiring criteria did not shift.[13]

Casuistry provides a disturbing illustration of the lengths people go to convince themselves they're being objective even when they're not. This pattern is one reason it's so important to educate people about the way bias works. If someone is able to give a convincing reason for why a man should be hired or promoted over a woman, people tend to understand that as proof that bias hasn't occurred.

Men's Successes Are Attributed to Skill, While Women's Are Overlooked or Attributed to Luck; With Mistakes, It's Just the Opposite

Everybody makes mistakes. Whether you accidentally sent out an officewide e-mail with a glaring typo or made the wrong call on a potentially lucrative deal, chances are good that, at some point in your career, you've messed up.

The problem is, as a result of our biases about what success looks like, women's mistakes tend to be given more weight and remembered longer than men's. One attorney said when she came up as a candidate for partner at her law firm, someone brought up a mistake she had made years ago, as a second-year associate. "The fact that I learned from my mistake—and that men who had been promoted had made similar mistakes—none of that mattered," she said.[14] Mistakes men make often are attributed to outside circumstances. The same is not true for women. Said one woman, "A man takes a big risk and makes a mistake, that's considered risky, but he's taking a chance; a woman does it, then it's just a big mistake."[15] It is particularly infuriating when advice books attribute women's failure to get ahead to the fact they are too risk averse. Talk about blame the victim.

A related pattern is that men's successes tend to be noticed and remembered, while women's are more likely to be overlooked and soon forgotten. This happens because when people's behavior conforms to our expectations, we tend to attribute it to some stable, internal trait and assume it reflects a truth about who they really are, whereas when behavior violates our expectations, we're more likely to attribute it to a fleeting external cause like luck.[16] What's more, people are likely to ignore or quickly forget information that disconfirms their preexisting hypotheses, so information about men's competence has more staying power than equivalent information about women.[17]

One of the most concrete and consistent examples of the uneven weight given to men's and women's successes is illustrated succinctly in a 2007 FedEx commercial called "The Stolen Idea," which features a meeting at a boardroom table.

"We have got to cut costs, people," says an executive. "Ideas?"

A nerdy-looking junior guy speaks up. "We could open an account on FedEx.com. Save 10 percent on online express shipping," he says with a self-deprecating shrug.

There's a moment of silence while everyone at the table looks at each other.

"Okay, how about this," the executive says, punctuating his idea with a karate chop. "We open an account on FedEx.com. Save 10 percent on online express shipping."

A murmur of approval passes around the table.

The nerdy junior guy cuts in. "You just said the same thing I did, only you did this," he said, waving his hands in demonstration.

"No, I did this," the executive responds, repeating the karate chop.

"Makes all the difference," someone says.

"Bingo!" someone else calls down the table.

The New Girl who pointed us to this ad works in a conservative field and said she sees this phenomenon all the time—but "almost exclusively by gender."

Ironically (or appropriately?), the commercial doesn't address gender at all—in fact, there's only one woman in the fictional conference room, and you only see the back of her head. But the advertisement does hint at several patterns that make women more vulnerable than men to this type of bias. One issue is the weight given to seniority. The executive who repeats the junior guy's suggestion is obviously one of the company's top dogs, and the other employees sitting around the conference room table have a vested interest (sometimes literally) in keeping him happy. It takes no more than a quick look at the numbers to tell that favoring seniority disadvantages women—look at law firms, where only about 15 percent of the attorneys at the top are female.[18]

What's more, seniority doesn't always help women. A managing partner at a law firm said she runs into the Stolen Idea at her firm all the time, despite being one of the highest-ranking attorneys at the firm. "You say something and then somebody else says it, and someone looks at them and says, 'Oh, that's a great idea.' I mean, that stuff happens all the time, still."

The body language of the two men in the FedEx commercial is also telling. The junior guy shrugs apologetically when presenting the idea; the executive speaks forcefully and punctuates his point with an aggressive chopping motion. The masculine man, in other words, gets credit for the feminine man's suggestion. This problem is that much worse for women, who need to be masculine to have their ideas heard but simultaneously can face social sanctions if they fail to be feminine, something we'll discuss more in chapter 4. Dominance and assertiveness are traits associated with masculinity; submissiveness and passivity are traits associated with femininity.

The Stolen Idea works along two levels: one, feminine women may be less likely to state an idea in a way that commands people's attention, making it easy to overlook. Two, since the traits consistent with leadership and idea generation are gendered masculine, there's a better cognitive "fit" for the man's assertion of a new idea than the woman's, making it easier for others to pick up on.

The patterns of bias seen in the Stolen Idea hold more generally as well, particularly when assigning compensation, rank, or responsibility. One successful rainmaker remembered asking a manager for a raise after a particularly lucrative year. The manager praised her for a job well done but said the committee wanted to wait until

---

SMOOTH COMEBACKS FOR ROUGH MOMENTS

Remember, as always, the three T's—timing, tone, and tier. If you're just out of college, you can't call the CFO a turkey-butt—but if you're the CEO, you might want to get straight to the point.

- Thanks for picking up on that idea.

- Interesting you should say that. That's exactly the point I was making.

- I think that's what I said. If you're disagreeing with me, I want to understand what you're saying.

- I'm thrilled you like my point.

- Exactly. You understand what I'm thinking.

- You may have been on your iPhone when I made that point.

- You turkey-butt. That was my idea.

the following year, to make sure her performance wasn't a fluke. He ultimately offered her a raise that was half of what she'd asked for. Another New Girl told us that shortly after hearing Joan talk, she was sitting in a meeting when she started noticing a pattern about how her colleagues were characterized. The women, again and again, were described as hard workers and team players.

"How she gets it done is by working harder and pitching in," someone said about one employee. "She pulls more than her fair share, and she does it all with a smile on her face." Another woman received more conditional praise: "Oh, she's a workhorse. She really knows how to drive for results, but I haven't seen her do strategy."

With the men, the assessment was much simpler: "Whatever he touches, he just crushes it."

This pattern comes out particularly strongly when men and women are put together on the same team and then evaluated separately. Even if a team is evaluated positively overall, studies have found that female team members will be evaluated more negatively than their male counterparts, found to have been less influential and taken less of a leadership role than the men.[19] This result is independent of actual contribution. People just assume women take the backseat because of stereotypes that men are more self-motivated and better leaders.

As a result of the cognitive disconnect between women and professional success, women's reputations can be extremely tenuous. When Carol Bartz was fired as CEO of Yahoo!, "everybody piled on," she said. One day, "they were coming over here en masse saying I was the best boss we ever had." And then, suddenly, "it was almost like I had never been there."

One attorney said she sees this whenever a woman at her firm has a significant achievement in a case she's litigating. "The woman's in charge of it all, and the woman's a hero," she said. "But then a cross-examination doesn't go as expected or something happens on direct. How quickly do you take her hero robe off?"

The answer, the attorney said, is "right away." Men's statuses are much more resilient. When people are provided with stereotype-affirming information, they are quick to replace the stereotype-countering information they had previously, forgetting women's professional successes—and men's professional failures— all too swiftly.

Objective Requirements Are Applied Strictly to Women but Leniently to Men

Generally, when we think of bias, we focus on the treatment of women: the associate who was kept off big cases and then considered too inexperienced to promote; the partner who was taken off a lucrative account when she got pregnant.

Directing our attention only to women leaves out a crucial point: often women's disadvantage stems not from the way they are treated but from the way *men* are treated. For every woman passed over for a promotion on account of her gender, there's a man who gets a leg up because of his. Marilynn Brewer, a prominent social psychologist, identifies this phenomenon as "in-group favoritism," noting that there's a difference between bias *against* an out-group and bias *in favor of* an in-group.[20] What we often think of as discrimination is actually, from another perspective, the fallout from someone else's good luck.

One way to reduce in-group favoritism is to require all employees to follow objective rules. This works great as a guard against discrimination—if the rules are followed and enforced objectively. But how often does that happen? Most hiring procedures involve some level of subjectivity. What's more, in many offices, little bureaucratic rules are broken all the time, often inconsistently— how many times have you "borrowed" a couple of pens from the supply closet or checked your personal e-mail at work? In-group favoritism often emerges in the form of leniency bias, which occurs when rules apply rigorously to members of an out-group but leniently to members of an in-group.

Former stockbroker Tameron Keyes, in her memoir *No Backing*

THE PRESIDENT SAYS IT BEST: LENIENCY BIAS ON TV

We were impressed that even President Josiah Bartlett, the fictional president on the hit television series *The West Wing*, can spot leniency bias when it crosses his desk.

In the tenth episode of the fourth season, the White House staff is grappling with the news that a highly successful female navy pilot is being court-martialed for disobeying orders when she refused to end an extramarital affair. Prominent women's political groups are causing a stir about her case—suggesting that she may have been unfairly targeted —but the staff, led by Chief of Staff Leo McGarry, encourages the president to keep the issue off his desk, for fear of stepping on the toes of military leadership.

Fed up with what he believes to be unfair treatment of the pilot, the president asks his personal aide Charlie, "Are we to live with the assumption that there are no men in the services who have committed adultery? I don't know what's worse, being stupid or pretending to be stupid."

Irritated, the president bursts into Leo's office. "Eisenhower and Kay Summersby, a subordinate. Hammond with the wives of *two* junior officers," he says, listing the names of male officers who were let off the hook after their affairs went public. "*So G.I. Jane gets a court-martial, and G.I. Joe gets a short film on hygiene?* That is all I have to say to you!"

Leo counters, "Nobody ordered Eisenhower to stop seeing Summersby."

"That's right. Because *men* don't give that order to other *men*!" the president shouts.

"Excuse me," Leo retorts, "but did you not fire our ambassador to somewhere-in-South-America-I-can't-remember because he was messing around with—"

"The daughter of the president of Brazil, which presented a political problem for me!" the president interjects. "Also, I didn't fire him. I asked him to resign, and I set him up in the private sector!"

Thank you, Mr. President. We couldn't have said it better ourselves.[c]

Down, remembers a couple of branch meetings during which her branch manager, who was responsible for her office, said that he was interested in his brokers' upward progress, not their absolute numbers. Shortly afterward, her sales manager, who worked under the branch manager, called her into his office and said she was out if she didn't make $10,000 a month each month until the end of her first-year contract. This same sales manager had walked around the branch and said, "Women shouldn't be stockbrokers. She's canned," Keyes told us. The branch manager's interest in upward progression didn't apply to her.

Leniency bias shows up in the policing of behavior, as well as work performance. One New Girl told us about her time as a partner in a firm where "the f-bomb [was] heard every other word." Yet, after using harsh language when a young, male associate ignored her seniority and chastised her, the New Girl found herself having to explain her tone to the managing partners, while the male associate got off without even a slap on the wrist. The New Girl felt that the same actions from a male wouldn't have raised any eyebrows: "It's exactly the same actions the males are taking, and the same words, and it is perceived in a totally different manner," she explained.

It's not usually quite so explicit, but many New Girls ran up against a similar double standard. An attorney told us about a time she advanced $500 of her own money to purchase thank-you gifts for powerful general counsel who were appearing on a national panel she was moderating. At the last minute, the attorney had to pull out of moderating the panel because her mother died unexpectedly. Given the pressures and emotions of the death, the attorney didn't get the expenditures for the thank-you gifts preapproved. Her supervisor refused to pay her back the full amount.

When she tried to challenge his decision, she got an e-mail back that said, in all caps, "YOU ARE NOT THAT F**KING SPE-CIAL. It doesn't make any difference that your mother died. You have to live by all of the same rules that your partners do" (the original did not have the asterisks).

Not the politest way of getting his point across, maybe, but okay —except for one thing. The other partners *weren't* held to the same rules. When the attorney shared her experience with co-workers, their responses were all the same: "What rules? Nobody has to do that."

Another female attorney said that when the men she worked with were far ahead of her in compensation within a few years of making partner, the reason given was that most of her clients were established clients of the firm. But one of the men, she said, had been handed a preexisting case that kept him going for years. "And I thought, 'Okay, I'm sorry, how was that different?'" the New Girl said. But she didn't say anything, she explained, because she felt that complaining would do more harm than good.

Women Are "Gossiping"; Men Are "Talking about Business"

All the types of Prove-It-Again! bias are some variation on the theme that information about professional women is understood and processed differently than it is for professional men. Nowhere is this clearer than when the same action is interpreted as business oriented by a man and frivolous by a woman. (Joan likes to refer to this as the assumption that "women are little bits of fluff.")

A consultant told us about the time she once took a break from a business meeting to talk to a female colleague. Partway through their conversation, a male co-worker walked up to them. "Sorry to interrupt you two gossiping, but I really need to talk to you," he said, pulling the New Girl aside. They hadn't been gossiping. The New Girl had been talking with her colleague about work. Their male co-worker assumed they weren't because of stereotypes of what women talk about (diets! clothes! who's hot!). It's hard to imagine him making the same assumption when approaching two men—unless talk of golf, hunting, and box scores is considered "gossip."

"In work settings a behavior such as frequent phone conversation is a good deal more likely to be seen as slacking off for a woman but productive for a man," notes social psychologist Madeline Heilman. "Similarly, waiting to make a decision rather than acting immediately may seem passive coming from a woman but prudent coming from a man."[21]

Even when people *aren't* talking about anything directly business related, men—and masculinized subject matter—tend to be given a free pass, several New Girls noted. Conversations about sports, for example, are a fully accepted form of professional small talk, which people understand implicitly as a means of building professional relationships. Conversely, conversations about children or shopping or any various feminized subjects are seen as a distraction from the real work at hand.

Perhaps the most dramatic study of this phenomenon concerns an analysis of letters of recommendation for medical faculty.[22] Letters for women were much more likely (34 percent compared to 23 percent) to contain "grindstone adjectives" such as "thorough," "hardworking," "organized," "conscientious," whereas letters for men were much more likely (13 percent versus 3 percent) to contain words like "achievement" and "accomplishment."[23] Perhaps the men were just better than the women, but another possibility

---

SMOOTH COMEBACKS FOR ROUGH MOMENTS

It might be better to dream about telling off your boss than to actually do it. But the jerk in the next cubicle? Let him have it with a smile!

COMMENT: "What are you ladies gossiping about?"
COMEBACK: "We're fantasizing—just not about football!"

COMMENT: "Complaining about men again?"
COMEBACK: "While that might be a rich topic of conversation, we were actually talking about something interesting."

is that the women's accomplishments often were attributed to hard work while the men's were attributed to brilliance. The women's letters were much more likely (16 percent versus 4 percent) to contain terms like "caring" or "compassionate" and to offer information about their personal lives.[24] Men's were much more likely to have information about their publications. Women were more likely to be praised for undervalued activities such as teaching and training. Men were praised for research, skills, and ability—the coin of the realm in academia.[25]

This kind of stereotyping is nothing new. In the 1940s, congresswoman Clare Booth Luce found her disagreements with other women written up in the press as "catfights."[26] In the 1990s, Supreme Court justice Ruth Bader Ginsburg interrupted colleague Sandra Day O'Connor during oral arguments, and O'Connor's rejoinder was printed in *Time* under the headline "Shut Up, Ruth" —never mind that a study of the justices shows that Ginsburg actually interrupted *less* than most of her colleagues in the ten years between 1998 and 2007.[27]

These characterizations are not confined to politics. One woman we spoke with recalled when she and one of her colleagues, also a woman, were pitted against each other in a competition over business. "We liked each other, we got along, we were friends. But we had to play this role, and this role happened to be me against her. So we just went at it just as you would against a guy," she said.

Except it *wasn't* the same as it would have been with a guy. Men have disagreements; women get into catfights.

A New Girl who works for a major company said she was replaced in a leadership position by a man who informed her that he was going to overhaul the entire department. He compared her leadership style to a Greek god ruling over her citizens. In contrast, he was going to be more of a Roman emperor, he told her. The crux of the issue, as he put it, was to "infuse the culture with strategic thinking, because it had previously been led by intuition."

After several months, the New Girl heard complaints from her former employees about their new manager's authoritarian style, but when she went back to ask him how things were going, he said everything was great. He said that he didn't have a tool for measuring his success. He just knew. "Is that sort of like leading with intuition?" she quipped.

Different ways of naming the same behavior have a huge impact on how the conflict and its participants are perceived. Sometimes when women are on the phone at work, it's for a personal call. Sometimes it's a business call. The same is true for men. But bias leads people to interpret the same action differently for men and for women, creating the illusion that men are more serious workers than women are and, once again, reinforcing the very stereotypes that drive the bias in the first place.

Why Biases Arise

Most of us are on automatic pilot most of the time. We couldn't function if we weren't.[28] Think about your morning routine. This morning, you probably woke up, got dressed, brushed your teeth, maybe made coffee. If you put cream and sugar in your coffee, it's because you know you like them, not because you tasted the coffee and decided anew that's how it would be best. If you drove to work, you probably spent the drive listening to music or thinking about a new project or rehashing a conversation you had the day before —not deciding on your route or thinking about when to hit the gas and when to hit the brake. Automaticity provides us with mental shortcuts so we don't have to spend all our time collecting information and making routine judgments.

We couldn't function unless we work on automatic, in most things, most of the time. At the same time, it's where many of our biases begin. Instead of starting from scratch when you meet the CEO of your company, you can start with some useful assumptions about what the CEO is like: smart, ambitious, and worthy of your respect. These aren't negative biases, but they're biases nonetheless. When you meet your child's kindergarten teacher, you'd be more likely to assume the teacher is compassionate, patient, and gentle. Again, not negative biases but biases nonetheless.

Biases start to become a problem when they lead to what Heilman calls "lack of fit"—when assumptions about a particular group clash with assumptions about the requirements for a given role.[29] This comes out strongly in the workplace, because the requirements for many, or even most, jobs are gendered. Social psychologist Peter Glick and his colleagues conducted a study in which they asked students to name any characteristics that came to mind when presented with a specific job title.[30] More than 60 percent of the time, participants listed gender when describing particular jobs; often, they listed gender first. Thus, nurses were described as female, nurturing, and helpful; paramedics were described as male, caring, and quick and alert.[31] Other studies have found that whereas most people use similar terms to describe the typical man and the typical manager, the terms used when describing women and managers overlap very little.[32]

The stereotypical requirements for successful professionals include leadership, assertiveness, sound judgment, and the ability to take control and make tough decisions. Sound familiar? That's because they're also the stereotypical requirements for successful masculinity. Successful femininity, on the other hand, is defined by nurturance, community orientation, and understanding. Prove-It-Again! bias reflects the gap between the assumptions about women and assumptions about professionals, which means that while men get the benefit of the doubt when it comes to professional success, women encounter unconscious beliefs that they're just not a good fit for masculine jobs and have to work twice as hard to get half as far. When it comes to the workplace, common cognitive shortcuts not only aren't useful; they actually lead to false conclusions about women.

If you have any doubts as to the role automaticity plays within your own cognitive processes, try taking the work-family version of the Implicit Association Test, which is easily accessible online.[33] The test presents subjects with male and female names and then asks them to associate a series of words associated with family (home, children, weddings, etc.) or a series of words associated with career (management, salary, office, etc.) with either the male or the female name. Both Rachel and Joan scored a strong association of Male with Career and Women with Family. Even though we're working to eradicate these biases, we share them.

Fortunately, you can lessen the harmful effects that your own and others' biases can have on your career. It helps to have an understanding of the cognitive foundation on which our biases are constructed. We've laid that groundwork. Now it's time to build a strategy that works for you.

*   *   *

Our initial assumption was that women would meet more Prove-It-Again! patterns at the start of their careers and then would graduate to Tightrope problems. But even women at the highest levels of their organizations face Prove-It-Again! problems.

"I bring in millions of dollars of revenue, and then—'What are you going to do for me tomorrow?'" said a top rainmaker for a major firm. "How many times do you have to knock the cover off the ball before they leave you alone? 'I hit a grand slam last year, so they shouldn't be bothering me for years' is what I'm thinking. But nope."

For professional women on the career ladder, Prove-It-Again! bias can make the climb feel like an eternity: two steps forward, one step back, all the way to the top. While this kind of bias can be discouraging, there's growing research showing ways to get around it.

3

Prove-It-Again! Action Plan

Because I am a woman, I must make unusual efforts to succeed. If I fail, no one will say, "She doesn't have what it takes." They will say, "Women don't have what it takes."

—CLARE BOOTH LUCE

Of the many strategies women have for Prove-It-Again! bias, perhaps the most straightforward one came from a general counsel at a Fortune 500 company: "The best strategy for proving it again is proving it again, right?" she said. "If somebody needs you to prove it again, pointing out that that's unfair is unlikely going to actually be successful, and proving it again gracefully is probably the best you can do."

A Catalyst study of women holding the title of vice president or above in Fortune 1000 companies found that a resounding 77 percent of respondents said consistently exceeding expectations was critical. More women attributed their success to outstanding performance than to any other cause.[1] And it's true: most women *and* men who make it to the top have worked extremely hard to get there.

So the most basic Prove-It-Again! strategy is to prove it again. But while hard work may be necessary for success, it's not always sufficient. In the previous chapter, we discussed the subtle biases that make women's achievements fade into the background while men's continue to shine. In this chapter, we'll address specific steps women can take to make their achievements stick.

Strategy 1: Trump the Stereotype

Prove-It-Again! stems from assumptions about how women will behave.[2] As we've mentioned, when we have relatively little information about people, we tend to depend heavily on stereotypes to describe them. Descriptive bias is a function of the shortcuts we use in order to think efficiently.

As a result, this type of bias tends to lessen as we get to know people better. When you think of a mother, chances are you think of a woman who is nurturing, selfless, and patient. When you think of *your* mother, you think of an actual human being with strengths and weaknesses and maybe a great sense of humor or a paralyzing fear of cicadas. A similar principle applies in the office. When people think of a businesswoman, they may think of a hard-driving, emotionless harridan—or an Ally McBeal–type ditz in teetering heels. One way to combat these stereotypes is to make sure people don't think "businesswoman" when they see you but rather think Joan or Rachel or Jennifer or whatever your name is.

When Madeleine Kunin first ran for governor of Vermont back in 1984, her campaign conducted a poll listing her credentials and the credentials of her opponent, John Easton, and released two versions. In the first, the candidates' names were shown at the beginning of the poll. In the second, their credentials were listed first. Kunin came out ahead in the poll in which credentials were listed first—but fell behind in the poll in which the candidates' names were at the top.

As a result of the findings, Kunin later ran a commercial with her accomplishments shown first and ran her name only at end, to level the playing field. She learned from the experience that voters were less likely to stereotype a female candidate if they had her accomplishments at the front of their minds. "If voters have a chance to absorb qualifications first, they are less likely to be influenced by gender stereotypes," she said.

This bit of real-world wisdom is borne out in the literature. As Madeline Heilman writes, there is no single global stereotype of women, and as a result, "providing defining information about women diminishes the ascription of traditionally stereotypic attributes."[3] Sometimes this is as simple as Kunin's strategy of leading with your accomplishments.

To ensure that everyone around you recognizes your competence, you need to have detailed information at hand to trump the stereotype that the typical woman is not suited for career success. So the single most important part of your Prove-It-Again! Action Plan is to keep careful records of your accomplishments with original documents in real time: "I did this pitch; we got that job." "Here's this metric; here's the number that shows that I met and

---

WHY YOU HAVE TO GET ORGANIZED:
YOUR ACCOMPLISHMENTS AT YOUR FINGERTIPS

Women's accomplishments tend to be overlooked, or attributed to luck — and, as we'll see in chapter 4, women have to be really careful about how they self-promote. The most effective way is to have the facts at your fingertips when you need them. To do that, you need to get organized. Here are four simple steps:

1. When someone gives you a compliment, make sure you have a record of it.

2. If it's in an e-mail, thank the sender by return e-mail and keep a copy.

3. If the compliment is verbal, send an e-mail thanking the person for the compliment, making sure you repeat enough of what was said so that someone reading the e-mail understands the compliment and the context in which it was given.

4. If you have a success measured by an objective metric — say you bring in a new client, make a big sale, or win a motion in court — *keep track of it in real time*. Keep a special file for this purpose. Don't put off the record keeping until later. Life moves fast.

5. *Do* spend the time to quantify or document your accomplishments, translating them into objective metrics if possible.

surpassed it." "Here's what the client or my supervisor said about my work." Commentary is unnecessary: let the facts do the talking.

This is a particularly effective strategy in workplaces with a relatively standardized, or at least universally accepted, evaluation system. One Fortune 500 vice president said that when she was a law firm associate, young lawyers were judged on how many hours they could bill and how much business they could bring in. "I satisfied the clients extremely well, and I worked harder than anybody and did more work than anybody," she said.

If you've received a verbal compliment, make your own paper trail. Often you can ask whoever gave it to repeat it in an e-mail: "I am just so flattered by what you just said, and I know my boss would like to know you said it. Any chance you could put it in an e-mail, to me or to him? Do you want me to shoot you an e-mail with the quote as I remember it as a reminder?"

"It's important to document all of the things that you do on the job, so that when it comes time for your performance review, you've got solid evidence," said a consultant.

One New Girl refers to this strategy as "selling your brand." "People think of you in sound bites, right?" she said. "If you don't work at it and convince people to want what you have to offer, if you don't talk about what you can deliver, you become a generic. And generics are cheaper." Another New Girl referred us to the Performance Image Exposure model, developed by businessman Harvey Coleman, which holds that performance is only one small component of success. The other two elements—Image, or deciding how you want other people to see you, and Exposure, or advertising yourself—are just as important and are often overlooked by those who think hard work alone will help them get ahead.

Strategy 2: Get Over Yourself

One of the most common strains of advice out there for women in business subscribes to what we like to call the "get over yourself" theory, which holds that women themselves are the largest obstacle they face in the workplace. (At the time of this writing, for example, one of the best-selling women's business advice books on Amazon was subtitled *How to Change the Patterns of Thinking That Block Women's Paths to Power*.)[4] The solution to women's problems, according to this school of thought, is for them to stop being so darn negative and just avoid those behaviors that keep women down.

Now, everything you've read in this book so far should be starting to make you think that, if you're a woman in the business world, changing yourself is not a silver bullet. But it's true that some traditionally feminine traits can impede women's workplace progress. And the fact is, in many environments, the self-effacement commonly expected of women disserves them.

"If you don't value what you bring to the table, it doesn't matter how much the external world changes. You're still not going to be a very good advocate for why somebody should hire you," said one New Girl.

If you explain away your successes and internalize your failures, it's much easier for others to do the same—at which point your negative opinions about yourself gain external endorsement. This creates self-fulfilling prophecies (technically known as *expectancy confirmation*), as negative stereotypes create a feedback loop that can lead people to conclude that stereotypes are accurate.[5] What's more, a lack of confidence in your abilities can lead to more mistakes, one executive observed. And when you take failure personally, people stop pointing out when you've done badly, because they don't think you can handle it. The overall effect is that people stop treating you as an equal and instead avoid giving you difficult assignments, said an executive, who gave the example of a soccer game to illustrate her point. "A male has a bad day, and he comes back in the locker room, and he says, 'That ref was completely against me' or 'Couldn't get a break' or whatever, and it's all externalized. He shrugs it off, right? But women come back, and they feel like, 'I don't understand. Why was he so against me? I can't believe I let everybody down.'"

The women at one major international law firm observed this pattern among their own, and changed it. "After returning from court, men would stand in the hall and start regaling a buddy in a loud voice," said an attorney at the firm. "You know—'I killed them. I was so smart, and the other side was so dumb. And this was great. And the judge was surprised, and I won.' And women would come back and go into their office and maybe say to a friend, 'Oh, squeaked that one through.'" "So we had a little experiment once," the attorney remembers. "We said, 'Let's all come back from court and let's do that. Let's stand in the hall and go, "Oh, I killed it."'"

One New Girl took this to heart when she and a colleague made a presentation outside their company. "We did okay," she said, "not great but okay." But to her colleague she said, "When people ask you how we did, let's tell them, 'We rocked it.'" So they did, and shortly afterward the head of the company met her in the hall and said, "Wow, I heard you rocked it." Lesson learned—get over yourself and rock it.

One New Girl, when she was interviewing for a new job, had just begun to take depositions by herself. (Depositions are interviews done in preparation for a trial.) But when she was asked whether she had taken depositions, she recalled, "I was, like, 'Yeah, of course.' And I just had the presence of mind to say that because I just dropped right in, and I got to start doing work that was appropriate for my level right away. But I had to skip the uncomfortable, 'Are you really sure you know how to do this?'" "Honesty is the best policy, but it may not be the best strategy," she mused. Of course, she didn't lie. She just displayed the confidence that she could parlay her experience into future successes. And then proceeded to prove herself correct.

Why do women need to do this? "I see men volunteering all the time for things that they don't necessarily know that much about, where a woman sort of feels like she has to have a PhD on the subject before she is going to be qualified to push herself forward in it," explained one woman. "Most women really want to be very, very certain about their answer before they will speak up," said a woman in high tech, whereas "a guy would say, if he's 75 percent confident, he'll throw it out, right?"

Most advice books scold women soundly for this behavior. But what women are doing is a rational response to gender bias: men are more willing to take risks because doing so is less risky. Recall the woman who explained this dynamic: "A man takes a big risk and makes a mistake, that's considered risky, but he's taking a chance; a woman does it, then it's just a big mistake."[6] The advice books are right, though: the women need to bite the bullet. Because many men will, as a result of the intense pressure they feel to "be a successful man"—a man with a successful career. Women don't have this kind of brutal pressure to give us courage; we'll just have to muster up the courage ourselves.

It's a good first step: get over yourself. Stop questioning your own abilities. Be confident and it will increase others' confidence in you. Doubt yourself and others will doubt you. There's a real risk in what one New Girl called "waiting to be perfect," and it's that you'll keep waiting forever. Get over your fear of taking risks, get over your inability to self-promote. Internal issues are a good place to start. But that's only the beginning.

Strategy 3: Know Your Limits

While proving it again is effective up to a point, it has some significant limitations. First, it's just not fair. Women shouldn't *have* to be more competent than men to get to the same place. As college president MaryAnn Baenninger points out, there are consequences to a society that "taught one sex that it had to work harder to gain access, and the other sex that access was guaranteed."[7]

Another problem is that women who prove it again and again often experience burnout, make mistakes out of exhaustion, or work so hard they just decide it's not worth it and quit. In 2010, women made up 47 percent of associates and about 15 percent of full-fledged partners, meaning that most women left partnership track before making full partner.[8] Of course, there are a lot of reasons for this discrepancy—some of the women likely sought careers outside the law firm rat race, and women are both more likely than men to leave the workforce when they have children and less likely to be promoted than men. But, based on Joan's experience of working with lawyers for three decades, some of them just got sick and tired of proving it again and again and again.

Another important point is that sometimes just sitting in your office and proving it through hard work isn't enough. One New Girl noted that when she was just starting out, her attitude was, "I'm not just going to sit here and whine and be a victim, I'm just going to do extremely well." But after years of attempting to prove it again and again, she found herself frustrated, isolated, and demoralized.

Another woman, who started out as a lawyer and eventually left law firms altogether to become an independent consultant, said Prove-It-Again! bias was responsible for her leaving her first job at a law firm. "I was overworked for, you know, three-plus years, and then ended up getting burned out," she said.

The experience of burnout holds outside of anecdote. Claude Steele, a psychology professor at Stanford, conducted a survey of women in Silicon Valley designed to assess how they reacted to being part of a male-dominated workplace.[9] The women from the settings in which they were the most underrepresented were more likely to get to work earlier, stay later, and engage in fewer activities outside of work. It's a logical response to feeling like you're behind, but Steele points out that the added burden of working harder to prove your worth can be stressful and distracting, isolating and inefficient, and can even lower the quality of the work you produce.[10]

Exacerbating these problems, when people are aware of the stereotypes against them, the resulting anxiety can actually impede the quality of their performance. The upshot is a vicious cycle in which people justify bias using the very phenomenon (lowered performance) that the bias causes in the first place. Steele calls this phenomenon "stereotype threat"; one New Girl called it "psychological kneecapping."[11]

Burnout is a particularly acute problem for women because Prove-It-Again! bias doesn't let up as they move up the professional level. In fact, unlike for men—who are often initially subjected to rigorous pressure to work hard that lets up as they gain seniority—the pressures on women can actually get worse as women advance in their careers. That's not news—that's the glass ceiling. One study found that women "have an easier time making the 'first cut' for a position or award, but they have a harder time making the final cut and actually being hired or winning."[12] As a diversity consultant observed, "The women work so exceptionally hard that it's really hard for anyone to be biased against them, because they are going above and beyond many of their male peers." But when employees begin to receive promotions, women often get left behind.

All of this isn't to say you shouldn't work hard, of course. Everyone who's reached the top has probably busted his or her butt to get there. But it's important for women to understand the outside forces working against them, so that the additional pressure doesn't take them by surprise. So prove it again—but know your limits. The only thing more important than giving it your all is making sure you have something left over for yourself.

Strategy 4: Address the Bias—With Kid Gloves?

If you feel you are dealing with a person of good faith who is capable of nondefensive self-reflection, sometimes the best thing to do is to try and confront it directly. We're not suggesting that you, say, accuse the most senior man at your company of sexism. But defending yourself against bias calmly and competently can be extremely effective.

Unconscious biases are unconscious, so sometimes simply bringing attention to them is enough to counter their effects. Once you've put together evidence of your accomplishments, you can go to a superior and make your case. One attorney told us she had laid considerable groundwork for a big lawsuit, only to find it assigned to one of her male partners. She went to a senior partner and asked him what she needed to do to get assigned to the case herself. She started with the positive, she said—she had an interesting docket and was generally happy with her caseload. At the same time, she was curious about why that particular case hadn't been assigned to her and wanted to know if there was anything she needed to do before she got the assignment. "And ultimately, I did get assigned to the case," the attorney said. "I mean, he just literally hadn't thought about it."

At one large firm, a hiring committee was choosing between ten candidates for a position, using headshots tacked to the wall to keep the candidates apart. One woman on the committee noticed that eight out of the ten top candidates looked almost identical: they were all balding white males in glasses. Even their shirts and ties were almost the same.

"Do you notice anything?" she asked her colleagues.

No one said anything.

"Because when I look at those pictures, I really notice some-thing," she persisted.

Finally, someone spoke up. "They all kind of look alike."

"And who else do they look like?"

There was another silence before someone finally said, "Well, us."

In helping the men in the room come to the realization them-selves, the New Girl avoided sounding like she was attacking them or even blaming them. But she made her point.

Accusing someone directly of sexism is more likely to make them defensive than to lead to productive dialogue, agreed one aca-demic, who got tired of hearing men and women compared based on shifting criteria within the hiring committee she served on. At one meeting, she watched as the committee compared a male and female candidate, both of whom had shortcomings. For the male candidate, however, the consensus was that he would grow out of his failings as he matured; for the female candidate, her failing was viewed as fixed and immutable. (Recognize that? "He's skilled; she's lucky.")

"I think we need to judge the candidates by the same standard," said the professor to her colleagues. "Either we look at what they've done and assume that's the way they're always going to be, or we look at what they've done and imagine how a person might grow out of that, but we can't be doing that for one and not the other."

She didn't make it a gender issue. She didn't point out that they were applying one set of standards to the man and one to the woman. But she did make it clear the committee needed to be consistent.

A note of caution: if you feel you are dealing with a bully, the gentle approach is not advisable. Confronting a bully is a big decision; if you do so, a bold approach often provides the most cover. A gentle approach risks tipping off the bully without providing any backup or witnesses and without enabling you to prove retaliation, should the bully take that path. How do you find out if someone is a bully? Let others be the litmus test; ask around. If someone is indeed a bully, someone else likely knows it.

Strategy 5: Play a Specialized or Technical Role

Very few of the women we spoke with said they had experienced little or no gender discrimination in the course of their careers. Of those who did, most either founded their own companies or developed a very narrow specialty, whether they worked primarily overseas, as an outside consultant in their respective industry, or in a very specialized role within their firms.

"I have a niche specialty, so every step of the way I could pretty much write my own ticket if I found a place that needed what I had," said one attorney. "I could say, 'I've got this expertise. I want to have this schedule. I want to have this salary.'"

An attorney we spoke with said she made an effort to be the one to find an answer whenever another attorney sent around an e-mail with a random question about the law. "By the end, I had established myself as the subject-matter expert in a couple of obscure things, but they were obscure things that came up just often enough that people would be directing people to me," she said. "People from all over the country would be e-mailing or calling, saying, 'Can you look at this for me?' 'Can you talk to a client for me?'"

Having a specialty—and excelling at it—is a great way to make your skills known both inside and outside the office and can be a good way to bring in business. The law provides an example. If another law firm finds a client with a problem in an area in which you specialize, it's not uncommon that the other firm approaches you to work with them.

This phenomenon is not limited to law. Many female executives become known as high performers by developing a special expertise, according to a Catalyst study: "Some successful women executives made a point of developing unique skills so as to become indispensable; others built their expertise by gaining external recognition."[13]

But this strategy comes with risks. As warned the National Association of Women Lawyers' annual report on retention and promotion, choose a specialty that's too restricted and you risk becoming what's known in law firms as a "service partner": "If a partner does not have her or his 'own' business, it means that her or his value to the firm inheres in the ability to service other people's clients. Perhaps it's because a given partner is the 'go to' person for Partner X, or perhaps it's because a given partner is a nationally recognized expert in some esoteric legal field. Either way, from the perspective of the firm, if a partner does not pull her or his weight as a rainmaker, that partner is viewed as a service partner."[14]

A related (and perhaps less risky) strategy is to take assignments abroad, where your primary signifier is often your foreignness and not your gender and where you can become your company's expert in a specific country. "It takes you out of boxes, because you don't have peers who are just like you who are competing with you," said a woman who worked in Europe with a healthcare company. "When I look back, I think that one of the secrets to my career was the fact that I was in places where I was free to be a little bit more me, to stand a little bit more on my own two feet and be a little less compressed by stereotypes."

A consultant who also works primarily abroad pointed out that when a company hires her, it simply doesn't make sense to treat her poorly. "When a consulting firm has paid a certain amount of money for me to come and work for them in Pakistan or Kosovo or Russia, are they then going to exercise gender bias once I've gotten there? It's very impractical. It's self-defeating," she said.

One final point. Being in an environment where you have to prove it again and again is exhausting. To survive and thrive, you need to keep your energy up. We don't just mean to exercise, though that's part of it. We mean your spiritual energy, or if that makes you uncomfortable, just call it verve. Recognize what gives you energy and what drains you, both in and out of work. As Joanna Barsh and Susie Cranston, authors of *How Remarkable Women Lead*, argue, it's necessary to move beyond a black-and-white understanding about how both work and home life affect your energy. While many of us see work as a place that drains energy, and home as a place that restores it, that's not necessarily true. "The right kind of work can be exhilarating—when you're so engrossed that you lose track of time. [Likewise] the wrong kind of family time can be debilitating."[15] Know what helps and hurts you, and be deliberate. We'll end this chapter with a wide variety of strategies others have used to keep sane.

* * *

Underlying all the strategies in this chapter is the same basic idea: because Prove-It-Again! is descriptive bias, it can be undercut by individuating information. Someone may have a stereotype about women in general, but the better they get to know you and your work, the more they will base their judgments on specific, rather than general, knowledge.

This is true for whatever part of your identity has you proving it again. All women are women, of course, but beyond that, women may find themselves subject to Prove-It-Again! bias for a whole series of other reasons: race, class, ethnicity, sexual orientation, disability status, and so on—what social scientists call status characteristics.[16] We'll talk in chapter 11 about how biases differ with regard to race, including the added challenge to women of color when it comes to proving it again. We don't have room in this book to take on the multitude of other status characteristics that make up identity, but it's important to emphasize that there are a ton of them and that we're mainly focusing on one.

"TAKING CARE"—OF YOURSELF!

We asked the New Girls what they do to keep themselves balanced and sane. Everyone's strategy was different, but everyone had a hobby or a philosophy that keeps them going. What's yours? Where do you find your energy and strength?

- "I keep going back to the Serenity Prayer. 'God grant me the serenity to accept the things I cannot change, the courage to change the things I can, and the wisdom to know the difference.'"

- "I try very hard to spend one hour each day outside. Some days I don't manage it, but most days I do."

- "Therapy. It accelerates change. You don't need to stay with your same problems. I had to pay money to sit with someone to give me permission to be happy, but it works."

- "Hiking, swimming, gardening, hot baths, and no work on weekends."

- "I try to live a life pleasing to God and to maintain a sense of myself as a spiritual person."

- "I like to disco dance. It's my way of moving my body and not caring what people think of me."

- "Spend time with friends who aren't in the same profession and friends of different ages. As you get older, you don't want all your friends of the same age group. The older ones start dying!"

- "How has nobody said 'drink' yet?"

PART II

The Tightrope

4

Spotting Tightrope Patterns

In the chat rooms around Silicon Valley, from the time I arrived
and until long after I left HP, I was routinely referred to as
a "bimbo" or a "bitch"—too soft or too hard, and presumptu-
ous, besides. —CARLY FIORINA

In 2008, as the presidential election approached, *Saturday Night Live (SNL)* featured a sketch in which Amy Poehler as Hillary Clinton and Tina Fey as Sarah Palin held a joint press conference to address the role sexism had played in their respective campaigns. The women opened with an introduction that segues into a riff on their respective political positions.

"I believe global warming is caused by man," Poehler says.

"And I believe it's just God hugging us closer," Fey answers.

"I don't agree with the Bush Doctrine."

"I don't know what that is!"

"But, Sarah, one thing we can agree on is that sexism can never be allowed to permeate an American election," Poehler says.

Fey nods at the camera. "So please stop Photoshopping my head on sexy bikini pictures."

"And stop saying I have cankles."

"Don't refer to me as a MILF."

"And don't refer to me as a FLURGE. I Googled what it stands for, and I do not like it."

"Reporters and commentators, stop using words that diminish us, like 'pretty,' 'attractive,' 'beautiful'—" Fey says.

"'Harpy,' 'shrew,' 'boner shrinker,'" Poehler cuts in.[1]

The sketch plays up the stereotypes that were repeated through the campaign coverage, which cast Palin as sexy, feminine, and unserious and Clinton as aggressive, masculine, and cold. Given the context, it would be easy to dismiss as a joke. Except these things actually happened. Palin's head was Photoshopped onto a picture of a woman in an American-flag bikini.[2] Fashion consultant Tim Gunn criticized Clinton's "cankles" and general fashion sense on national television.[3] Both liberal Bill Maher and conservative Tucker Carlson have called Palin a MILF in public.[4] FLURGE is a made-up word, but commentator Andrew Bacevich referred to Clinton as a harpy in the online magazine *Salon*.[5] Regardless of your political leanings or your opinion of either woman, the sexism that emerged in the 2008 presidential campaign (and again in the lead-up to the 2012 election) was pretty shocking. The public reception of both Clinton and Palin illustrates the "damned if you do, damned if you don't" quality of femininity. So how do you win? If you're criticized if you're "too feminine" and you're criticized if you're "too masculine," then what's the "right" way to be a woman?

This is the Tightrope women walk every day. Nearly three-fourths (73 percent) of the women we interviewed reported Tightrope problems, with women of color 9 percentage points more likely to report them (77 percent) than white women (68 percent). Nearly twice as many women interviewed reported "too feminine" problems as they did "too masculine" problems (66 percent versus 34 percent). (This is interesting, because "too masculine" problems have received far more attention.) Veer feminine, like Palin, and you're dismissed as frivolous and lacking in substance. Veer masculine, like Clinton, and you're a bitch who's impossible to work with. Palin and Clinton are two extreme examples, but the Tightrope affects almost all women at some point in their careers. As Shelley Correll, a sociologist at Stanford, said to Joan in an interview, "You have to be recognized for your competence. You have to have influence. You have to get other people to be able to go along with your ideas. You need to gain access to informal information or insider information. And you have to do all of this while avoiding being threatening, not upsetting the hierarchy, and creating the sense that you fit in in the organization."

As a woman who works with the investment banking industry observed, if women "play a traditional female role, which is more consensus building and more gentle in terms of team dynamics and looking out for the team, they're considered just too wimpy to have what it takes to succeed in this aggressive culture. On the other hand, when they jump in and they play that kind of investment-banking aggressive, they are labeled as a bitch immediately."

"There's different rules that women have to follow," a professor agreed. "You have to smile more. Your behavior is judged on a different standard. You have to be nice as opposed to assertive and bitchy."

The Double Bind

While women judged as masculine often will be considered for the same opportunities as men, they may also be judged incapable of the parts of the job that require emotional intelligence.[6] Women who are seen as very feminine, on the other hand, tend to be judged as low on competence but high on warmth and are often treated kindly but not taken seriously. If you're "too feminine," you won't get the same opportunities as men in the first place. If you're "too masculine," you'll be penalized for lacking in social skills. Think about Palin and Clinton: both women lost in the 2008 election, but Palin ended up on the reality TV circuit, while Clinton ended up as secretary of state.

Tightrope bias is named for the precarious balance women are expected to strike between masculinity and femininity. While we sometimes assume that men are masculine and women are feminine, the truth is that masculinity and femininity are independent of (albeit frequently correlated with) biological sex. Think of David Bowie or Boy George, both men famous for a style that's usually called androgynous but that's actually just feminine, from their makeup to their glitter to their skintight clothing—or Annie Lennox, who favors short hair and pantsuits and sings in a low voice that's hard to identify as male or female.

People tend to conflate sex and gender and assume that all men are masculine and all women are feminine. That's not how it works. Many feminists, including us, make a distinction between gender and biological sex. Gender is the collection of characteristics that constitutes the social identity of men and women.[7] To vastly oversimplify a complicated theory, social theorist Judith Butler proposes that all gender is at some level a performance.[8]

Understanding gender in this way, rather than as a natural binary, highlights that everyone performs gender somewhat differently, and most of us, regardless of biological sex, have some characteristics typically coded as "masculine" and some characteristics coded as "feminine." People also enact gender differently depending on their circumstances: "Certainly, individuals cannot decide *whether* they want to bring gender into being. But they do have some choices about *how* to bring gender into being," write Devon Carbado and Mitu Gulati in an essay about gender identity at work.[9] David Bowie's Ziggy Stardust persona worked well in his 1972 concept album, but it's an understatement to say it would feel out of place in the boardroom.

In popular culture, women are often grouped into two camps: the femme and the tomboy. Femmes tend to be more traditionally feminine, and tomboys more traditionally masculine. On *Mad Men*, sultry Joan caters to men's stereotypes of women to rise to the top in the feminine position of head secretary (and, spoiler alert, ultimately uses her sexuality to ascend even higher). Peggy, on the other hand, is career oriented and fiercely independent and fights her way into a position traditionally held by men. On *30 Rock*, Liz Lemon is the pajama-wearing head writer; Jenna is the diva obsessed with her looks. Or take Betty (tomboy) and Veronica (femme) from Archie comics. In fact, the femme/tomboy distinction has deep roots, going back at least as far as Shakespeare and perhaps before: see the contrast between feisty Katherina and tractable Bianca in *The Taming of the Shrew*, or in *Pride and Prejudice* between headstrong Elizabeth Bennet and her sweet, trusting sister Jane.

While masculine women and feminine women face different kinds of Tightrope bias, it's important to remember that we're all working through the same issue, which is that success is stereotyped as both male and masculine. As Tina Fey said, the Hillary-Sarah sketch on *SNL* shows the two women experiencing "different sides of the same sexism coin."[10] And while some women are stereotyped as "too feminine" and others as "too masculine," any attempt to remedy one problem risks triggering the other.[11] What that means is that the problem lies not with women but with the underlying assumption that women (and men!) need to conform to a set of expectations that deny important parts of their identities.

MASCULINE TRAITS	FEMININE TRAITS
Aggressive	Affectionate
Ambitious	Cheerful
Competitive	Compassionate
Forceful	Gentle
Leadership abilities	Gullible
Independent	Shy
Individualistic	Soft-spoken
Decisive	Sympathetic
Self-sufficient	Tender
Risk taking	Understanding

This list of masculine and feminine traits is taken from the Bem Sex Role Inventory, the standard test used for assessing perceptions of gender roles.[a]

Either a Bitch or a Doormat

Dozens of studies in the past ten years have shown that, when people are presented with resumes for a male and a female candidate —names changed but all other information the same—the male candidate is generally preferred over a woman with identical credentials. Probably the most famous study involved the resumes of two Silicon Valley entrepreneurs, Howard and Heidi Roizen. Heidi Roizen, as it turns out, is a real person, and the resume was actually hers. Howard Roizen is her fictional alter ego—identical to Heidi in every way except that he's a man.

Stanford Business School professor Frank Flynn gave one of his classes a case study on Howard Roizen and another on Heidi Roizen, changing only their sex and gender identifiers. While the classes rated Howard and Heidi as being equally competent and accomplished, Heidi was deemed to be more "selfish" than Howard and therefore less hireable.[12] Keep in mind that their accomplishments were *exactly the same*. How could something as simple as a name change create the illusion of a whole new dimension of Roizen's personality?

As psychologist Susan Fiske and colleagues write, women—like racial and ethnic minorities—often have to make a choice between being liked but not respected or being respected but not liked. "One envies and respects high-status groups (e.g., rich people, Asians, Jews, businesswomen) for their competence, but one does not like them. And one disrespects low-status groups (e.g., housewives, people with disabilities, Latinos) for their incompetence, but one may like and patronize them."[13] Because of the link between masculinity and status, this means that more masculine women tend to be higher status but at the same time less well liked. More feminine women tend to be of lower status but better liked.

Fiske refers to the bias against masculine women as "hostile sexism" and the bias against feminine women as "benevolent sexism." People's reactions to tomboys are often hostile and defensive; reactions to femmes tend to be patronizing and protective. Both sets of reactions impede women's progress. In fact, in a survey of attitudes in 19 different countries, Fiske and coauthor Peter Glick found that in countries where men tended to display benevolent sexism, they were more likely to display hostile sexism as well.[14] This section discusses both how to avoid the benevolent sexism of being shunted into undervalued, dead-end, traditionally feminine roles and how to avoid the hostile sexism that emerges when you violate people's expectations by refusing to remain in the feminine sphere.

Handmaidens and Good Girls

Some women are very comfortable acting in traditionally feminine ways. Career advice targeted toward women tends to assume that *all* women are like this, which is why much of it tells women we just need to man up.

It is true that some traditionally feminine behaviors tend to hold women back. Modesty is a good example. Studies show both that women tend to present themselves more modestly than men and that a modest self-presentation tends to undermine perceived competence.[15]

Other traditionally feminine behaviors signal deference and subordination, so it's not surprising that they make one seem less commanding. High-status people speak louder and more rapidly than low-status ones, maintain a high level of eye contact with lowered brows and a backward body lean, and are more likely to point.[16] Low-status people are soft-spoken, slump, and make little eye contact.[17] It's pretty clear which style is masculine and which is feminine.

A particularly dramatic example (one that highlights gender as a performance) concerns posture, as documented in a fascinating study, "Power Posing," by Dana R. Carney, Amy J. C. Cuddy, and Andy J. Yap.[18] The study documented that traditionally feminine postures, like sitting in a chair with legs crossed and hands folded, are "low power pose[s]."[19] The authors found that high power posers, male or female, experience increases in testosterone, decreases in cortisol, and increased feelings of power and tolerance for risk. Low power posers not only *looked* less self-confident. They literally *became* less self-confident. (For more on the subject, check out Cuddy's fabulous TED talk.)[20]

Think back to middle school and high school. Being accepted was pretty important. Many of the habits we developed at that time, from our voice pitch to how we sit to how assertive we act, stemmed from an understandable desire to seem normal. But some behaviors seen as normal for women are, in fact, characteristic of low-status groups.

"Men in mixed-sex groups talk more, make more task suggestions, display more visual dominance, use less tentative speech, and are more influential than women," reports sociologist Cecilia Ridgeway, an expert in how status beliefs affect behavior.[21] ("Visual dominance" means looking people straight in the eye.) Men also interrupt more. These patterns do not appear in same-sex groups given a gender-neutral task.[22]

"I think females are less likely to speak up," observed a scientist. She said she prefers to talk to colleagues one-on-one rather than raising issues in meetings, because she worries about "the question or comment being perceived as nonrelevant or dumb."

While women are often exhorted just to speak up, this reluctance may be tied to a woman's quite realistic sense of having more to lose than a man might in a similar situation. Indeed, as a black woman, this same scientist wondered if her "level of timidity" was even higher than that of white women. African American women, as will be discussed in chapter 11, trigger two sets of negative competence assumptions.

Women tend to use tentative, deferential speech forms, especially with men. These include verbal hedges and disclaimers ("I'm not sure if this is correct, but . . .") and posing statements as questions ("Don't you think . . . ?").[23] Verbal deference may feel natural and comfortable for women, but studies show they only do it when men are around.[24] The *I wonder if*'s disappear in women-only groups.

Even more confusing is the feminine mandate to be nice, which has generated huge amounts of discussion and advice.[25] Women are expected to be warm, friendly, collaborative, and nice.[26] Men—not so much. "When men assert themselves, it's quirky, funny or amusing. When a woman does, it's a temper," said a professor quoted in Pamela J. Bettis and Natalie G. Adams's wonderful study "Nice at Work in the Academy."[27] Men are expected to be aggressive, outspoken, unemotional, and competitive.[28] A lab scientist made it clear that the road can be bumpy for women who don't get the memo. "I think that men can get away with 'I don't have time for that; don't bother me with that,'" she observed. "Whereas I and some of the other women in the lab, that would not be acceptable. We're expected to be nice."

The mandate to be nice can also serve to ensure that women behave as helpmeets, taking on the kind of important-but-under-valued tasks that have to be done but that no one gets much credit for doing. "People that don't work hard at being nice just don't realize how much they are taking advantage of other people," a graduate student and full-time administrator told Bettis and Adams.[29] Nice work also can become exhausting.

Look, we're not telling you to be mean. But feminine women get shoved in all kinds of boxes: the Good Girl, who does what she's told and never raises a fuss; the Service Partner, who helps out where she's needed and never takes credit; the Assistant, who finds herself buried in paperwork she can't say no to; the Workhorse, who works hard and keeps her head down and hopes to be rewarded later; and the Flirt, who (everyone knows) isn't afraid to use her sexuality to get what she wants.

The label that rarely attaches to these women is *leader*. As long as women are relatively nonthreatening, they're often rewarded for hard work and cooperation. At the same time, the very qualities that make them successful at lower-level work can keep them out of the running for more prestigious positions. One woman who spent years as in-house counsel at a major corporation said she had seen countless women get shoved aside because they never escaped the feminized roles they adopted as junior employees. "The young ones come up, and as long as they preen and they do all the things that the male executives expect of them, they will last, until they're more seasoned and senior, and then they're no longer the protégés of the men. They're somehow competition, and they're kicked to the curb."

In a lot of professional jobs, long hours and considerable grunt work are expected of all junior employees, regardless of sex. But while men find that they are naturally elevated to higher-status positions, women can end up in a never-ending Groundhog Day of service roles. "If you've been a handmaiden for three years and now you're trying to break out, you're really going to have to prove it," one New Girl said, "because not only are you behind, you're now wearing a sign around your neck saying, 'Handmaiden.'"

"Ambitious women tend to operate as the dutiful daughter," noted an executive officer. "The good girl, dutiful daughter is often who gets promoted but not necessarily who you want to be in charge."

Doing the Office Housework

Even women who aren't interested in traditionally feminine behavior often find themselves pressured into feminine roles. "You definitely see women corralled into these helping kinds of things. Women would get leaned on for the sort of, 'Can you run this?' 'Can you volunteer to do this?' 'Could you serve on this committee?' It didn't translate into pay or advancement. It was just, 'You're a helping kind of person,'" said one New Girl. "And I think if you were to say, 'No, I really can't make that commitment,' then you would be seen as not a team player." The same thing did not happen to men, she said. "They weren't seen as uncooperative. They weren't seen as not a team player. They were seen as, 'Well, of course you should be [compensated]'—if they were even asked in the first place."

And there's the rub. If the men aren't even asked to take on dead-end work, they don't have to deal with the delicate political question of how to turn it down. "They were basically counting on you not to assert yourself." That's what's meant by gender policing. Another New Girl put it like this: "There's a very subtle expectation that [administrative tasks] will be taken up by women"—what she referred to as "housework." One woman, who's a high-level partner at a major professional services firm, said when someone's birthday rolls around, she's still expected to bake them a cake.

Carol Bartz, former CEO at Yahoo! and software company Autodesk, said she was once at a small dinner at Steve Jobs's house for then-president Clinton, along with about ten other Silicon Valley executives. They mostly knew each other, but because of Jobs's association with Pixar, there was an entertainment executive there who didn't know who Bartz was. He came up to her and asked her to get him a cup of tea. "I just said, 'Gee, does it look like I'm the one who gets the tea?'" she remembered. Another CEO who knew Bartz leaned over and explained Bartz's position to the thirsty gentleman.

When Madeleine Kunin was a Vermont state legislator, she became a part of the state's powerful joint fiscal committee, which makes financial decisions for the state while the legislature is out of session. At the first meeting, the committee members voted to decide who would fill various internal executive positions, such as chair and vice chair. One of the other members spoke up to nominate Kunin as secretary.

"No," she answered.

"Well, then," he joked. "We should make you chairman of the Entertainment Committee!"

Kunin declined, controlled her anger, and then expressed herself to that legislator later in the hallway. He dismissed the comment as "only a joke."

One attorney said that when she worked at a law firm, she was constantly asked to take on extra tasks around the office with little or no extra compensation or credit. "Could you serve on this committee? Could you take this supervisory role?" other attorneys would ask her. "It seemed like saying no would not be perceived well, even though it should have been totally legitimate to say, 'No, this is going to take up my time, and it's not worth the investment of time that it would take to do it right, and you're not giving me credit for it.'"

Several women we spoke with said that, despite all their accomplishments, they were still expected to answer phones, make copies, or top off coffee when it runs low. One attorney who said she feels most comfortable in a skirt and heels said even that basic display of femininity meant her co-workers had trouble picturing her in a position of authority.

"Even if people know that you are a very accomplished lawyer who has negotiated multistate, multimillion-dollar agreements and are very well respected by those who know your skill set, they can't see you in a substantive role," she said. "Can't do it. And even if they do start to see you in a more substantive role, it is hard for them to accept you without having a negative assessment of you."

Tomboys

So it's clear that being more feminine can lead women to be shunted to the side and seriously affects their career advancement. The solution should be pretty obvious: man up. If women who act feminine aren't taken seriously, maybe women who act masculine will be.

Except that's not quite how it works.

One general counsel said that in her experience "strong, independent, decisive" women often got stuck with reputations as difficult to work with—which in turn led to decreased opportunities; "They don't get referred business from other lawyers in their law firm. They don't get the associates that they might want to work with. They don't get those associates to work with because they have this bitch reputation."

"Women pay a price for counter-stereotypical behavior, even though it may be required for a successful career," writes psychologist Laurie Rudman.[30] She calls this "backlash." When women manage to be successful at male-dominated jobs, they can overcome stereotypes that women can't fill traditionally masculine roles but instead face a "perceived violation of feminine 'shoulds.'"[31] While they are more respected than their feminine counterparts, they are also more disliked. Women who show agency and leadership, who take control of their environment, and who aren't afraid to make their accomplishments known are often viewed as competent but described in disproportionately negative terms. Many others have similar findings. A study of female managers by Madeline E. Heilman and Tyler G. Okimoto found that "bitter," "quarrelsome," and "selfish" were considered highly characteristic of female, but not of male, managers.[32]

Women who achieve success in the workplace face "social rejection, taking the form of dislike and personal derogation."[33] This kind of backlash not only can hurt women socially but can also negatively impact women's evaluations and their chances for raises or promotions. As women climb the corporate ladder and take on more traditionally masculine roles, these problems often get worse, leading them to be called "*bitch, ice queen, iron maiden,* and *dragon lady.*"[34]

Ann Hopkins, the plaintiff in the landmark 1989 gender discrimination case *Price Waterhouse v. Hopkins*, is a classic tomboy. When she came up for partnership at the accounting firm, she was denied —despite her undeniable qualifications—on account of her interpersonal skills. One colleague described her as macho; another told her to take a course at charm school.[35]

The Supreme Court ruled in Hopkins's favor, holding that the burden fell on Price Waterhouse to show that the firm would have denied Hopkins the promotion to partner even if she had not been a woman, a ruling that was a major victory for antidiscrimination law. Unfortunately, this kind of backlash still happens today. One New Girl, a former vice president at a Fortune 500 company, was coached repeatedly that she needed "not to be so outspoken" and that she "needed to be less apt to call it the way it was." She also remembered a conversation with a supervisor about another woman in their department, who was being demoted to a less prestigious position because she was hard to work with. The New Girl didn't think it was fair that this woman, who was one of the best lawyers in her department, was being transferred and asked her boss why the decision had been made.

"Well, it's her rough elbows," her supervisor answered.

This answer, the New Girl thought, was a classic example of a double standard. "You've got a man downstairs who has the worst rough elbows on the planet, but when he displays those, they always say, 'Yeah, but he's such a good lawyer.'"

Being a Bitch

Some women just don't care that much if other people don't approve of their personal style.

"I'm sure people have said that to me a million times: 'Boy, you act like a guy' or 'Why aren't you more feminine?' or something. And I'm sure I said, 'F**k you, asshole,' and forgot about it like five minutes later," one self-professed tomboy told us.

That's one approach. But for those of us with thinner skin, these insults can be really hurtful. What's more, the backlash against women perceived as bitches can have real effects on career opportunities. One attorney said colleagues often complained about how difficult it was to work with aggressive or competitive women: "Oh well, she's a big athlete. She's a real pistol. I mean, it's great in the courtroom, but my God, it's hard to live with her."

Another New Girl, the managing partner of a national law firm's state practice, remembered the time the firm chairman requested an in-person meeting to discuss the budget. After traveling thousands of miles to see her, he arrived and plopped down into the chair across from her. The New Girl was expecting a discussion about growth and opportunities following a successful seven-figure year. Instead, the chairman revealed the real motivation behind the meeting. Her e-mails, he told her, were too harsh. In fact, they were mean. Given her myriad responsibilities, she frequently sent quick e-mails to save time. She was the chair of the firm's mentoring program, the default purchaser of gifts for the office staff, the one who took the left-behind women lawyers out to client lunches, and the person everyone at the firm came to see when they had personal problems. But somehow, that wasn't enough. The chair told her she needed to spend more time engaging in locker-room talk with the boys. "You're out of your cotton-picking mind, boyfriend," she told the chair.

Quite a number of the women we interviewed felt comfortable with being thought of as a bitch. An executive said, "I tend to push hard on my staff, and I have high expectations. And I think there is an element of people thinking, 'Oh, what a bitch.'" A vice president at a Fortune 500 company said she realized early on that she was never going to be liked by all her staff. "Some people on my own staff called me a bitch," she said. "All good leaders, I think, make unpopular decisions. So I would get that whole thing about the bitch whenever I would do something that wasn't popular."

This isn't to say that women never act bitchy. Hell, men sometimes act bitchy, and so do women. As one New Girl pointed out, the first step in avoiding being perceived as a bitch is to not *be* one. "First of all, I ask myself, 'Are you being a bitch?' And sometimes I am. I have learned that you do not need to be an asshole in any way to be effective."

But even when you're not acting bitchy, you may be labeled a bitch for behavior that would go unnoticed for men. While men may be called "assholes" or "dicks," the threshold of unacceptable behavior for men is considerably higher than for women, and for men poor behavior is often excused with a "boys will be boys" eye roll.

In a *Saturday Night Live* skit called "Bitch Is the New Black," Tina Fey defended Hillary Clinton against people who called her a bitch. "Maybe what bothers me most is that people say Hillary is a bitch," Fey said. "Let me say something about that: Yeah, she is. So am I. . . . You know what? Bitches get stuff done."[36]

"The 'what-a-bitch' thing doesn't happen at lower levels, unless it's a peer, because men would say they're not important enough to really care about," said an executive who's been called a bitch more than once. "You only are going to be called a bitch when you can actually do something to them."

In other words, being labeled a bitch is sometimes an unavoidable side effect of doing your job, which means you may have to make a choice: when it comes down to it, would you rather be a bitch or a doormat?

Backlash

Remember in the previous chapter when we told you that one way to overcome Prove-It-Again! bias is simply to prove it again? That's a good strategy, but it needs to be approached with caution. Because ambition is stereotyped masculine, successful women violate expectations for how women should act, which leads to a greater risk of prescriptive bias.

One woman who works in the health-care industry said she was once passed over for a promotion because she intimidated a male colleague. She had taken an assignment abroad and needed to download several of her responsibilities to a man two levels her senior. But her explanations overwhelmed and intimidated him, she said, and when it came time for her to get promoted, the senior colleague stood in her way. The woman who had advocated most strongly for the New Girl eventually had to tell her that she hadn't gotten the promotion. "All of your bosses wanted you promoted, and it's clear in the sessions that you manage up really, really well," the woman explained. "The problem is you intimidate your peers or the people just above you, and they're worried that that will translate into intimidating people who report to you."

Another woman received feedback early in her career that she was too aggressive, and then, when she made that adjustment, was told the opposite. "Early in my career, I was told that I argued too much, that I needed to pick my battles," she said. "And in some ways, I think I went way too far to the other extreme because, now, the feedback that I get is that I should talk more, make a point."

In one study of backlash in hiring, researchers found that women who said things like "I like to be the boss" and "I like being in charge" were rated as more hirable than women who said, "I like to have plenty of input from the people who work with me"—but as less hirable than comparable men and as having relatively low social skills.[37]

So women need to be seen as competent both at work and at womanhood. As psychologists Laurie Rudman and Peter Glick write, the balancing act many women face is difficult and demanding, "akin to driving over rough terrain while keeping one hand on the wheel and the other reassuringly on passengers' backs."[38]

Sexual Harassment

The issue of sexual harassment provides some of the roughest terrain women need to master. While there wasn't even a word for it until the 1970s, sexual harassment is now such an established form of discrimination that almost every office has a sexual harassment policy. And yet sexual harassment remains a fact of life for many professional women. Who among us hasn't been leered at by a supervisor or heard male co-workers saying inappropriate things about a woman who's not there?

The New Girls reported a wide array of experiences of harassment, from being asked out repeatedly by male co-workers to hearing them objectify other women in the office. "Man, did you see that one that came in to interview? She's hot. I want her for my assistant," is an example of common banter, according to one woman we interviewed.

There are two schools of thought regarding why sexual harassment by men against women happens. One is that it's motivated by male sexual attraction or desire. The other is that it's motivated by power.[39] If sexual harassment stemmed solely from male desire, Professor Jennifer Berdahl has observed, then the women who are the most feminine in looks, dress, and demeanor should be subject to the most severe problems.[40] But that's not what she found. In

---

SMOOTH COMEBACKS FOR ROUGH MOMENTS

In our first meeting, we asked the New Girls how they deal with sexual harassment. These are their comebacks.

When male co-workers are making jokes or inappropriate comments about a woman who's not there:

"I take a mother role: 'You don't want to go there,' or 'Think about what you just said,' or 'What are you thinking?'"

When a married or involved co-worker makes a pass at you:

"I know your wife. She's my friend. You're married. There is just no way that I would ever consider that. So let's not ever go there again."

"You would hate yourself, and we could never be friends. Neither of us wants that."

When "just-one-of-the-boys" joking goes too far:

"You'd do her? That's a shame. She's way out of your league. I hear she goes for guys who don't treat her like a piece of meat."

"Eeeewwww."

When men are sharing a picture of a hot girl:

"You know, that's cute, but it just doesn't do much for me."

a study that spanned both college campuses and workplaces, masculine women reported higher levels of sexual harassment than feminine women did, and sexual harassment was found to be more frequent in male-dominated workplaces than in female-dominated workplaces. What this means, Berdahl proposes, is that "sexual harassment is driven not out of desire for women who meet feminine ideals but out of a desire to punish those who violate them."[41] In other words, one of the functions of workplace sexual harassment is to police women into a specific form of femininity.

Sometimes sexual harassment is driven by one bad actor or a small group of people. Then there's institutional sexual harassment: when a corporate culture is built around male bonding and facilitated by the sexual objectification of women. It's pretty rare these days for people to think it's a good idea to hold meetings in strip clubs, but it's certainly not unheard of for a group of guys to make a trip to a strip club as an unofficial after-work outing. This is worse in some industries than others: one New Girl who works in tech said that the custom of hiring attractive young women to help with industry events is pervasive. "You go to these trade shows, and it's all about the booth babes," she said. At one event, her company had a bar at its booth, along with female servers. A corporate officer decided the women weren't attractive enough and demanded new ones.

That said, many women find themselves in situations in which sexual banter or jokes form the fabric of office bonding—and some women just like a dirty joke or two. This presents women with difficult dilemmas about where to draw the line between harassment and banter. Indeed, drawing that line can be a Tightrope issue in itself. Up to a certain point, what constitutes sexual harassment is mostly subjective; an off-color joke may be just an off-color joke to one woman, while to another, it's an offensive display of aggression. The line between joking with someone and being sexually harassed is often a matter of personal boundaries rather than a hard-and-fast rule, so it's important to be clear when you've left your comfort zone. Also noteworthy is a study by Jennifer Berdahl and Karl

WHEN DOES SEXUAL HARASSMENT MAKE FOR A STRONG CLAIM?

"It needs to be pretty bad before you make a complaint of sexual harassment. The guys who get accused of it just go completely ballistic usually. So I think you need to have a pretty strong claim before you do something really formal about it," said employment lawyer Kathy Dickson.

Legally, there are two kinds of sexual harassment. *Quid pro quo* harassment is when a supervisor or boss conditions a job benefit on sexual favors: if your boss says, "No promotion unless you sleep with me," that's a strong claim. Usually, quid pro quo suits are brought by the woman being harassed, although they may also be brought by her female colleagues, who argue that the quid pro quo dynamic in their office creates a situation in which all the women get the message that they will never get anywhere if they do not submit to the supervisor's advances.

Hostile environment sexual harassment is what Joan calls the "porn on the walls" type, after the case of *Robinson v. Jacksonville Shipyards, Inc.*, 760 F. Supp. 1486 (1991), in which women sued on the grounds of a sexualized atmosphere that, they said, made it impossible for them to function, including lots of pornographic pictures on the walls of their work site. It may include offensive and unwelcome touching, like grabbing a woman's breasts or butt, forcibly kissing her, full-body hugs, and the like, or an offensive and hostile environment, such as multiple lewd jokes, constant comments on women's bodies — "That dress makes her tits look huge," "I'd like to tap that" — or over-the-line "teasing" designed to embarrass and humiliate women who are present. A single dirty joke or offhand comment isn't enough: in order to be illegal, hostile environment harassment must be "severe or pervasive."

Aquino that found that sexual interactions with co-workers may well have negative outcomes even for those employees who enjoy or don't mind it. Whether they enjoyed the experience or not, study subjects who experienced more workplace sexual behavior also reported increased rates of withdrawal from work, including neglecting tasks and thinking about quitting.[42]

For those women who enjoy a certain level of banter, it can be hard to know where to draw the line. One New Girl said she enjoys banter with the boys—but she speaks up when things go too far. "I'm not going to take these kinds of personal conversations about drinking or dating or whatever and feel like I'm discriminated against or like it's any sort of harassment. That doesn't feel real to me. It feels like people interacting and getting to know each other. On the other hand, when there's a true issue of gender bias, I feel like because I'm thought of as one of the guys, I'm expected to dismiss it."

Lesbians

For lesbians, cultural prescriptions as to the "right" levels of masculinity and femininity often feel particularly weighted. The stereotype is that lesbians tend more masculine than straight women, but that's by no means true across the board. Stereotypes of short hair and loose pantsuits aside, the only way to tell a woman is a lesbian is if *she* tells *you.*

Some lesbians attempt to duck the effects of sexual orientation discrimination by choosing not to talk about their sexual orientation at work, which can mean anything from actively hiding a partner or obfuscating weekend plans to simply not volunteering information.[43] This strategy, however, can have unintended consequences: considerably more closeted gay people report feeling "stalled in their careers" than those who are out at work, and the sheer energy it takes to keep such a big secret may impact productivity.[44]

For lesbians who are out at the office, benefits may include having more room than straight women to push boundaries of acceptable gender performance. One woman quoted in a study called *The Double-Glazed Glass Ceiling*, about professional lesbians, said she's noticed that the straight women in her office have a harder time negotiating and asserting themselves than she does. "A lot of the things that in a woman would be seen as aggressive, I kind of get a 'get out of jail for free' card from the men because, 'well she's a lesbian,'" she said.[45]

Another woman in the study said she had observed that women of all sexual orientations take on the persona of a "power dyke" —slang for a professionally successful lesbian. "The power dyke is a very common look around the office, straight or gay, because it's the stereotype of a very strong woman. If you look at the stereotype of a power dyke, a woman who wants to escalate very quickly through the organisation, who doesn't act like a man, but has a very male quality, a corporate quality."[46]

Whether it's because lesbians face less backlash for not being ladylike or because they tend to have fewer family responsibilities and more help or simply because they are more likely to be in higher-paid jobs historically held by men, lesbians have a wage premium of anywhere from 6 percent to nearly 25 percent compared with women as a whole, and lesbians tend to be overrepresented in traditionally male domains.[47] One theory is that, whereas straight women tend to be in relationships with male partners who earn more than they do, there's no such assumption with lesbians, which means that they don't subordinate their careers to their partners'.[48] Another is that they tend to be more comfortable with behaviors traditionally typed masculine than straight women are; the other side of that coin, of course, is that they may also just face less backlash for masculine behaviors and therefore gain more from them.[49]

The effects of intersecting identities are never easy to dissect. Butch lesbians may be disliked and discriminated against for their "display of 'inappropriate' gender mannerisms," or they may get a free pass on some of the backlash straight women face when they act masculine. They may face both of these reactions in the same day.[50]

The Tightrope is a particularly good illustration of the fluid interplay of advantage and disadvantage when women's axes of identity intersect. In the context of Tightrope bias, some lesbians may have something of an advantage over straight women, but that doesn't mean they don't face different types of bias as well—or that their identity as a lesbian will trump their identity as a woman at any given moment.

Dress for Success

There's nowhere that the lose-lose nature of Tightrope bias is clearer than in the literature about how professional women should dress for success. As law professor Katherine T. Bartlett writes, "The 'dress-for-success' literature makes chillingly clear the tightrope women are expected to walk. Women are cautioned to avoid both the 'imitation man' look and the feminine look, both of which detract from their authority."[51]

Dress "too masculine"—a shirt and tie, a pantsuit—and people may think you're not competent at being a woman. Dress "too feminine"—pastel colors, cleavage—and people may think you're not competent or professional.[52]

This double bind is a byproduct of our assumptions about workplace competence: attractiveness is linked to masculinity for men, and therefore reinforces stereotypes about the relationship between masculinity and professional success. (Think Brian Williams.) For women, on the other hand, attractiveness is linked to femininity and can actually trigger negative competence stereotypes. Think about Erin Brockovich. Sure, she's a smart, hardworking, resourceful single mother. But that's not the point. The point is that you can see her bra through her shirt. She dresses like "a dumb slut"—*but she's not!* And there you have the gimmick.

One consultant who worked with a major firm was told at her review that she wasn't going to be taken seriously if she kept looking so good.

"Do you think I dress inappropriately?" she asked her reviewer.

"You're just very attractive," he told her. "You dress beautifully, but that means people aren't focused on you. They're focused on the way you look."

On the other hand, dressing "too masculine" can also lead to backlash. One woman who moved into a relatively conservative workplace said she learned to blend in with her female co-workers by adding a scarf to her pantsuits. "I'd never worn scarves," she said. "I hate wearing scarves. They sort of choke me. But I learned to like them, and I liked the color and all of that. I had to do it."

A New Girl who works in the South says women at her firm don't do business casual, even when it's permitted, because of the challenges it presents to their credibility. "Business casual is a disaster for women here," she said. "You lose some credibility and professionalism just by putting on a sweater and a pair of slacks."

So what's a woman to do? Damned if you dress up, damned if you dress down: that's the Tightrope. That said, every truly successful woman has her own style. For every Hillary Clinton, who once referred to her campaign staff as "The Sisterhood of the Traveling Pantsuits," there's a Ruth Bader Ginsburg, who came to an interview with Joan wearing a pair of dainty lace gloves.[53]

One litigator said that back in the 1970s, she wore pantsuits to court. At the time, a woman in pants was quite the statement, and a male clerk came up to her one day and said in astonishment, "You're wearing a pantsuit!"

The New Girl looked at him calmly. "So are you," she said.

For another New Girl, who favors skirt suits, stilettos, and colorful clothing—"I've never worn a f**king blue suit," she said —it's become a joke among her male colleagues that they always have to wait for her because she has trouble walking in her shoes. High heels are a touchy subject among feminists, but this New Girl pointed out that her shoes actually tip the power balance in her favor. "Who's really in control of the situation?" she said. "They're waiting for *me*."

Another woman said when she graduated from law school, "the way I survived was basically keeping a low profile. Nose to the grindstone, not wearing makeup, wearing my glasses, and bow ties, and doing really good work." It wasn't until several years later that she learned there was another possible approach. "I met this female federal district court judge," the New Girl said. "And she was the one who told me that it was okay to wear makeup, and not only was it okay but it was a good weapon, and that I should be wearing sling-backs in the courtroom to keep the courtroom focused on me. It wasn't that it was a sex thing. It was more that, as a lawyer, you need to command attention. And you might be at a disadvantage as a woman, so you need to use every weapon that you have. What the hell? So, I did. I started doing that, and it made a huge difference."

"Did I go through the bowtie phase, the Oxford shirts and the bow ties and the navy suits?" asks one executive. "Of course, everybody did. But, man, as soon as I felt I could wear a dress with a jacket—and then without a jacket—I felt like my life had changed."

We're not going to tell you what to wear to be successful, because every woman has different tastes and every workplace has different expectations. Wear what makes you feel comfortable, confident, and professional. But there may be times when it's advantageous to dress the part.

Look around your office to see what other women do. Ask a senior woman you trust for her advice. And, as always, the bottom line for avoiding Tightrope bias is to balance the masculine and the feminine. Wear jewelry with your pantsuit. Wear skirts with clean tailoring. Wear whatever you want, but know that you're sending strong signals with your clothing, so make sure they're the signals you want to be sending.

Find Your Voice

There's more of a consensus on speaking voice than on clothing, but it's no less charged an issue. Most of the women we spoke with agreed that it was best to "speak lowly and slowly," as one put it.

You may not even think about your voice pitch as something you can change, but most of us use different pitches for different situations. One consultant told us her husband always knows she's on the phone with a client because she uses her "Mrs. Business" voice.

For a particularly vivid example of the different registers available to one woman, compare a clip of former British prime minister Margaret Thatcher speaking from the beginning and the end of her career. When she became the leader of Britain's Conservative Party in 1975, she famously took voice coaching at the National Theatre to lower her voice.[54]

And it's not just pitch that plays into Tightrope bias. As linguist Deborah Tannen notes in her book *Talking from 9 to 5*, "Conversational rituals common among men often involve using opposition such as banter, joking, teasing, and playful putdowns, and expending effort to avoid the one-down position in the interaction. Conversational rituals common among women are often ways of maintaining an appearance of equality, taking into account the effect of the exchange on the other person, and expending effort to downplay the speaker's authority so they can get the job done without flexing their muscles in an obvious way."[55]

Because male is the default setting in the workplace, what Tannen calls "conversational rituals among men" dominate office conversation. Women are more likely than men to downplay their confidence in a decision, more likely to apologize even when they didn't do anything wrong, and less likely than men to boast of their achievements.[56] All of these patterns can put women at a serious disadvantage when it comes to negotiations.

One former investment banker said all of her first-year reviews said she needed to speak up more in meetings. But when she tried, she found she couldn't get a word in edgewise: the men would interrupt her or each other, and she just couldn't find a place to jump into the conversation. "I still remember the day that one of the VPs taught me to step on the end of a sentence," she said. "This one VP sat me down and said, 'Here's what you need to do. When [your co-worker] is almost done, you start to make your point, and if he doesn't stop, you just say, 'Oh, I'm sorry. I thought you were done.'"

We tend to think of our voice and our speech patterns as in-grained characteristics, like height or eye color, but the fact is we change them, either consciously or unconsciously, countless times over the course of our lives and even our days. Try paying atten-tion to what your voice sounds like in different contexts. Do you use the same pitch when you're talking to your boss, your co-workers, your partner, your children? Do you sound the same right after you wake up and once you've had your first cup (or four) of coffee? Record yourself and listen to the playback—do you sound the same on the recording as you do when you hear yourself talk? Another technique is to think of a domain in which you feel con-fident and authoritative—in which you interact with others (and men) as an equal or even a superior—for many women, this might be in the home or family context; if you bring that same self-image and persona to work (one of confidence, power, authoritativeness, or comfort) and imagine you are that same person in a meeting, this can help you speak up more comfortably and confidently.

Think back to Judith Butler's idea of gender as a performance. We're always constructing our gender identities. While we don't want to tell you to express your identity in one particular way, we do think it's important to understand that the process is always happening. You need to take conscious control of how you present yourself. Know your own voice(s)—and use them.

Projecting Credibility and Confidence

Sitting through a session with Cara Hale Alter, president of com-munications-training company SpeechSkills, is enough to make the world's most confident person self-conscious. She points out the countless little cues we send without even noticing, many of which have a huge effect on others' perceptions of our credibility: the amount of time we hold eye contact, for example, which Hale Alter says should be between three and five seconds (that doesn't sound like much, but try it—it starts feeling a little strange somewhere around second one and a half); or "tail-wagging," Hale Alter's word for swaying around in place, popping your hips, and nodding your head, which she says amounts to apologizing even when you haven't made a mistake.

SpeechSkills gives presentations to both men and women, but once again, there are specific things women need to pay extra attention to. Hale Alter recommends that you distribute your weight evenly on your feet as much as possible and avoid small signs of discomfort, such as self-touch (when you, for example, rub the palm of your hand with your thumb or play with the fabric on your pants) or smiling too much.[57]

Many of the New Girls said they've developed a special consciousness about how they present themselves in professional situations. "I've developed ways of standing a little bit closer, of standing my tallest, of looking up and squaring my shoulders, and not feeling loomed over," said one executive. A former attorney who now works as a consultant said when she's in meetings, she tries to make sure her "body takes up some amount of space, rather than sitting there closed off."

Once again, it all comes back to the Tightrope. Hold yourself in ways that signal weakness, uncertainty, or submission, and you're priming stereotypes of femininity. At the same time, women who carry themselves like men—think Janet Reno or Sue Sylvester from *Glee*—are often derided as butch and subject to backlash for being manly. Rachel is six foot one and has towered over most women and the majority of men she's ever worked with. At the same time, her speaking voice is pitched relatively high, and she wears a lot of skirts and dresses. While many advice books for women might criticize these behaviors as excessively feminine, Rachel has found that they help offset the defensive reactions to her height. Joan, who's also tall for her generation, keeps her hair short and generally wears pants. But she always wears jewelry and has some very excellent shoes.

No matter the balance you settle on for yourself, the most important thing to keep in mind is that, more than anything else, people can sense your confidence level. Whether you tend masculine or feminine, the confidence you project sends strong messages about how seriously you expect to be taken. Not that any of us actually knows what we're doing all the time—but as one officer at a Fortune 500 company said, act like a duck: "Glide on the surface and paddle like hell underneath." "How you ask questions, where you sit in a room, how you dress and carry yourself, all say, 'I like me,'" she said. "That doesn't mean I'm arrogant or insufferable. But it does say there's no self-loathing here."

* * *

Walking the Tightrope can make you feel off-balance. It may require you to rethink some of the givens of your personality— things you laid down in middle school or high school and have considered closed questions for years, things like how you pitch your voice, how you stand, or how you strike a balance between niceness and authority.

Men are much less likely to have to do all this reworking, which (again) shows why office politics is often trickier for women than for men. If you find yourself baffled about how on earth you are going to negotiate the tight space women are offered in your particular job, consider consulting a career coach who can help you find a way to walk the Tightrope without losing your sense of integrity and authenticity.

5

Tightrope Action Plan: Neither a Bitch . . .

When a man gives his opinion, he's a man. When a woman gives her opinion, she's a bitch. — BETTE DAVIS

During a particularly rough week in the 2008 presidential primary season, a voter in New Hampshire asked notoriously controlled candidate Hillary Clinton how she was holding up. She teared up. "It's not easy," she said, her voice breaking.[1] The next day, in a stunning upset, she won the New Hampshire primary. More than one pundit attributed her win to her uncharacteristic display of emotion.[2]

Crying is a huge taboo for professional women—at one meeting, one New Girl asked the others how they handle tears in the office. The answer was unanimous: just don't.

But Clinton is the exception that proves the rule. From the beginning of her political career, Clinton has struggled with masculinity problems. After Bill's election, the Clintons bragged that the American public had gotten "two for the price of one," and Bill put her in charge of what was to be one of the key initiatives of the Clinton administration: health-care policy.[3]

As a result, Hillary got eviscerated in the press. And so she adapted. Her hair offers a particularly good illustration of her negotiation with masculinity: at the start of the Clinton administration, she sported a pageboy held back with a black velvet hairband. Too severe, was the rap: not feminine enough. So, ever the learner,

Hillary abandoned the hairband. She went to her hairdresser and got a shorter, fluffier, more feminine cut. (Note that, as she has entered her own as secretary of state, she sometimes indulges in a no-nonsense ponytail.)

This chapter is for women like Hillary, who are naturally assertive. It's also for women who have been told to "man up" and have found that following that advice led to feedback that they are "outspoken" or "coming on too strong." Both groups encounter backlash for violating prescriptions that women should act feminine.

An important proviso before we begin: telling a woman to act more masculine or more feminine is not in our job description; there's no right or wrong way to be a woman. All the advice in this chapter and the next is only relevant if you encounter a problem you are seeking to solve. If you are tomboy-to-butch or happily rocking stilettos and it's working fine for you, go in peace. But if you are masculine and are encountering backlash or are very feminine and are not being taken seriously, then consider the advice in this chapter and the next *if you decide the job is worth it.* In reading this book, some of the strategies may well cause you to wrinkle your nose or want to go take a shower. Just skip over that suggestion and move on to the next. You may decide it's just not worth changing how you express yourself in order to fit in. After all, keeping your job at the cost of losing yourself makes no sense.

Strategy 1: Be Likable?

For years, the conventional wisdom has been that women don't get ahead because "women don't ask," based on a study that found that 57 percent of men, but only 7 percent of women, negotiate their starting salaries.[4] Many organizations seized on the "women don't ask" phenomenon and started training women to negotiate harder.

This is irresponsible.

You hear all the time that women don't ask but almost never that women who do ask are seen as less desirable hires or as unappealing people to work with.[5] A 2005 study performed several experiments that documented this. The first two were paper-and-pencil tests. One found that both males and females were less likely to recommend for hire female candidates who negotiated for extra compensation and job benefits. The second showed that people were no less likely to want to work with men who negotiated but much less likely to want to work with women who did. Whether the candidate asked simply or assertively had no effect.[6]

The third experiment involved a video of men and women negotiating. Only here did a difference emerge between male and female evaluators. Women did not penalize women who negotiated, but men did—even though the men saw the women negotiators as equally competent as those who did not negotiate.[7]

Women who demonstrate "the same confidence applauded in men" often find themselves facing hostility that can prove a serious impediment to advancement.[8] Nice girls don't get the corner office, as the eponymous book advises, but one study that analyzed the gender differences in our perceptions of agreeableness found that "nice girls might not get rich, but 'mean' girls do not do much better."[9]

Studies suggest that women need to combine competence with likability.[10] This came out in Joan's interviews. "Women need to understand that women who are perceived as bitchy to other women get a bigger demerit than men who are perceived as assholes to other men, because men who are assholes are just competitive and women who are bitchy are no good," said one Fortune 500 executive.

A study conducted by some of the leading researchers in the field tested four different speaking styles for effectiveness. Some speakers tried to persuade subjects using a "high task" style: they spoke relatively rapidly, with few hesitations, and maintained a neutral facial expression, relaxed body posture, moderately high eye contact, and calm, moderately intrusive hand gestures. Other speakers used a "dominant" style: their voices were louder, firmer, and angrier; they maintained more eye contact and had a stern and threatening facial expression and a stiff, backward-leaning posture. Still others used a "social" style: they used a somewhat more pleading tone of voice and a friendlier facial expression, leaned forward more, and used moderately calm hand gestures. A fourth group used a "submissive" style, using the softest, shakiest, slowest voice, with hesitations and stumbles.[11]

No surprise: the "submissive" style was least effective for both men and women. Both men and women who used the "dominant" style were disliked—but likableness affected women more negatively than men. Men found women who used a "high task" style less likable, more threatening, and less influential than men who used the same style.[12] Likability was an important predictor of influence, particularly with men.

What worked best for women was the "social" style. The study's conclusion: "social behaviors enhance influence when combined with competence, whereas submissiveness interferes with influence."[13] Women, to be influential, need to be likable.

Many high-level women reported in our interviews that they spend quite a bit of time expressing interest and concern about the lives of those who work for them. It's expected of women. What's galling is that it's not expected of men. If you decide not to do it, no judgment here. Joan spent years refusing to do this kind of emotion work, most notably mothering of students, on the grounds that she did that at home. She now feels differently. Partly it's that she no longer has small kids at home. Partly, it's part of her rapprochement with femininity—Joan's transition from tomboy to femme is well under way. And part of it is her belief that the solution is not to have women stop reaching out to people but for men to start doing so.

A former CEO made reaching out part of her leadership style. "What most male leaders don't have," she said, "is a real level of empathy. I'm a toucher. I always start a meeting with picking up from the last personal conversation we had. Like, 'We talked about your son, he was having trouble in school. How's he doing?'" Sometimes, she said, "If I see somebody who seems to be detracted, distracted, and edgy and whatever, I'll say, 'You don't seem to be yourself. Is there something wrong? I mean, can I help? Do you need some time?'" They won't necessarily pour their hearts out immediately, she said. "Although most people really want to. But, once you establish that it's okay with me, oh, my God, they'll just jump onto my psychiatrist couch and let me know what's going on. And then I'll go to their manager (obviously without divulging any confidences), and I'll say, 'So-and-So is having a little trouble at home. I think they ought to have some time off' and whatever. And then they'll come back to me and say, 'Well, how did you know that?' And I said, 'Well, I asked.'"

Strategy 2: Balance the Masculine and the Feminine

The single most important message of this chapter is that, while women have taken on masculine roles, feminine mandates remain.[14] So, while men can succeed by sticking consistently with the masculine, women need to mix the masculine with the feminine.

As a New Girl who works in human resources moved up the ranks from a lower-level employee into the C-suite, she learned the importance of adapting her approachable and "highly collaborative" working style to the increasing gravitas expected of someone in her position, likening the ability to balance between masculine and feminine traits to speaking two different languages. "You have to translate. You have to become bilingual and keep the intent of the way of working that's made you highly successful and translate that."

Much of the advice in this chapter boils down to a single word: balance. No one acts either masculine or feminine 100 percent of the time; the trick is to recognize that the balance changes depending on the situation. You're not going to act the same way in a big investor's meeting as you would when a junior employee stops by your office looking for help.

The balance that truly successful women achieve taps into the best parts of masculinity and femininity. A film executive quoted in Alice Eagly and Linda Carli's *Through the Labyrinth* said successful women have learned to be "tough and compassionate, aggressive and morally and emotionally responsible, decisive and creative" all at the same time.[15] It's pretty clear which of those characteristics are gendered masculine and which are gendered feminine. But it's also clear that, gendering aside, they're simply the traits of a good leader.

Strategy 3: Stand Your Ground, with Softeners

Know thyself. Women need to have higher self-awareness than men do, according to sociologists Olivia O'Neill and Charles O'Reilly.[16] In a study tracking female MBA graduates for eight years after business-school graduation, they found that the most successful women were those who displayed masculine traits tempered with high levels of self-monitoring. In fact, the study found that masculinity was positively correlated with success for the high self-monitoring women and negatively correlated with success for the low self-monitoring women.[17] Fortunately, the formula for avoiding the bitch label is simple, even if putting it into effect can be complicated. Just as women who tend feminine need to balance their feminine traits with masculine traits, women who tend masculine need to balance the masculine with the feminine. Softeners can be any of a wide variety of feminized behaviors.[18] Wearing high heels, makeup, or dresses can work, if you're into that. If you aren't, you can make a personal connection with your colleagues or speak in a high voice or smile a lot or just hang pictures of your kids in your office. Take your pick or pick your own.

One vice president at a major corporation said she learned over time that sometimes it could be more effective to listen than to talk. "Even though I had a point of view, I didn't need to voice it. I could figure out a better way of coming around the back side," she

---

STAR GAZING: MIXING THE MASCULINE AND THE FEMININE

How do these stars get away with their characteristic masculine behavior?

Fiercely independent and autonomous (Angelina Jolie) . . .

Assertive and confrontational (Mae West) . . .

The strong silent type (Marlene Dietrich) . . .

. . . they are all visibly feminine

---

said, "because I might actually voice it on the front end and just completely derail whatever it was I was trying to get to."

"As focused as I am, I will soften that around the edges," an executive said. "If I had to choose and somebody had to say, 'She's aggressive' or 'She's lucky,' I always figured it would be better for me if people thought I was lucky rather than aggressive, because it would give me more freedom to operate."

Remember the Prove-It-Again! pattern in which men's successes are more likely to be attributed to skill, and women's are more likely to be attributed to luck? Well, this executive found a way to use that to her advantage. It's a risky strategy, because allowing people to believe you're lucky rather than competent can put them on a hair trigger to challenge your authority when your "luck" runs out. But if you're confident in your competence and how it's perceived in your workplace, being self-effacing about your success can soften people's reactions to you.

Another strategy is to figure out how to frame a traditionally masculine behavior as feminine. One consultant said she realized that the best way to become successful at her company was to be a rainmaker and that her ability to connect with people was her greatest strength when it came to developing potentially lucrative relationships. At the time she began growing her business, the most successful rainmakers were called hunters, for the way they

---

AVOID THE PITFALL OF THE OFFICE MOTHER STRATEGY

Playing the office mother is one way for women to inject warmth into their leadership style. But handle with care: make sure you lose the selflessness that's expected of mothers. The challenge is to preserve the warmth and authority associated with motherhood, while avoiding the ever-sacrificing Madonna — which leads straight to a never-ending round of office housework.

"captured" their clients. "And I always said, 'No, no, no, I'm a gardener. I grow things,'" she told us.

Women mix the masculine with the feminine in a million different ways. There's no one answer. It's up to you to find a softener that feels authentic to you. If it doesn't feel authentic, it won't work.

Strategy 4: Laugh It Off

The benefits of using humor in the workplace are both well documented and obvious. Humor provides a good medium through which to present new ideas and can serve both to create group cohesion and camaraderie and to establish dominance in a group.[19] If you're the only woman in the room, it can help establish a rapport to set people at ease in a sensitive situation and can signal that you don't intend to sit passively on the sidelines. It can be a great way to let men know that their behavior is unacceptable without coming off as, well, humorless. And in the same way that picturing your audience in their underwear makes them seem less intimidating when you're giving a presentation (or so goes the old piece of advice), having a sense of humor can help you maintain your equanimity in the face of things that seem infuriating or unfair.

One attorney told us about a time she walked into a courtroom and realized she was the only woman there out of some 60 lawyers.

Instead of trying to ignore a fact that both she and everyone else present had clearly noticed, she said, "Oh, I must be in the wrong place. This must be the 'How to Break through the Glass Ceiling' seminar." Everyone in the room laughed. The comment let them know that, while the New Girl recognized that she was very much in the minority, she was confident enough not to be bothered by it. At the same time, her joke signaled that she had enough of a sense of humor not to take herself too seriously. In one neat stroke, she countered both the stereotype that women are too timid to compete with men and the stereotype that women in masculine roles are bitches.

A former Fortune 500 general counsel said she frequently used humor as a softener when dealing with her subordinates. "I'm not just bang, bang, bang; business, business, business," she said. "I like to crack jokes."

"You always have to say whatever you're saying with a smile on your face or with a touch of humor," agreed a financial professional. "That's where the self-deprecating charm comes in, and the dry humor."

Keep in mind, though, that self-deprecating humor needs to be used delicately, so it doesn't just sound like you're putting yourself down. One New Girl said she used to make fun of herself as a softener, until one day her mentor just said, "You know what? I just wish you would stop doing that, because it undermines

---

RIFF OFF AN ESTABLISHED SCRIPT

"One style I have seen work is the big sister with the big personality."

"Be warm Ms. Mother 95 percent of the time, so that the 5 percent of the time when you need to be tough, you can be."

"As a young woman law professor, when the class threatened to get out of hand, I turned the light switch on and off—the way a kindergarten teacher does she wants to calm things down. I made a joke out of it."

you." "She was like, 'Why would you degrade yourself?'" the New Girl remembers.

Deborah Tannen notes that the most common form of humor among women is self-mocking, whereas the most common form of humor among men is "razzing, teasing, and mock-hostile attacks."[20] Self-deprecation, in other words, is actively feminized, so it needs to be used with care. Too much self-deprecation can undercut your authority.

But, said one New Girl, regardless of how you show your sense of humor, it's always a good survival tool. "Instead of saying these people are bad or these people are wrong, it's that they're silly, and they're funny, and they're buffoons," she said. "And if you can see them in that way, then they're little instead of big."

Strategy 5: Manage Your Anger

On any given day at the office, there are always going to be a million little things that could tick you off. A junior employee missed a deadline, a colleague teased you about gossiping when you were actually talking business, the copier ran out of toner. But for most of these things, the issue might not be worth spending the political capital it would cost to raise them.

Sallie Krawcheck, who was recently ousted from her position as head of the wealth-management division at Bank of America, has spent most of her career on Wall Street and has seen some of the worst stereotyping it has to offer. "I can't count the number of times I have seen men slam something on a table, even throw something," she said in an interview with *Marie Claire* magazine. "You sort of do a mental eye roll and move on. I can count on one hand—on one finger—the number of tantrums I've seen a woman have. As she was having it, I remember thinking to myself, Bitch. So if *I'm* having that view, it's hard to imagine that someone else isn't having the same view. Women need to operate in narrower emotional channels than men."[21]

WHAT'S BEEN YOUR EXPERIENCE WITH ANGER?

"How else do things change? They change because you care enough, and you care because you're angry, because a principle sacred to you has been violated or threatened.

"If things make you pissed, then figure that out. Like, 'Okay, this makes me pissed about my job: I'm going to go on maternity leave. I saw what happened to the three girls ahead of me on maternity leave. I saw what happened when they came back. That makes me angry. It makes me angry that they got shitty assignments. It makes me angry that they eventually left the firm. It makes me angry they don't have role models in this firm.' So what can I do?

"I can either tolerate the same thing and do the same thing they did, . . . or I can do the hard thing and try to institute social change."

"I guess if I spoke to a lot of our senior men like I really wanted to, I would have been out the door long ago," one New Girl mused.

The typical advice for women is to bury their anger, which reflects the unhappy fact that anger is much harder to navigate for women than for men. We don't think burying your anger is necessarily the best choice—and frankly, it's not always possible. Anger is a human emotion as inevitable as happiness or hope.

But you do need to make sure you're intentional about how you *show* your anger. Angry women can trigger stereotypes of high-powered females as ball-breakers or, alternately, as hormonal nutcases—making it all the more important for women to remain in control of their anger rather than allowing it to control them. Women of color face a series of additional challenges in the form of racialized gender stereotypes like the angry black woman. We'll get more into the specifics of how these stereotypes affect women of color in chapter 11, but anger is a stumbling block for women of all races and ethnicities.

According to business professors Victoria Brescoll and Eric Luis Uhlmann, it's particularly important for women to offer a concrete external attribution for their anger.[22] Explaining why a situation makes you angry subverts stereotypes by tying your anger to an external cause. Instead of being cast as an "angry woman," you become a woman who is angry.

It also helps to show anger sparingly. "If you're usually a relentlessly positive person, and you are really angry, I think it gets people's attention," said one professor. She added that it has the most impact when you can avoid diluting it with other emotions, such as panic or insecurity. One attorney told us she rarely gets angry, but when she does, she makes sure it's clear on her face—a trick she picked up in the courtroom that's just as applicable in the office. Because it happens so infrequently, she said, it tends to get people's attention and make it clear that there's a problem.

"So, if I have a witness who is prevaricating all over the place, I employ a stony visage," she said. "Jurors will look up, if they're sleeping, and judges will put their pens down. Everybody will look at me like, 'Is she going to lose control?' But I do it very clearly. And what it does to the witness is unsettle them. And that's the object. If I can unsettle the witness, then I can get under the skin of this fabric, and we usually hear what really needs to go on. And then, he'll usually say yes to whatever I tell him."

"Just really pick your battles and think about, long term, does it matter?" an executive said.

While some of the women we spoke with said their strategy was to "never let them see you sweat," many other women said anger, deliberately deployed, was a good negotiation tool—or even just plain necessary. The strategy that you use depends a lot on your personality; Ursula Burns, the CEO of Xerox, said she values authenticity above all else. "One of the things that I was told early on is that you should never let them see you sweat," she told the *New York Times*. "I remember hearing that and saying: 'Oh, my God! I think that they have to see you sweat.'"[23]

One New Girl remembered being given her salary for a new position, which was a promotion. She had previously been involved in human resources management and knew what comparable salaries looked like. She believed the amount being offered was significantly lower than was appropriate.

"Is that it?" she said to the manager who told her.

The man was taken aback. "Yes, that's it. I thought you would be happy."

"I'm not," she said simply.

"Well . . . do you want to talk about it?" the manager responded.

"Best I not talk about it now," she said, ending the conversation and leaving his office. The manager, she later learned, scrambled to address her concerns, stepping in on her behalf to lend support for her getting more money.

Note that the New Girl wasn't hiding her anger. Instead, she was signaling very clearly that she had control over it. Said one New Girl, "It's very important to let people know that you know you're being angry. I say, 'I know that I seem really angry here, but I am angry.' Saying it that way makes me sound a lot more firm and bold but not so shrill and what have you."

When you do show anger, it's important to do it in a way that doesn't humiliate the subject of your wrath. (This is also a good way to be a better human being.) From a strategic standpoint, it's particularly important for women to allow subordinates to save

---

WOMEN ARE WORSE NEGOTIATORS FOR THEMSELVES THAN FOR OTHERS: WHY?

In a study of people participating in an executive training program, women negotiated $141,643 for their own salaries — but when negotiating for others, the salary figure climbed to $167,250. Why? Two reasons come to mind. One is that women themselves are probably aware, at some level, of the penalty imposed on women for self-promotion — so when negotiating for themselves, they hold back. Even if they don't hold back, the pushback against self-promoting women probably makes women negotiators less effective when negotiating for themselves than for others.[a]

face. Tannen writes that men have been found to be more cautious about criticizing a superior than criticizing a subordinate, while for women this pattern is reversed, perhaps because displaying anger at a male subordinate risks violating two separate prescriptions: first, the prescription that men should hold more authority than women, and second, the prescription that women should be understanding and forgiving.[24]

One way to deliver constructive criticism is to have this conversation behind closed doors, said one executive, rather than hashing out the issue in public. Another executive said being clear that you find the situation—and not the person—unacceptable can go a long way toward maintaining diplomatic relations. This goes back to the earlier discussion about internal versus external attributions for anger.

"It's very important to distinguish between 'This situation is making me angry. This is not a viable solution. I don't think this is going to work' and 'You're a bad person,'" the executive said.

Enlisting the person who has annoyed you to help reach a solution to the problem is also a strategy that we heard over and over again. Specifically, framing your anger as a question, rather than a statement, helps soften it and comes with the additional benefit of forcing the person you're angry with to really think about his or her actions and motivations. If someone has made a decision you don't agree with, instead of saying directly that the decision was wrong, you can ask him or her to help you understand it. This approach avoids casting blame on any individual, which can keep people from getting defensive.

One executive said she started out relatively combative but soon realized it was more effective to frame her criticism as a request for help. "Instead of saying, 'You've a bad guy, and you've got to change your behavior,' I was saying, 'I'd like to do this, and I could use your help. What do you think?'"

Strategy 6: Let the Facts Speak for Themselves

The principle of self-promotion is simple: you can't expect to get credit for accomplishments no one knows about. But for women, things get complicated fast. For one thing, women are socialized to be self-effacing and to underplay their accomplishments—and when they do advertise their achievements, they're often subject to backlash that self-promoting men don't face.

Fortunately, the New Girls had lots of ideas on how to make sure other people know just how awesome you are, without making it look like *you* know you're awesome, too. One longtime attorney said she was always "fond of guerilla stealth."

"I don't come out leading with my accomplishments," said a woman in the finance industry. "I let the accomplishments kind of come out in the course of the interaction. Not being a 'toot your own horn' person defuses the situation."

Another New Girl remembered being in a meeting with leading lawyers from around the world when the subject of how to globalize law firm relationships came up. Her firm had relationships with several international corporations at the time, so she talked about her role in handling those relationships. "And I was doing it for two reasons," she said. "One was to actually forward the discussion, but the other was to credential myself."

One attorney said that whenever there was good news in a case she was working on, she made sure to disseminate it quickly to her partners, which allowed her to "stay on top of the message" and meant that an update on good news was seen as just that—news —rather than as self-serving. Making sure your team's achievements are recognized is part of being a good leader—but if you're savvy, it's also part of making sure your talents as a leader are recognized, too. Sociologist Cecilia Ridgeway notes that women in mostly male groups gain higher status and influence if they appear group-oriented than if they appear self-oriented.[25] Call it strategic femininity.[26]

There are other subtle ways of advertising your achievements that don't come off as bragging. In a *New Yorker* profile titled "A Woman's Place," Sheryl Sandberg remembered the first year she was invited to *Fortune* magazine's Most Powerful Women Summit. At first, embarrassed by the title, she refused to put it on Google's Web-based calendar. (She was working as a business-unit general manager there at the time.) The conference's organizer chided her for being timid and failing to own her power, which Sandberg described as an "Aha!" moment.[27] Something like listing prestige engagements on your company's Out of Office page is a great opportunity for sneaky self-promotion, because if questioned, you can always hand the responsibility to someone else. A sociology professor said she always tells people to display the awards that they've won and make sure their resume is widely available. If you're asked to share a bio about yourself, she said—on your company's website, perhaps, or with other attendees before a conference—don't be afraid to go a little over the top. People will usually assume someone else wrote it for you, and anyway, chances are that everyone else's will be over the top, too.

Strategy 7: Use the "Strom Thurmond Principle"

One of the more irritating realities of the workplace is that some men expect women to behave in specific, feminized ways. You can try to avoid working with these men or simply ignore their expectations, if you're not interested in catering to their bias. But several New Girls said this kind of old-fashioned sexism can actually be a way to approach men who otherwise may dismiss powerful women altogether.

One New Girl, lobbying on a client matter, needed to meet with Strom Thurmond, the legendary conservative whose record included staunch opposition to racial integration. As a liberal woman, the New Girl knew she wasn't in the best position to get through to him. Normally matter-of-fact and professionally garbed, the New Girl selected a pink suit and heels for the meeting and carefully coordinated her makeup to her clothes. It worked. Senator Thurmond gave the New Girl his full attention, and she ended up with his cooperation. "If you really want to influence someone, you have to start where he is and move him forward," the New Girl said. "You can't stand here and say, 'Come to me.'"

The Strom Thurmond principle is that when men are very committed to traditional masculinity, it's sometimes possible to use that to your advantage. Acting feminine can be a way to get traditionally masculine men to let down their guard enough to hear what you're saying. Some people are willing to do this. Others aren't. It works because, to quote legal theorist Catharine MacKinnon, "one genius of the system we live under is that the strategies it requires to survive it from day to day are exactly the opposite of what is required to change it."[28] If it makes you feel icky, don't do it. If it feels like a warm embrace from your Barbie days, it may well work for you.

Another example of making masculinity work for you is to flatter men by invoking associations with chivalry—what kind of a man would turn a blind eye to a damsel in distress?

"Being beaten by a woman is kind of a different thing than being beaten by a man," said one executive. "I've always been very conscious that men like to feel responsible for your success. So then the question is, how do you take it to that next level, where they want you to have success that they may not have envisioned and can't control?" The answer, she said, is to signal loyalty to those who have helped you out. "I've never been afraid to be gracious," she said. "And I don't mean, like, smarmy gracious, but I mean to actually acknowledge in a very heartfelt way that a lot of what I have is because of what they've given me, instead of resenting that somebody else had to give it to me."

Strategy 8: Round Up a Posse

As a young law professor, Joan got an e-mail from her colleague Peter with the subject line "Leti did a good thing." Peter described how Leti, another professor on the faculty, had helped a student get a prestigious public-interest fellowship. A few months later, Joan got another e-mail—this time from Leti, about one of Peter's accomplishments.

Both Leti and Peter had a reputation for being team players rather than self-promoters. They didn't *have* to be self-promoters—they had formed a posse, a group of men and women who trumpet each other's achievements and publicize each other's work. Having a posse brag on your behalf helps keep backlash at a minimum, because not only does it get your name and your accomplishments out there, it also makes clear that you have allies and supporters of your work. In return, of course, you do the same for them.

"It's much easier to speak up and promote someone else than yourself," noted sociologist Shelley Correll in an interview with Joan. "Women who are connected to each other and to supportive men and get in the habit of promoting each other—this is the way women's competence gets noticed without it looking self-promoting."

A posse can also help with, for example, Stolen Idea bias: one New Girl (we'll call her Caroline) said she had a supervisor who would notice when one of her contributions was overlooked and "would literally say, 'I want to go back to something Caroline said a minute ago that we didn't seem to give fair vetting.'" If Caroline had tried to say that herself, it might have looked like whining. Having someone else stand up for her allowed her to keep her distance from the issue and gave the challenge greater weight.

*　*　*

For many women—particularly feminists of Joan's generation—advising women to act more femininely borders on heresy. After all, femininity may be associated with submissiveness, for all the reasons we discussed—and when many of the New Girls were starting out, it almost always was. But it turns out that there are a lot of qualities associated with femininity that can help you significantly, if you use them strategically.

The takeaway from this chapter is that feminine behavior isn't always weak. Adopting certain feminized qualities can make you a better co-worker—and a better person. We're extremely lucky in that as women we're able to take the best qualities traditionally ascribed to masculinity and femininity and combine them. In the next chapter, we'll discuss some traditionally masculine behaviors you can play with as well to find the balance that works for you.

6

Tightrope Action Plan: ... Nor a Bimbo

I don't mind living in a man's world as long as I can be a woman in it.
— MARILYN MONROE

The February 2013 issue of *Cosmopolitan* magazine includes an article in which Mika Brzezinski—a cohost of MSNBC's *Morning Joe* as well as author of the women's business advice book *Knowing Your Value*—provides readers with "The 5 Best Work Rules I've Learned." In Rule Number 3, "Don't Be Left Holding the Mop," Brzezinski recounts a conversation she had with Elizabeth Warren: "Elizabeth Warren, the newly elected senator of Massachusetts, shared with me that she 'held the mop' for too many years. You're probably thinking, Huh? But it makes sense: Early on as a Harvard professor, she took bad teaching shifts because the men said no. There's a fine line between paying your dues and knowing when to say no."[1]

The January 2013 issue of *GQ* magazine, on the newsstands at the same time, contains an "Office Party Survival Guide," which promises readers "eight face-saving tips for surviving the night with your job, reputation, and arrest record intact." Tip Number 2 may seem familiar, if a little off: "2: Never Offer to Help with Planning or Cleanup—You may as well tattoo the word *lackey* across the small of your back. Real company men leave the piddly-shit details to others so that they have more time to think of bigger, bolder ideas. What if we sold a hot dog inside a taco shell? Think about it."[2] The advice is basically the same; the tone is totally different. In fact, "Just Say No to Office Housework" is our Strategy 1 for this kind of Tightrope bias. But it's clear in the contrast between the tone in *Cosmopolitan* and *GQ* why saying no can be so tricky for women. When *GQ* says "real company men," what it really means is "real . . . men." The small tasks and sacrifices that keep the workplace running are all too frequently left to—and expected of—women.

The difference between "Don't Be Left Holding the Mop" and "Never Offer to Help with Planning or Cleanup" is all in the framing. It turns out this is the most important part. If you were to walk into your office blustering about tattoos and tacos, you're more likely to end up with a reputation as a jerk than with a raise and a promotion. The strategies that follow provide ways to get what you want while avoiding some of the backlash that women may face if they depart from the roles expected of them.

Strategy 1: Just Say No to Office Housework

The "mop" that Elizabeth Warren refers to in the Brzezinski article is well-known to many professional women. People often assume women are a perfect fit for office housework; what, exactly, this means varies a lot from industry to industry. In law firms, it's serving on low-power committees like the diversity committee and the associates committee. Committee work is office housework in academia, too: time-consuming and undervalued. Of course, organizations *say* that this committee work is valued, but research shows it's just not.[3] And then there's the stuff that even *looks* like office housework: taking notes, answering the phone in a conference room, being asked to order lunch or go get something in the middle of a meeting.

All junior-level professionals have to do ministerial tasks, accurately and uncomplainingly, but here we are talking about something different: when women, but not men, are assigned ministerial tasks that are often time-consuming and undervalued.

**WHAT WOULD THEY SAY IF SOMEONE ASKED
THEM TO GET COFFEE?**

Liz Lemon, from *30 Rock*: "What the what?"

Joan Holloway, from *Mad Men*: "My pleasure, gentlemen."

Ally McBeal, from *Ally McBeal*: "I'll have my secretary do it."

Smurfette, from *The Smurfs*: (silence)

Leslie Knope, from *Parks and Recreation*: "How much chocolate syrup do you want in it?"

Kima Greggs, from *The Wire*: "You f**king with me, son?"

Carrie Matheson, from *Homeland*: "I don't have time for that! An American POW has been turned."

It's well-worn advice but worth repeating: if you're going to find any kind of balance on the Tightrope—or anywhere in life—you'll need to learn to say no. Women from all careers and job levels are often relegated to service roles, as one component of Tightrope bias is the expectation that they will do traditionally feminine tasks simply because they are women. The only way to interrupt this pattern in your own life is to stop saying yes to assignments or requests that take up your time without advancing your career.

"Would you ever just say, 'No, stop doing that. You really need to stop saying yes to me?'" a career consultant pointed out. Of course not. If you have someone who's constantly willing to do menial tasks, you're not going to tell them to stop.

Another New Girl told us about a vice president who sat her down at her first job after business school and told her, "You have to have a mindset that you work for yourself." "Every company that you work for, what they ideally want is they want you to work 24 hours a day, seven days a week," the woman told her. "It's a natural thing that any good company wants from good employees, and it's up to you to draw the boundaries. A company is never going to draw the boundaries, and don't expect them to. You have to draw the boundaries."

It can be hard to know how to say no without burning bridges or seeming like you're not a team player. (Note the sports metaphor—the "not a team player" label is particularly weighted when applied to independent women, as it implies they're doing a bad job both at femininity and at masculinity.)

"At the end of the day, you have a fantasy of saying, 'I'm not going to do this anymore, I'm going to say no,' but then you go back to work the next morning, and you end up doing the same thing again," one New Girl said.

Many of the women we talked with said the best way to opt out of menial assignments is to provide an alternative way to get it done. A female marketing director at a law firm noticed that male partners often asked the female marketing staff, in a very offhand manner, to take notes during certain types of planning discussions. She coached the women on her staff to take preemptive steps by speaking privately with the male group leader before meetings, when they could suggest in a neutral way that it might be helpful and a good educational opportunity to ask junior associates (several of whom were male) to attend the planning discussion and to be responsible for a meeting report.

The trick is to say no without triggering the charge that you are "not a team player." If you can convince your employer that they're better off letting you reach your full potential, rather than wasting your resources doing menial tasks, you can maintain your community orientation without getting pushed to the sidelines

"It's a persuasion game to some extent," said a senior partner at a major law firm. "How could I explain why what I wanted to do was better for them than what they wanted me to do?" She said she managed to escape being bogged down in extra projects by allowing herself only one "scut-work assignment" a year. Instead of simply saying no to projects she didn't want to take on, she would provide alternative solutions for getting the project done and explain the

---

SMOOTH COMEBACKS FOR ROUGH MOMENTS

These are some things New Girls have said when they were asked to do things way below their pay grade. Of course, if you're more of a minimalist, there's always a classic "Sorry. No."

COMMENT: "It's Stephen's birthday tomorrow. Can you bring in cupcakes?"

COMEBACK: "Do you really want somebody who's being paid what I'm being paid to make cupcakes?"

COMMENT: "Hey, the coffee's out. Do you think you could make another pot?"

COMEBACK: "Let's make a rotational list. We can put all our names up and take turns."

COMMENT: "Can you order sandwiches for the meeting today?"

COMEBACK: "The receptionist's right out front. She knows where we usually order from."

---

other work she had that prevented her from accepting scut work. For example, she said, if she were assigned what she called "take-care kind of stuff," she would explain that she had a lot of work for important clients, with whom the firm wanted to maintain a good relationship. Then she would suggest an alternative solution for the task at hand. By framing what she wanted as good for the firm, the attorney managed to balance the masculine imperative toward results with the feminine imperative toward selflessness and got what she wanted without seeming self-centered or rude.

Strategy 2: Make the Housework Work for You

Being able to say no is a nonnegotiable requirement if you want to get ahead. But you don't need to say no all the time, and you may not be able to. Sometimes work that isn't high profile or prestigious is nevertheless important, like organizing a diversity committee or a mentoring program. Not only is it sometimes okay to take on undervalued jobs, there are ways to work it to your advantage.

One task many women have complained about is being asked to take notes during meetings, a gendered assignment that harks back to the days when the only professional role a woman could have was as a secretary. At the same time, one New Girl pointed out that the person who takes notes holds the power of the pen. If she doesn't agree with something someone says, she doesn't have to include it. If no one brings up a point that she thinks is important, she can add it into the record. Obviously, there are limits; don't step over the line into the unethical. But just because a job is gendered feminine doesn't mean it can't be powerful.

Feminized work can also be used as a springboard to more concrete forms of power. One attorney in charge of her law firm's women's initiative used the visibility that role gave her to run successfully for an elected position on the Executive Committee.

This strategy, however, takes planning and intentionality. Something like a women's or diversity initiative is often treated as an afterthought. One woman who works at a professional services firm said she often ends up doing traditionally undervalued work, but she's found that negotiating forces people to recognize the value in what she's doing. "By saying no, it means that they realize it's hard to find people they can trust to get it done," she said. "It lets them come to their own realization that, 'Actually, this must be hard. . . . There must be some skill to it.'"

The tendency is to assume that women do office housework because they enjoy it, which buys into stereotypes of women as nurturing and inherently selfless. But nice work is *work*: it takes time and resources, and it can be done badly or well. Really pushing back on why people think you're the best person for a particular job makes them think about the skill that goes into it and sheds light onto an area of work that might otherwise remain invisible.

In order to ensure you're getting the credit you deserve, here are five things you can ask for when you're taking on a new project:

1. *Take something off your plate.* If you're already busy, don't take on a new project without taking something else off your plate. If the work you're already doing is too important to pass on, the person giving you your new assignment is likely to see that and back off.

2. *Get credit for the time you spend on the project.* Depending on how your company counts work—billable or nonbillable hours, compensation credits, etc.—the credit is going to look different, but you need to make sure that the hours you put into the project are somehow reflected.

3. *Negotiate for a higher-status team member to help you out.* That way you can build a valuable connection with someone at your company, and his or her reputation can lend gravitas and prestige to the project.

4. *Ask for a direct report to a higher-up.* Again, this will help you make connections with powerful people at your company and give you a chance to talk about your project with someone who has real influence.

5. *Secure a budget.* First of all, if you don't have money, you're not going to be able to get anything done. But what's more, the funding you get also tells you a lot about how seriously your company is willing to take your project. It's no secret: money is power.

6. *Establish a sunset and a succession plan.* Working on a low-prestige project for a year or two is fine—particularly if it's something that matters to you. Just make sure you don't get stuck there after you need to have moved on, and have a succession plan in place so you don't get stuck in a dead-end indefinitely.

More generally, while deciding whether to take on a new assignment, there is a series of questions you can ask yourself, an HR manager told us. "If I want to be able to be seen as a credible voice at the table, then what do I need to do in order to do that? If I don't want to get caught in these double binds, then how do I need to move and act? Do I become part of it, or do I stand outside of it and say, 'Not for me, folks'?"

You need to answer these questions honestly. There's no black-and-white answer about what work is personally or professionally rewarding. If your workplace really values diversity, you can leverage a role as a diversity officer into genuine political power. If all your superiors care about is the bottom line and your goal is to advance in your organization, then you'd better make it clear that's where your priorities lie as well.

HOW TO CONVINCE YOURSELF TO HIGHLIGHT YOUR ACCOMPLISHMENTS

Think of it this way: Most people are fair. But they are also busy.

Expecting them to take time out of their busy schedules to ferret out what a totally fabulous job you are doing is not really fair to them. It's demanding too much of their time and attention. You need to make it easy for them by providing the information they need to know what you're up to.

Another point: Remember that men are much more likely than women to highlight their accomplishments. They do this for two reasons. First, men are under such pressure to be "successful men" that many feel they have no choice but to act ambitious. Also, men are socialized into "mine's bigger than yours"–type banter that may make it feel more natural for them to brag. Many men won't think twice about putting themselves out there. If you want to be in the game, you need to do the same.

Be careful, though: bragging is often seen as more unseemly in women than in men. Look back at chapter 5 for tips for how to highlight your accomplishments without triggering backlash.

Strategy 3: "Doormat Nice" versus "Gender-Neutral Decent"

We're not going to tell you to stop being nice. But we are going to urge you to think about what being nice means.

One woman interviewed for "Nice at Work in the Academy" deftly separated decency from doormat: "I don't want to be known as nice. Polite, respectful, considerate, compassionate, maybe a person who steps back and takes a second look before making a judgment call, but not nice."[4]

The key is to keep the one and lose the other. Another woman made the decision starker: "The first choice is to be nice to everyone and do whatever they want. And you know, just fit in and that kind of stuff. The second one is to be better than everybody and then you don't have to be nice."[5]

"As you evolve in your career, you realize you're just not going to be friends with everyone and that's okay," an in-house lawyer told us. "It doesn't mean you can't work well with them. I am the prototype of the 'girl who wants to be liked,' and so my personal challenge is it makes me uncomfortable even to say that, but with experience I've come to peace with the idea."

Remember, this is work, not a popularity contest. If you have to choose between being respected and being liked, go for the respect every time. If the coin of the realm at your job is that being nice means being self-deprecating, don't go there. As an athletic director who had been fired told the authors of "Nice at Work in the Academy, "If you have to choose between competent and nice, choose competent."[6]

Strategy 4: Stop Apologizing

In *Talking from 9 to 5*, Deborah Tannen discusses the role that ritual apologies play in everyday speech. Women, and men to some extent, say things like "I'm sorry" even when they know they haven't done anything wrong: for example, when other people don't understand them, when giving criticism, as a sign of solidarity. It doesn't necessarily mean the speaker is sorry—but it can send the message, albeit inadvertently, that you're in the wrong even when you're not.

Tannen links this tendency to women's training to "take the one-down position" in social interactions.[7] Women's conversational patterns tend to lead them to put themselves down, with the implicit understanding that their conversational partner will lift them up again. For example, say you had an appointment for a phone call with someone in a different time zone. The scheduled time comes and goes, and no call. An hour later they call and explain that they were confused by the time change.

"Oh, I'm sorry," you say. "I should have been clearer about which time zone I was working with." The expected response to such a statement is then for the caller to deny your apology and issue one of his own. Women, Tannen writes, are more likely to use this style of conversation and expect their apologies to be interpreted in this way. Men, on the other hand, are generally taught to "avoid the one-down position and develop strategies for making sure they get the one-up position instead."[8] While Tannen is careful to point out that neither strategy is inherently more or less valid, the divergence in style ends up disadvantaging women, who are left issuing an apology and looking weak as a result.

One New Girl said she is consciously unapologetic when she had already decided on a plan of action. "You don't have to ask for somebody else's feedback before you're going to tell them something you know you're not going to change your mind on," she said. "I actually think about it and try to adopt the grounding of 'I'm not going off on a harebrain unless I have the facts and have thought it through and understand that what I'm about ready to utter is right.' And if it's right, I'll say it to anybody."

A former vice president at a Fortune 500 company said she noticed the younger women at her company being forced into positions subordinate to men. When one of them came to her for advice, the vice president told her to stop apologizing—advice she didn't hesitate to give because "there's no way she could become so aggressive or outspoken that she'd cross that line." "Don't apologize. Don't try to go back and prove it over and over and over again. Take the stance here that you've already proved it, okay? And approach it that way, because if you allow them to, they will back you down every time and make you keep proving it."

You don't need to remove apologies from your repertoire. Apologizing sometimes is what decent people do; it can be a perfectly valid softener and a good way to avoid backlash. And keep in mind that it's okay (and even speaks well of you) to apologize when you

---

CRY ME A RIVER

We all know there's no crying in baseball—but what about at the office? The majority of the women we spoke with said they avoid it at all costs. But a few said it could actually be a source of power.

One of the New Girls told us her physical response to anger is to cry. Instead of trying to suppress it, she's clear about what it means: "When I'm crying, it's because I'm pissed. This is what it looks like when I'm mad," she tells people when she starts to cry. "I mean, when I'm crying it's not a weak emotion. It's the strength of anger."

Crying tends to make the men in the room uncomfortable, but this New Girl said she's found she can use that discomfort to her advantage.

Most people generally take a dim view of crying in the workplace, finding it unprofessional or even manipulative. And yet Facebook COO Sheryl Sandberg recently garnered a lot of attention for admitting, "I've cried at work. I've told people I've cried at work."[a]

The tension around crying ultimately comes down to power and how much of your power you want to give away. If you're as powerful as Sandberg, you can afford to give away a little of your power. Just make sure you have some to give away first.[b]

actually make a mistake or even occasionally—to the right audience—as a show of solidarity. Just be sure to apologize because you've done something that warrants an apology, rather than as a general social lubricant. If you're the type who tends to come off as arrogant or antagonistic, it could help you to apologize more. If you feel like you're being marginalized or not taken seriously, take a second look at your conversational style, and stop apologizing when you're not in the wrong.

Strategy 5: Flirt—Carefully

Whenever the topic of office flirting comes up during a New Girls' Network meeting, the conversation picks up. Flirting is a big part of how women relate to men and masculinity, and the question of when, if ever, flirting is okay at the office always garners some pretty impassioned responses.

"How many people flirt occasionally at work?" Joan asked at one meeting.

Every single woman there raised her hand.

"I *only* flirt in the workplace," one New Girl said.

Although the subject of workplace flirtation is a taboo one, the fact is that most people admit to doing it. In a *Harper's Bazaar* poll on workplace behavior, 86 percent of female respondents said they would "happily flirt with a male colleague if it meant they got their own way"—a finding that prompted UC Berkeley researchers to conduct their own study on whether flirting does, in fact, help professional women get ahead.

The findings of the study were mixed. The female negotiators who "engaged in flirting behaviors"—smiling, leaning forward, touching their faces or hair, and speaking animatedly—were found to be more likable than the male negotiators and no less competent. At the same time, they were found to be less authentic and more manipulative, consistent with the finding that "flirting is perceived as superficial and exploitative of one's appearance and sexuality."[9]

USING YOUR SEXUALITY AT WORK

Lillian Kraemer, who was first in her class and a member of the *Chicago Law Review*, stormed into the law review office, throwing books everywhere and berating her (male) colleagues. She was trying, and failing, to get a job at a Wall Street law firm.

"You guys are all getting jobs," she said. "I'm never going to get any jobs. I rank higher in the class than you do. What am I going to do?" Someone suggested she go talk with Soia Mentschikoff, one of the early woman law professors and the first woman to teach at Harvard Law School.[c]

"Where do you stand in the class?" asked Mentschikoff. When Lillian said she was first, Mentschikoff's advice was this: "Wear a little black dress that subtly does something for you and a small silver pin."

"What do you mean? What does that have to do with my ability to be a lawyer?" Lillian demanded.

"Lillian," Mentschikoff replied patiently, "have you tried wearing a little black dress and a small silver pin?"

"No."

"Well, try it and come back and tell me what happens."

Lillian did as she was told and immediately received several job offers. "From that day to this," Kraemer said, "I have never interviewed in anything other than a black dress and a small silver pin, and I have never not gotten an offer since that time."[d]

This took place in 1964. How much have things changed? A 2010 article on *Glamour.com* suggests a "trusty sheath dress" for summer interviews.[e] In 2012, legal website *Above the Law* published an interview that quoted NYU professor Anna Akbari saying, "In interview situations in particular, women should always wear a skirt or dress, as it is heavily favored over pants by interviewers (many of whom are men)."[f] We like to think these strategies are overly cautious—but do you want to risk it? Some will. Some won't.

Merriam-Webster's Dictionary defines flirting as "to behave amorously without serious intent."[10] At the risk of sounding didactic or just plain obvious, *without serious intent* is the operative phrase here. If you want to put a man at ease, a little bit of playful banter and a smile can be a good way to establish a rapport. We've found that it's best after that to set clear boundaries; what exactly that means depends on your personality and situation.

"I think it works because there's humor in it," said one New Girl of her flirtatious style. She said she learned how to flirt from her mentor, a private equity manager with a penchant for low-cut shirts.

"She would go see a client, and depending on the client, there was a little less cleavage showing for some and a little more for others. And she just said, 'That's me.' She was voluptuous. I learned from her that I could be flirty and there was nothing wrong with being flirty. And I only once ever had a client cross the line and perceive that flirtiness as anything but having fun," the New Girl said.

Playful smiling, teasing, and joking—as long as everyone involved is comfortable—can be an accepted form of currency in the workplace. Condemning anything that could be construed as flirtatious, one New Girl said, "takes away a potential tool that can be very effective."

"Flirting? I'd call it efficiency," said a banker quoted in a *Forbes* article on the subject.[11]

At the same time, if you're not comfortable with flirting in the workplace, don't do it. As one New Girl said, "If you don't flirt in life, don't flirt at work." It's not going to make other people comfortable if you're doing something you're not comfortable with —and with flirting, you need to be highly attuned to the reaction you're getting, and stop immediately if either you or the other person begins to be uncomfortable.

*   *   *

This chapter and the one preceding it were some of the hardest we had to write. Telling readers the "right way" to be a woman is exactly what other advice books do—and what we're trying to avoid. Gender is one of the most complex parts of identity, and it's not for anyone else to decide what it means to you.

In fact, some of our biggest disagreements as coauthors came up as we were working through the Tightrope. Joan was adamant that the advice be separated along "too masculine" and "too feminine" lines; Rachel felt most women face challenges from both directions and favored a more integrated approach. In some situations, we even saw different types of bias: where Joan saw "too masculine" bias in the outside pressure placed on women to perform menial tasks, Rachel saw "too feminine" bias in the devaluation of important nice work. (This type of difference, we'll discuss later, is pretty consistent with the generational divide among feminists.)

These are the tensions that will always come up in discussions of Tightrope bias, and we hope to continue to work through them. The end goal is that we stop gendering basic traits like assertiveness, anger, or community orientation and seek out ways to be balanced and effective humans without worrying about how that impacts the presentation of our gender. Until then, it's helpful to understand the stereotypes that shape how our behavior is processed and interpreted and to understand how to work them to our advantage.

PART III

The Maternal Wall

7

Spotting Maternal Wall Patterns

What is the rudest question you can ask a woman? "How old are you?" "What do you weigh?" "When you and your twin sister are alone with Mr. Hefner, do you have to pretend to be lesbians?" No, the worst question is: "How do you juggle it all?"

— TINA FEY, *BOSSYPANTS*

In 2003, the *New York Times Magazine* published an article called "The Opt-Out Revolution" detailing eight women educated at Princeton who dropped out of the workforce after having children. In the wake of the feminist revolution, the article implied, women were rejecting successful careers, driven by personal choice or biological imperative to stay home with their children.

"I don't want to be on the fast track leading to a partnership at a prestigious law firm," says Katherine Brokaw, who holds degrees from both Princeton University and Columbia Law School. "Some people define that as success. I don't." She had left the workforce shortly after the birth of her first child and was, at the time the article was published, a stay-at-home mom to her three children.[1]

The article quotes several other women like Brokaw—highly educated, highly skilled women trumpeting their choice to leave the workforce. They all affirm their decision to drop out of the workforce to have kids, citing their joy in motherhood or an irresistible biological pull. You have to read far into the article before it begins to seem like maybe the "choice" these women made wasn't so much of a choice after all.

"I wish it had been possible to be the kind of parent I want to be and continue with my legal career," Brokaw muses, "but I wore myself out trying to do both jobs well."[2]

In a country where the workplace is structured around an ideal worker who's on call 24/7 and motherhood is characterized by the model of a mother always available to her children, it's hard to balance work and family. No news there. What's more controversial is to call this phenomenon gender bias, but when 82 percent of American women—and 76 percent of women with an advanced degree—have children at some point in their lives, how can we call it anything else?[3] Some women drop out of the workforce, abandoning careers they've spent decades building and becoming economically vulnerable in the process. Other women keep working and become subject to criticism about their parenting or their commitment to their jobs or both, placing them in the uncomfortable position of being the broken ones, the women missing the gene that drives women back to the home, where, the story line goes, mothers belong.

"Women with families who have made it to senior positions, they're considered freaks," said one consultant. "In fact, we call ourselves the freaks." Of the mothers we interviewed, 59 percent reported Maternal Wall problems.[4] Mothers of color were more likely (63 percent) to hit the Maternal Wall than white mothers were (56 percent). But remember that most of the women of color interviewed were scientists; these findings may reflect racial differences or hostility to mothers in science or both. Fully 68 percent of scientists with children reported Maternal Wall bias.

These new findings about the prevalence of Maternal Wall bias, combined with prior findings about the strength of Maternal Wall bias once it is triggered, contain some good news and some bad news.[5] The bad news has been discussed: once Maternal Wall bias is triggered, it can have very strong negative effects. The good news is that not all workplaces are infected by it. Just over 40 percent of the mothers we interviewed reported no Maternal Wall bias. So if you encounter it, beware—but also be aware that you could probably go elsewhere and find someplace without this bias.

Opt Out or Pushed Out?

The problems mothers face in the workplace are as perennial as journalists' search for a good story, which is probably why the opt-out story line just won't go away. In the summer of 2012, former State Department official Anne-Marie Slaughter published an article in the *Atlantic* magazine, titled "Why Women Still Can't Have It All," that quickly became one of the most read stories in the magazine's history and brought new life to a debate that had slipped into the background. Slaughter, who left a position as Director of Policy Planning at the State Department to be more available to her troubled 14-year-old son, argued that the current structure of the workplace makes it impossible for most women to be professionally successful and happy with their family life.

Slaughter's article marked a new and welcome attention to the forces that push women off the fast track. All too often, the decision to leave one's career is framed as motivated by a biological *pull*, erasing the effect of the bias and discrimination that *push* mothers out of the office and into the home.

"There's a misconception that it's mostly a pull toward motherhood and her precious baby that drives a woman to quit her job, or apparently, her entire career," said former teacher Sarah McArthur Amsbary, who was quoted in "The Opt-Out Revolution." "Not that the precious baby doesn't magnetize many of us. Mine certainly did. As often as not, though, a woman would have loved to maintain some version of a career, but that job wasn't cutting it anymore. Among women I know, quitting is driven as much from the job-dissatisfaction side as from the pull-to-motherhood side."[6]

In a 2006 study of Wall Street, sociologist Louise Marie Roth examined a sample of 76 MBA graduates who began working at

Wall Street securities firms in the early 1990s. She found that 32 percent of women she studied were motivated by family responsibilities to leave their high-powered trading roles for less demanding jobs; 36 percent of women described experiencing some form of pregnancy discrimination or seeing it in action against someone else.[7]

"When I was pregnant, people I sat immediately with, they just did not think that I should come back to work," said a trader. "So they were mad at me if I did, and would say right to me, one of my bosses and another MD, would say, 'Who's going to raise your children? Don't you think that you're the best person to raise your children?' They would give me lectures every day. 'This is a serious thing. You're bringing someone into the world.'"[8]

So do women really "opt" out—or are they pushed out? Pamela Stone, author of *Opting Out? Why Women Really Quit Careers and Head Home*, quotes marketing executive Patricia Lambert, who left her job after she realized her decision to go part-time had pushed her off the fast track: "I decided to quit, and this was a really, really big deal because I never envisioned myself not working. I just felt like I would become a nobody if I quit. Well, I was sort of a nobody working, too. So it was sort of, 'Which nobody do I want to be?'"[9]

Two-thirds of the women Stone interviewed for *Opting Out?* had tried to adjust their job or work schedule in order to accommodate family responsibilities before deciding to quit. A study of Harvard graduates found that women who work in non-family-friendly jobs were more likely to quit after they have children.[10] Women were less likely to leave professions in which family-friendly policies are more available and less stigmatized than were women in professions in which the opposite was true. Women with MBAs were more likely to quit than to switch to a family-friendly job—though MBAs working in family-friendly jobs before motherhood were no more likely to quit. Women with law degrees were more likely than MBAs to shift to a family-friendly job—something Joan takes particular pride in, given her 15 years of work, with Cynthia Thomas

Calvert, to create quality part-time schedules for women lawyers.[11] "A woman's work environment plays a causal role in 'pushing' her out of the labor force at motherhood," concludes the study.[12]

Stone also noted that 40 percent of the women she talked to dropped out after their first child—meaning that 60 percent didn't drop out until after their second child, sometimes continuing to work until their older children were as old as 15.[13] Contrary to the perception that women who leave the workplace are prompted by "a 'last straw' moment like an epiphany," Stone found that "it was deliberate and thoughtful, long and protracted, complex, and except for the women who had always intended to stay home, difficult and doubt-filled."[14]

While none of the New Girls left the workforce for good, several took a step or two back for a period of time to spend more time with their children. One New Girl remembered confiding in an older male mentor about the difficulty of balancing work and family demands. He suggested she reduce her hours and step back some. "Nobody at my firm had ever done that, and I had never been tempted to. Ever," she said. But the mentor was persuasive, and she did end up going part-time. It was the right thing for her family, she said. "But, it was such a career bender it was unbelievable." The New Girl ended up moving to a new firm, and even then she has trouble shaking the stigma that had attached to her. "It lasted for a very long time, even though I never worked in the new firm part-time for a day in my life," she said.

"What I found most disturbing was the more active pressure for women to change career paths," another lawyer said. She remembered one young associate whom she described as "terrifically talented." When the associate had her second child, the head of her group approached her and suggested that she consider switching from the partner track to a counsel role, which involved less responsibility and limited career mobility. He assured her that she could get back on the partnership track when she felt less overwhelmed. But, the New Girl said, in her experience people who took a break rarely returned to their prebreak roles.

The Big, Bad Wall

And so we come to the Maternal Wall.[15] A study conducted by sociologists including Stanford's Shelley Correll found that when subjects were given identical resumes, one but not the other belonging to a mother, nonmothers received 2.1 times as many callbacks as equally qualified mothers and were recommended for hire 1.8 times more frequently than mothers.[16]

When Correll first saw the results of the study, which were published in a paper called "Getting a Job: Is There a Motherhood Penalty?," she said excitedly to Joan: "I have been studying these kinds of gender biases for years, and I have never seen effects this large."[17]

The magnitude of the bias against mothers makes it a rewarding research subject, but that's not good news for working mothers. The Maternal Wall may well be highest in academia. "She had a Caesarian section, and three days later she was teaching," recalled a scientist of her colleague. "I don't want to be perceived as not doing my job because I have a kid."

Said one New Girl about a female colleague, "People would say in pitch meetings, 'She has four children,' as if she was a Flying Wallenda or something, and she would get very irritated. 'Why are you talking about my children? Why aren't you talking about my competence?'" Another professional noted being shocked by a woman she met in 2010: "this very young woman who confessed to me that in her workplace she could not put pictures of her children in her office because she felt that evidence of motherhood was an automatic detriment to her career, that people would make assumptions about her commitment."

These were not flattering assumptions. Recent studies have shown that mothers are subject to descriptive biases that lead others to see them as warm but not competent.[18] This translates to an acute form of Prove-It-Again! bias: mothers are seen as more feminine than women without children, making them less likely to be hired or promoted than equivalent men or childless women.[19]

If all women are forced to toe the line between being seen as "too masculine" or "too feminine," the Tightrope is even trickier when women have children. Mothers are both more likely to be sidelined for being seen as prioritizing family over work and more likely to be seen as deficient in their devotion to work. Few people these days would dream of calling a job unsuitable for a woman— and yet people encourage mothers to step back from demanding environments all the time.

"I've heard partners say, 'I'm not going to use this associate on any of my cases, because she has four kids at home,'" said one attorney.

Another New Girl remembered an associate at her firm who had fantastic reviews, a solid book of business, and was well liked by her peers—but who was nevertheless denied partnership two years in a row. When another partner asked why the associate had been overlooked yet again, the response was simple: "Oh, she has two kids."

"The ideal worker is expected to be unreservedly devoted to work, while the ideal mother is expected to invest similarly intense levels of devotion to her children," explains Stephen Benard and his coauthors. "As a result motherhood is perceived as incompatible with high levels of work effort."[20]

The reason that discrimination against mothers is often viewed as culturally acceptable is that it frequently shows up as benevolent, rather than hostile, sexism. Benevolent bias can be ignored or overlooked because it's grounded on genuinely good intentions. But that doesn't mean it doesn't have serious negative effects on women's careers. As Supreme Court justice William Brennan famously said, benevolent sexism (which he called "romantic paternalism") "put[s] women, not on a pedestal, but in a cage."[21]

"I Had a Baby, Not a Lobotomy"

"Since I came back from maternity leave, I get the work of a paralegal. . . . I want to say 'Look, I had a baby, not a lobotomy!'" said a

Boston lawyer quoted in a well-known study by law professor Deborah Rhode.[22] Because mothers are stereotyped as nurturing and family oriented, that image comes into conflict with stereotypes of professional women as cold and career driven. As a result, regardless of the actual quality of their work, mothers can find themselves working even harder than childless women to prove their competence and commitment again and again. Joan's Center for WorkLife Law clinic runs a hotline for mothers who have faced workplace discrimination. One of the callers' major complaints is that they have to prove themselves all over again after they get back from maternity leave.

A consultant at a major firm told us about an opportunity that came up for her to go abroad for a project while she had young children. It was a good opportunity for advancement, and it was only six months in duration. But when she expressed interest to the partner she was working with at the time, he was quick to tell her that pursuing the project would be a mistake. "No, no, no," he said. "You don't want to do that. You've got your young kids. I know what that's like. It wouldn't be a good thing for you."

An attorney told us she had observed a similar thing happen to a young woman in her office, who came up in a conversation about potential candidates for an open position. "The discussion was about, 'Well, she wouldn't be able to do that job, because she has kids and she can't travel. And, you know, she shouldn't be away from home that long. And this job wouldn't suit her,'" she said.

The job that the committee decided the young woman wasn't capable of filling happened to be a prerequisite for promotion. They all agreed that she had the competencies and skill set to perform her duties. They just assumed that she wouldn't—or shouldn't—want to travel because of her family responsibilities. It's hard to imagine the same thing being said to a similarly situated man.

As we discussed in chapter 2, Prove-It-Again! bias occurs as a result of the close association between leadership and masculinity. Because mothers are seen as even more feminine than women as a general category, the lack of fit is even greater for women with children. When women have children, they can find themselves suddenly shunted from the "career woman" category into the "mother" category, leading to a ramping up of negative competence and commitment assumptions.

Prove-It-Again! bias against mothers is much the same as Prove-It-Again! bias against other women—only more so. For example, just as women's mistakes are noticed and remembered while their male peers' are overlooked and soon forgotten, people are particularly primed to remember instances when mothers' family duties interfered with their work and to hold it against them. Men or childless women, for whom such absences are likely to be seen as a fluke rather than part of a pattern, get off the hook much more easily.

One attorney said that when she became a partner, she gained access to all her old performance evaluations. In her second year as an associate, she had missed one meeting to take a child to the emergency room, and for years afterward that featured prominently in the assessment of her commitment. "After that incident, year after year, there was a question about my ability to become a partner, my commitment to the law, and whether, because I had three children, it would just be too much." "I traveled all the time, I was in the court all the time," she said. "I missed *one meeting* because I had to take my child to the emergency room, and that kept getting highlighted in my evaluations."

The other Prove-It-Again! pattern that comes out particularly strongly for working mothers is that even when they're actually working, there's a tendency to assume that any absence is due to family rather than work responsibilities. "I think it is definitely true that if a woman is not in the office, there is an assumption that she is doing something with her kids, whereas that is not true for the guys," said one New Girl.

Motherhood leaves some women feeling they have to start proving it all over again. One career counselor observed, "There are women who do an incredible job after the first pregnancy. And still there's a doubt. Every pregnancy they have to re-up their commitment because maybe this is the one that's going to take them out."

All this sounds depressing. Don't despair. Remember that this does not happen everywhere. Other women return to the office after maternity leave to find supportive colleagues and policies. Keep that in mind if this section rings too true.

Walking the Tightrope—With a Stroller

Bias against women often is subtle. Bias against mothers often is not. If you're a working mother, chances are you've had someone tell you, "I just don't know how you do it." It's meant as a compliment, but it rubs many women the wrong way.

"Whenever I hear somebody say that, I want to smack them," said one New Girl. "Maybe I'm overly sensitive about it, but I always feel there's this sentiment underneath the comment that says, 'You must be completely messing up.'"

Another woman, a partner at a professional services firm, said that when her children were younger, she often left conversations with the men she worked with feeling like she was being "slammed in some way." "I can't tell you how many men have said to me things like, 'Oh, my wife is at home because, of course, she feels that her children come first.'"

Mothers face two double binds. One is an exaggerated form of masculine/feminine Tightrope bias. Because mothers are stereotyped as nurturing and, well, maternal, behavior that departs from that expectation may meet backlash. One Fortune 500 executive remembered getting angry with a colleague while she was seven months pregnant: "I started just giving him my mind."

"Hold on," the man said to her. "You're pregnant!"

"I'm not raising any wimp in here," she answered.

Mothers also face an extra double bind in addition to the masculine/feminine Tightrope all professional women walk: good workers put their job first; good mothers put their children first.

"If you're being a good lawyer, you're not a good mother, and if you're being a good mother, you can't be a good lawyer," one woman said dryly. "If you're staying all night at work, there's no way you can be a good mother. And if you're asking to go home early or trying to get permission to work from home, there's no way you can be a good professional."

This is a type of prescriptive bias, explain the authors of "Cognitive Bias and the Motherhood Penalty": "Employers discriminate against mothers because they believe mothers *should* be home with their children. Mothers who demonstrate high levels of commitment to paid work violate prescriptive stereotypes about the appropriate place for women."[23] This study found that mothers who are seen as particularly accomplished are penalized at work because they are seen as bad mothers.

Said one New Girl, "I mean, I'm not even a mother myself and I see it all the time. The kind of 'Oh, she must be off with her kids,' or people saying, 'She doesn't see her kids. This is no kind of a life.'"

Maternity Leave

In the ninth season of the television show *Friends*, character Rachel Greene has a baby and takes maternity leave from her job at Ralph Lauren to care for her. In the episode "The One Where Rachel Goes Back to Work," Rachel and the baby's father, Ross, stop by the office to introduce her co-workers to their daughter. When Rachel ducks into her office to pick up some of her things, she finds a strange man at her desk.

"Who the hell are you?" she asks him.

"I'm Gavin Mitchell, the person who's taking over your job," he answers.

"Wait a minute," she says. "What do you mean, you're taking over my job?"

"Well, while you were on your baby vacation, I was doing your job."

Rachel panics and decides she needs to come back from maternity leave two weeks early, in order to make sure she still has a job when she comes back. She goes to Ross and tells him what happened.

"Listen," she tells him. "Sudden change of plans. My maternity leave just ended. They told me that if I didn't come back today, they were gonna fire me."

"What? No, that's illegal. I'm gonna have the Labor Department down here so fast they won't even—" Ross begins.

"All right, all right," Rachel interrupts him. "Calm down, Norma Rae. They didn't actually say that. I'm just afraid if I don't come back right now this guy's gonna try to squeeze me out."[24]

Friends is a sitcom. And because it's a sitcom, Rachel and Gavin make up by the end of the episode (and make out in the next one). Rachel keeps her job and her previous responsibilities.

OUR FAMILY-HOSTILE PUBLIC POLICY

Roughly 95 percent of developed countries have 14 weeks of more of maternity leave, as do about half of African countries, 30 percent of Asian-Pacific countries, and about 25 percent of Latin American and Caribbean countries.

The United States is the only developed country that has no nationally mandated paid maternity leave. The United States is joined by only three countries: Liberia, Swaziland, and Papua New Guinea.

The United States also lacks many other provisions that help reconcile work and family in other countries. These include worker protections such as mandatory vacations, part-time parity (proportional pay and advancement for part-time work), limits on mandatory overtime, and the right to request a flexible schedule. The United States also lacks high-quality, subsidized child care, after-school programs, and adult day care. It even lacks paid sick days.

As a result, Americans report higher levels of work-family conflict than do the citizens of other industrialized countries.[a]

Often that's not how it works in real life. One consultant remembered a former supervisor who became frustrated because some of his employees on maternity leave refused to give him a date for their return. "It kind of colored his whole view of women that go on maternity leave," the New Girl said.

Women on maternity leave often fall victim to an "out of sight, out of mind" mentality. "Then when they come back, it's 'Oh, my, gosh, I forgot about you. Now, we have to do something with you.' And the issue is that people expect that they're not going to have much time available, so they don't put them on the big assignments," the consultant said.

Another New Girl said in her experience women can sometimes run into problems even before they've had a child—or after they've had one child and proven that they can have a family and maintain a commitment to their work. "'Nobody knows what's going to happen.' That's a very common statement in one way or another," she said. "I hear: 'Well, the case is going for one or two, maybe three years, and this is a really critical management position. And I just don't know if we can give it to her, because she might leave. She might change her mind. She might have another kid.'"

Part of this attitude toward women on maternity leave is cultural. The United States is one of a very few countries without federally mandated paid parental leave, alongside only Liberia, Papua New Guinea, and Swaziland.[25] The Family and Medical Leave Act, passed in 1993, guarantees up to 12 weeks of unpaid leave for reasons including pregnancies and adoptions, but only for women who have been employed for more than 1,250 hours in the year prior to the leave by a company with more than 50 employees. Some employers, particularly large companies, offer paid leave. Estimates have put the percentage of American mothers who receive paid maternity leave as low as 11 percent, although professional jobs are much more likely to offer it than are hourly jobs.[26]

The lack of federal paid parental leave signals the attitude prevalent in the United States that it's a privilege, not a right. Even in those jobs where paid leave is available, it may be stigmatized.

Supervisors may feel that taking leave shows a lack of commitment to the job, or they may be worried that once a woman goes out on leave, she won't come back.

This is one of those issues that's mostly structural, meaning that it's hard for you, as an individual, to change it. Sure, you could not take your leave, but that's definitely not the solution we're trying to propose. At the same time, it's important to know that the bias exists, so that when you run into obstacles, you know *it's not your fault*.

Flexibility Stigma

One solution to Maternal Wall bias is to implement policies that enable women (and men) to be productive at work while still retaining some flexibility in their personal life, from implementing flex-time policies to allowing employees to work from home. Unfortunately, these policies often work on paper but not in practice. While 79 percent of companies in one national survey reported that they allow at least some of their employees to change starting or quitting times, usage rates typically are low, with somewhere between 10 and 20 percent of employees participating in either a formal or an informal agreement to vary their hours.[27]

In other words, the vast majority of companies already *have* flexible policies, but the vast majority of employees don't use them. For example, the pharmaceutical company Novartis actually had such a good written flex-time policy that it was on *Working Mother* magazine's list of the 100 best companies for mothers when it was hit with a massive discrimination lawsuit. The women who took advantage of the company's excellent recorded policies were retaliated against and sometimes actively pushed out.

The failure of flexibility programs is a prime example of why we wrote this book. Ideally, we will continue through trial and error to create a system in which flexibility isn't stigmatized unnecessarily.

FAMILY RESPONSIBILITIES DISCRIMINATION

In 2004, a class of sales representatives from pharmaceutical power-house Novartis filed *Velez v. Novartis*, a lawsuit alleging, among other things, that the company discriminated against pregnant women and mothers. The evidence against the defendants was striking: several women reported being questioned repeatedly about their child-care arrangements,[b] one reported being told to get an abortion, and another said she was urged during a training session to avoid getting pregnant.[c]

Michelle Williams was excluded from the company's Management Development Program because she had just had a baby and her supervisors weren't sure she was still interested in the opportunity.[d] While on maternity leave, Joan Durkin was harassed about her sales numbers by a manager whom another employee quoted as saying, "the Novartis maternity leave policy is a 'good deal' and that managers should put pressure on sale representatives before they go out on maternity leave to prevent them from becoming 'lazy.'"[e] Jennifer Ryan Tselikis's manager told her he preferred not to hire young women at all, explaining, "First comes love, then comes marriage, then comes flex time and a baby carriage."[f]

In a 2007 decision, the judge noted that pregnancy discrimination is "a form of discrimination against women" and granted certification to a class that included those women whose pregnancies or child-care responsibilities resulted in disparate treatment. In 2010, after years of litigation, a federal jury not only awarded the named plaintiffs $3.36 million in compensatory damages, it also found the company's behavior so egregious that the company was fined an astounding—and, in the world of employment discrimination lawsuits, extremely rare—$250 million in punitive damages.[g] The case ultimately settled for $175 million and paved the way for a new set of discrimination lawsuits.

But for now, it's important to know that it *is* stigmatized so you can understand why you're facing the problems you're facing.

The *American Lawyer* looked at the top 100 law firms and found that those *without* a flexibility program often had more than two times the number of women equity partners than those with a flexibility program.[28] Consulting firm Deloitte & Touche has worked for over 15 years to make workplace flexibility a cornerstone of its human resource strategy, and yet at a recent panel one representative of the company noted that his entire department, with two exceptions, consisted of men married to homemakers.[29]

A study by Jennifer Glass showed a complicated—but never positive—relationship between mothers' use of work-family policies and wage growth. Taking advantage of companies' child-care assistance programs tended to show only a small adverse impact on mothers' wages, while reduced work hours showed a large negative effect, even if mothers subsequently returned to their workplaces full-time. Use of flexible work arrangements showed no significant impact on wage growth, but use of accommodations that diminished "face time" led to potentially serious wage penalties. The only way to diminish the wage penalty associated with reduced work hours was to leave one's current employer and start working full-time at a new job. "Whatever productivity gains are produced by these policies are more than offset by the negative reaction of employers to those who are not continuously available for work," Glass concluded.[30]

One consultant who had worked with a law firm that had a very well-developed flex-time program said the women who took advantage of it tended to be so grateful for the accommodation that they didn't feel that they could complain when they ended up shunted to the side when it came to important assignments. "They understand that there are certain things that are off-limits to them because of their hours and that there's certain type of projects that just don't work," the consultant said. "But they also see something else, which is that some people aren't utilizing them as well as they could and they certainly don't value what they are bringing. It's not just that they're in a more limited situation but that it's more limited than it needs to be."

In professional settings, "time becomes a proxy for dedication and excellence," note sociologist Cynthia Fuchs Epstein and colleagues, so that employees who can't be available 100 percent of the time often are seen as less dedicated and competent than those who can, regardless of the actual quality of their work.[31]

Moreover, once you're in the flexibility ghetto, it can be hard to escape from, said one woman who worked part-time at her law firm after having a child. "You feel as though there's this 'PT' written on your back so long as anyone in your firm knows you once went part-time," she said.

The Invisible Husband

An unspoken assumption throughout a lot of the research on Maternal Wall bias is that mothers come paired with fathers—fathers who can provide enough support for families to live comfortably on a single paycheck and/or fathers who can provide help with child care and leave mothers available when work demands it.

This assumption is clearly unreasonable when spoken out loud. As of 2009, more than half of all children born to women under 30 were born to unwed mothers. The picture changes dramatically when you look at women in that age group with college degrees, for whom only 8 percent of children were born out of wedlock, although in this group minorities—women of color and lesbians in particular—are less likely to be married when they have children than are white, straight women.[32]

Professional women without the support of a husband or partner face unique challenges. The opt-out debate, for example, doesn't really apply to them—they can't exactly quit if there's no one else to support the family, discrimination or no. They're also usually breadwinners by default, meaning that one frequent justification for women's lower earnings disappears. Single mothers often

---

THE INVISIBLE HUSBAND IN CHILDREN'S BOOKS

Many beloved children's books illustrate the Invisible Husband problem. The charming *Goodnight Moon*, by Margaret Wise Brown, includes a mama and baby bear rocking in a chair—no dad in sight.[h] The classic *Where the Wild Things Are* starts off when rambunctious Max gets scolded by his mom:

> The night Max wore his wolf suit and made mischief of one kind and another
> his mother called him "WILD THING!"
> and Max said "I'LL EAT YOU UP!"
> so he was sent to bed without eating anything.[i]

The mother-as-disciplinarian also appears in *The Cat in the Hat*:

> "I know some new tricks," said the Cat in the Hat. "A lot of good tricks. I will show them to you. Your mother will not mind at all if I do." Then Sally and I did not know what to say. Our mother was out of the house for the day.[j]

And . . . dad? Nowhere to be found.

---

support families on their own, so it can't be argued that they don't need the higher pay given to male breadwinners with lower-earning wives, and yet single mothers nonetheless earn somewhere between 34 and 44 percent less than comparable men.[33]

Childless and Child-Free

Some women are childless—they wanted to have children but never did or never could.[34] Other women are child-free: they didn't want kids. Both groups can hit the Maternal Wall, according to psychologist Madeline Heilman, who writes, "Although there may be no relevant information available about the social and family life of a woman applying for a job, it is likely that it will be inferred that she is 'looking for a husband' or 'planning a family,' in either case putting her work second to family concerns."[35]

As one woman who worked for decades in corporate America observed, everyone assumes that young women will have children at some point. "And so you can't see them staying. Therefore, you're not really going to put as much effort into them."

Of course, some of these young women never do have children, but the New Girls without children said they faced stigma and unwanted inquiry about their personal lives, as well as measurable backlash and even lowered wages. For example, while mothers face a wage penalty because people assume their family responsibilities take precedence over work, women without children may face a wage penalty because people assume they *don't* have responsibilities outside the office. One New Girl, now a hedge fund manager, said when she was a young consultant, her firm hired a graduate student to come work for them. The New Girl had been working for the company for three years, but even though she had considerably more experience and seniority than the new male hire, he was offered a salary higher than hers. She went to the senior partner she worked for and asked him what was going on.

"What's the deal?" she asked him. "Is he more valuable because he's never worked here before?"

Flustered, the partner explained that the new hire had a wife and two children. "What do you do with all your money anyway?" he asked the New Girl.

"For all you know, I'm supporting my parents," she said.

The partner was chagrined, and the New Girl ended up getting a raise. (Again, sometimes addressing bias is as simple as pointing it out when it's happening.) But assumptions about the value of time of women without children frequently lead them to feel undervalued. As we'll discuss in later chapters, this is a major contributing factor in the Tug of War. Women without children are seen to have near-infinite time to spend on their jobs, as well as on care work inside the office. At the same time, researchers Caroline Gatrell and Elaine Swan write, they are seen to be insufficiently nurturing, excessively masculine, and "not quite normal."[36]

One lawyer, who told us she had never wanted to have children, said she faced assumptions that there was simply something wrong with her throughout her career. "People thought I didn't have kids because I worked too much, because if I wanted to be successful in my job, that meant I made a trade-off and decided I didn't want to have kids," she said. "That was the assumption. And so, therefore, some people who feel that all women should have kids thought there was something wrong with me, that, you know, I wasn't the good woman."

THE NO-CHILD PENALTY

"Janet [Napolitano]'s perfect for that job. Because for that job, you have to have no life. Janet has no family. Perfect. She can devote, literally, 19–20 hours a day to it."[k]

A British study found that women without children work the most unpaid overtime.[l] Men without children put in the highest levels of overtime—8.3 hours a week. But they tended to get paid for it. Nearly one in four women (24.2 percent) reported unpaid overtime, the highest percentage of any group of workers.

Why? Many women without children report the assumption that they are always available to take on more work because they have "no family" and "no life." But of course this is false. Everyone has a family —and many people today often form circles of close friends who play many of the same roles family traditionally plays. The assumption that women have "no life" is a carryover from an earlier age when "childless spinsters" were considered somewhat pathetic. Hence National Governors Association chair Ed Rendell's comment about Janet Napolitano, quoted above, when she had just been nominated to be President Obama's secretary of homeland security.

Fatherhood Helps Men . . .
Unless They Share the Care

Eight days before her child was due, a very pregnant Cherie Booth Blair argued in court on behalf of England's Trades Union Congress, a confederation of labor unions, that a law covering parental leave should be backdated, allowing women—and men—who already had young children when the law was passed to take time off to spend with their families. Several months earlier, she had hinted that she wanted her own husband, British prime minister Tony Blair, to take time off when their child was born.

"I am pleased to report that in 1998 the Prime Minister of Finland took advantage of his right to parental leave," Booth Blair said at a press conference. "I, for one, am promoting the widespread adoption of his fine example."[37]

Although Tony Blair hesitated, he ended up taking two weeks off for the birth of his son, Leo. This option isn't even available to most American men, but, as researchers Adam Butler and Amie Skattebo note, the Blair family's internal debates about the prime minister's family responsibilities sparked a wider debate about the use of paternal leave.[38]

Mothers, on average, make significantly less money and work significantly less than women without children do. For men, the opposite is often true: the birth of a child correlates with an increased salary and more time spent at work for white and Latino fathers.[39] In the past, married men were actually provided an institutionalized "family wage" premium. This is illegal, but it still happens today—Joan hears regularly from women who were told point-blank that their male colleagues received a raise because they have a family to support. Men may also receive more subtle advantages in the form of lowered performance and punctuality standards. Because fathers are assumed to be breadwinners with families to support, they are stereotyped as more committed to their jobs and allowed greater flexibility.[40]

Former Vermont governor Madeleine Kunin said in an interview with Joan that she was struck by the double standard for men and women during the blizzards that hit the East Coast in December 2010. New Jersey governor Chris Christie took the last plane to leave the state before the blizzard struck and was in Disney World with his family while his constituents were stuck in their cars overnight on the Garden State Parkway. His explanation? "I know my responsibility as a father." His wife, he explained, wouldn't let him cancel the trip.[41]

"My question," Kunin said. "Could a woman governor say this? *Would* a woman governor be able to say, 'I know my responsibility as a mother' and not pay a political price?"

As a woman governor herself, Kunin knows what she's talking about. Seriously. Imagine it. Imagine a woman governor explaining that she shirked her gubernatorial duties because her role as a wife and mother called. She wouldn't be governor for long. She certainly wouldn't be encouraged to run for president by her party a short year later.

At the same time, being a mother has its perks. There's maternity leave, for one. And while mothers with caregiving responsibilities may face stereotypes, bias against fathers who take time for their families' care may be even more severe. A 2003 study found that men who ask for family leave suffer more negative reactions than women who do.[42] A 2004 study reported that men who took even a short time off due to a family conflict were given lower recommendations for rewards and poorer overall performance ratings.[43] Meanwhile, according to a 2007 study, if a father does not send signals to his boss or colleagues that he has caregiving responsibilities, having children actually helps his career. He is given a higher starting salary than a childless man and is held to lower performance and punctuality standards.[44]

While the flexibility stigma affects men as well as women, the mechanism is somewhat different. For men, the stigma stems from Tightrope bias: when men depart from the expectations we have

---

BEWARE OF THE BAGEL TRAP

Martha Minow, the dean of Harvard Law School, once told Joan a story about her sister. Just after her sister got married to a man she had been with for many years, she woke up one Sunday morning and insisted her husband go get bagels and lox. Why? That's what her father had always done.[m]

She's far from the only woman to have fallen into the trap of expecting her spouse to act like her father did. Having a baby triggers traditional gender expectations even more than getting married does.[n] Couples often report that it negatively impacts the quality of their relationship.[o] Conflict over the division of labor is a key reason.[p]

One reason for this problem is that gender pressures on women to be the perfect mother—one who is always available to her children—descend once a baby is born.[q] These pressures are worth resisting. Studies show that fathers who take substantial parental leave significantly change their relationships with their children.[r] Children do better when both parents remain involved in their care.[s] So remember: part of being a good mom is to let go enough to let your partner develop parenting skills. Give him (or her) room. Don't hover.[t]

Gender pressures on men also play a role. Pregnancy and childbirth typically is an anxious time for fathers, who often feel the full weight of the breadwinner role descend on them.[u] Remember, conventionality pressures a man to be a good father by increasing his work hours so he can "support his family."

---

for appropriate masculinity, they face a backlash that harms their performance ratings and results in a lower salary. While men with families are expected to do what it takes to support their families financially, men with family caregiving responsibilities are seen to be insufficiently masculine and looked on with suspicion. A study by psychologists Laurie Rudman and Kris Mescher asked subjects to rate a male employee who did or did not take a family leave to care for a child or parent. If the employee took leave to care for a child or parent, he was less likely to be recommended for rewards such as a promotion, a raise, or a high-profile assignment than a male employee who did not take any leave.[45]

The men were penalized because they were seen as bad workers, but poor performance was not what drove the negative perceptions. They were seen as bad workers precisely because they were thought to have traits traditionally viewed as feminine: being weak, insecure, emotional, or naive. In other words, the flexibility stigma is a femininity stigma.

This finding has been confirmed by the three other studies. One, by Joseph Vandello and three colleagues from the University of South Florida, found that men and women are equally likely to want a flexible schedule and to place a similarly high value on that option. (Only compensation ranked as a more valued goal for both sexes.) But men were much less likely to say they planned to ask for one. Why? Many men feared that asking for a flexible schedule would make them seem more feminine—and, when they believed that, they were likely to shy away from asking for as much flexibility as they actually desired.[46]

A final study surveyed actual workers rather than students in experimental settings and examined unionized public-service workers rather than professionals. It found that, in a female-dominated workplace, men who did more child care received the highest levels of "masculinity harassment": taunting triggered by perceptions that someone is insufficiently masculine. In workplaces dominated by men, caregiving fathers faced more general harassment: being teased, put down, or excluded.[47]

The conclusion is one that Supreme Court justice Ruth Bader Ginsburg highlighted long ago: women will never achieve equality until men do.[48] In fact, perhaps the single most telling question one can ask of a prospective employer is whether the *men* take parental leave. If men routinely take leave—not for a day or a week but for the same amount of time women typically take leave—that's a pretty good sign that leaves, and perhaps flexible schedules, are less stigmatized than they often are today.

*   *   *

Once women become mothers, they often find they have to start proving themselves all over again—just when they are exhausted and barely keeping afloat. With shocking regularity, Joan hears from lawyers who return from maternity leave to find they are given little or no work. Of course, if they end up not meeting the annual hours goals set forth by their law firm, they find themselves in deep water.

This is a particularly corrosive effect of the Maternal Wall: women hit it when they are vulnerable—when they have just returned from maternity leave and are already ambivalent about leaving their babies or a little later, as they struggle on the front lines with babies and jobs, or when they have a second child or a third. If the pressure becomes overwhelming and they drop out, it's presented as their own choice.

In other words, the current system is perfectly engineered to damn women into feeling guilty no matter what they do. The bottom line is that women—and men—need better choices. Too often, today's workplaces are perfectly designed for the breadwinner-housewife workforce of 1960. That has to change. To quote one New Girl, "Look at your daughters and ask yourself, why is it that you're encouraging her to do really well on her standardized tests? Why is it you're encouraging her to stay up all night to do fabulous essays so she gets into the best college? Why is it you want her to be a champion soccer player? Where is that leading her? If we can't fix the road ahead of her, she is going to go running into the wall that so many of us have run into."

8

Maternal Wall Action Plan

There's no way to be a perfect mother, and a million ways to be a good one. —JILL CHURCHILL

Staying home with children is a choice many women make. Women should have that choice. So should men. However, this is a book for professional women, so we'll be focusing on how to deal with the obstacles that emerge for those women who *do* stay the course at work.

Of all the types of bias we discuss in this book, Maternal Wall bias is the closest to the surface—and also the least challenged. Few people these days will suggest out loud that a woman's gender should bar her from opportunities at work or that a woman's inherent emotional needs mean she's not as good an employee as a man. For mothers, all bets are off: when women have children, it's common for supervisors and co-workers to encourage them to take a step back. Articles in national magazines expound on the maternal instinct and suggest that women's innate values simply don't align with the contemporary workplace. According to a 1997 study by Diane Kobrynowicz and Monica Biernat, there's a lot of overlap between the characteristics ascribed to the "good mother" and the "good father"—except only the good mother is described as "always available to her children."[1]

All of the strategies in this chapter are designed to address the overwhelming tension between this cultural mandate and the expectation that the good employee always be available to her job. This tension runs so deep that it reaches even those women who don't have children at all. Understanding this tension as a form of gender bias is important as we work to move beyond it. Luckily, there are ways to alleviate some of the pressure in the meantime.

Strategy 1: Let People Know That You Remain Committed to Your Work

As with the other types of bias we've presented, dealing with and minimizing your personal work-family conflict is only half the battle. Descriptive bias, as we discussed in chapter 1, emerges from a lack of information that leads us to make automatic assumptions. One source of frustration we have heard time and time again is that supervisors pass over mothers for opportunities without ever asking them whether they are interested.

Fortunately, there's an easy way to address this problem. While the ultimate solution is for people to stop making unfounded assumptions, in the meantime, as a working mother, it helps to be crystal clear if and when you are available and willing to take on a project.

One New Girl described a colleague who had a mentoring relationship with a more senior man, with whom she was talking about a big opportunity that had come up overseas. The mentor began to get excited for her but then stopped himself.

"Oh, but you've got a husband and kids," he said.

The younger woman was quick to point out the problem with her mentor's assumptions. "Hold the phone. Wait a minute," she said. "What did you just do there?"

The mentor, the New Girl said, quickly understood the implications of his statement and was horrified by what he had done—"I'm mentoring this woman. I'm committed to her career, and I potentially just blew it because I potentially took an opportunity off the table for her," he realized.

The mentor ended up being very supportive. But he needed to be reminded that just because the woman he was mentoring had a family, that didn't mean she had to be exempt from any opportunity that would affect them.

As one New Girl said, "It becomes absolutely critical that you are very clear about what you want to do, where you're headed, your long-term commitment. You've got to hit the underlying assumptions about what's going on here. You have to show you're committed, that you have no fears yourself about your ability to do a great job and have wonderful children, that you are willing to travel, you've got your life set up appropriately, that you want the assignments that will prove your problem-solving ability."

By now you know that the first step to countering description bias is to give the people around you information about *you*, so they don't make assumptions based on stereotypes of the typical woman—or, in this case, the typical mother.

So, when you return from maternity leave, let the people around you know you remain committed to your career. The best approach is, before you leave to have or adopt your baby, to put a date on the calendar on which you will call your supervisor and have a conversation about your reentry plan. If you become ambivalent and torn about when and whether to return after the baby is born, don't hesitate to talk with a career coach—or, for that matter, to do some couples therapy if the topic of who will do what when gets heated.

Before that date rolls around, talk with one or more people at your office whom you trust about how best to handle your reentry. Ideally, someone in your organization has the responsibility to facilitate mothers' return from maternity leave—that makes it easy. If not, ask someone you trust who has been through it. Ask what the pitfalls are. Brainstorm how to navigate them. Learn who, if anyone, in your environment has old-fashioned ideals about whether, and how much, mothers should work.

Then, when your target date rolls around, call your supervisor and ask to meet. During that meeting, say specifically that you intend to continue in your career. Identify what kinds of assignments you would like when you return, and discuss how to get them. If you feel comfortable doing so, slip into the conversation what your child-care arrangements will be. If your family depends on your salary, say so. If your husband is willing to follow you if the right job comes up for you, say so. If you have career goals for the next year, discuss them. Do whatever feels comfortable that will clearly signal that you intend to continue your career.

Strategy 2: Tolstoy Was Wrong

You also need strategies to combat prescriptive bias. There's plenty of it around. In Allison Pearson's best-selling book *I Don't Know How She Does It*, narrator Kate Reddy is at her child's Christmas pageant when one of the other mothers comes up to her and starts chatting. "Any second now she will ask me if I've gone part-time yet," Kate predicts dryly to the reader. Sure enough, the woman comes up to Kate, and before you know it, she's asking, "So, are you working part-time now? No? Still full-time? *Good heavens!* I don't know how you do it, honestly. I say, Claire, I was just saying to Kate, I don't know how she does it. Do you?"[2]

Comments many working mothers report hearing that attack their choices or their ability to be good mothers can feel like a slap in the face—and they can make you want to slap back. But remember that mothers aren't held to the same standards as other women. They're held to even higher standards of feminine behavior, and if anger is often met with backlash for women, the response can be even more negative for working mothers. A 1990 study of business students found a "plummet" in the performance evaluations of women managers when they became pregnant. Subjects reacted negatively toward a pregnant manager because they expected her to be "nonauthoritarian, easy to negotiate with, gentle, and neither intimidating nor aggressive, and nice."[3] In other words, pregnant managers were expected to act docile and feminine and encountered pushback when they behaved in the assertive, directive ways required by their role as managers.

In the face of hostile prescriptive bias of the "I don't know how

---

SMOOTH COMEBACKS FOR ROUGH MOMENTS

From misunderstanding-on-purpose to a quick sarcastic barb, there are a lot of ways to let people know they're out of line with their comments about your personal life.

COMMENT: "I don't know how you work so much. My wife could never spend so much time away from the kids!"
COMEBACK: "I focus on what my kids need. It seems to work out for all of us."

COMMENT: "How do you get it all done? You must be so overwhelmed."
COMEBACK: "Well, the house elves make it a lot easier!"

COMMENT: "You must really miss your kids when you're away from them!"
COMEBACK: "I do miss them. You must miss yours, too."

COMMENT: "Why would you want to come back when you have three babies at home?
COMEBACK: "Well, if you are offering to pay my mortgage . . ."

---

you do it" ilk, keep it light. A lawyer quoted in a 2006 American Bar Association report described hearing these comments often: "I get that a lot: 'Don't you feel bad leaving your kids at home? Don't you miss them?'"[4] What's a girl to say?

Tell them that Tolstoy was wrong. Happy families are *not* all alike. Tell them that you are sure that whatever decisions your colleague has made are right for his (or her) family and that the decisions your family has made are right for yours.

It's also worth noting that discrimination against mothers is illegal. In *Mommy Wars*, screenwriter Terri Minsky remembers telling an executive she worked for that she was pregnant. "You're as useful to me now as if you had a brain tumor," the executive replied.[5]

That kind of comment is gold to plaintiffs' attorneys, for whom it represents evidence of sex discrimination. If a supervisor says that kind of thing to you, that's a big deal. Consult chapters 12 and 13.

Strategy 3: Get Over Yourself, Squared

Having children can be a full-time job. So can, well, having a full-time job. It's definitely possible to do both and to do both well. But there's no question that it's hard—particularly in the face of social pressures to be the perfect mother and the perfect employee —to balance being a professional woman with being a mother. It's also hard to give up your career. There are no easy choices, and it's important to give yourself and the women around you credit for that.

One New Girl said she was having lunch with an older woman who was a high-powered executive. The New Girl had just gone back to work after having her second child, and the older woman asked her how she was doing.

"Oh, I'm doing great," the New Girl replied.

"No, really," the woman persisted. "How are you doing?"

The New Girl looked at her and said, "I don't know how people do this."

"They don't," the woman replied.

"That experience was so powerful to me, because there I was feeling completely inadequate," the New Girl remembered. "All these other women around me seemed to be blithely going through life balancing this work thing and the kid things and whatever, and I was totally overwhelmed."

A businesswoman told us the advice another working woman had given her: "You just can't do all the little things your mother probably did. And you have to pick and choose and decide what's going to give you joy and passion and will be important to your children and what just doesn't matter that much."

Remember: the emotional tone of how you approach family life is more important than making sure your child's Halloween costume is perfect. And for all the guilt that's heaped on mothers who fail to live up to the ever-soaring standards of helicopter parenting, the fact is that a lot of the little things really *don't* matter that much. Helicopter parenting not only isn't required to be a good mother, it can actually harm child development, according to data from the National Institute of Child Health and Human Development.[6] While parents these days may feel pressure to make sure their kids' every minute is accounted for—piano lessons, soccer practice, gymnastics, Girl Scouts, and so on—many experts think that a lack of free time and independence can stunt children's imagination and self-sufficiency. It's also worth noting that this intensive scheduling is a relatively new phenomenon. Ironically, the type of micromanaging that's become expected in a world where many parents both work full-time was almost unheard of in the caregiver-breadwinner families of the past. Joan's mother, in the 1950s, just sent the kids out to play in the yard. She may have been a stay-at-home mother, but she would no more have gotten down on the floor to play with a baby than she would have flown to the moon.

That doesn't mean it's not important to be available to your children—it just means you should resist the pressure to be Super-Mom. There's nothing wrong with buying cupcakes from the bakery for the kindergarten class. A store-bought Halloween costume is not the end of the world. Hire a babysitter once a week and go out on a date—this is *really, really* important. Holding yourself up to an unrealistic standard of being always available to your children can leave you in tatters, and remember: emotional tone is often more important than utter Betty Crockerdom. There's going to be some external pressure from your children regardless of how deftly you juggle: "Emily's mom makes her a sandwich every day when she gets home from school. Why aren't you ever home to make me sandwiches?" It can be painful to feel like you're disappointing your child, but keep in mind that children grow up, and things get easier.

Joan tells younger mothers that the clouds part when the youngest child is four—and when the youngest is 12, you get your life back. She's speaking from experience: as a law professor, writer, and founder of multiple programs on work-life balance, Joan has been working—sometimes working *a lot*—on work-family issues since Rachel was born. Although Joan was always home for dinner and made the effort to chaperone field trips and be there when it mattered, her job was a near-constant source of tension. There were business trips, law review deadlines, book tours, visiting professorships in Charlottesville and Cambridge and San Francisco. When Rachel was a child, she never hesitated to point out the irony in the fact that Joan worked so much on advancing work-family balance for other women.

It wasn't until Rachel was well into her teens that she began to appreciate Joan's work—if at first simply because of the horrifying realization that, had Joan not been able to funnel much of her nervous energy into her job, even more of it may have been directed to tracking Rachel's already closely watched movements. And when Rachel went off to college, she began to understand Joan as a human being *and* as a mother. But it took Rachel a long time to understand how vital it was to Joan to have a career doing work she felt was important.

Despite the stress caused by work-family tensions, numerous studies confirm that having a job keeps women happy and healthy.[7] Sharon Meers and Joanna Strober, authors of *Getting to 50/50*, document a series of studies that show, among other things, that women who had been homemakers for most of their lives were more likely than other women to report poor health and that women who quit work after having a child had 30 percent more psychological distress compared to women who returned to work.[8] As Meers and Strober explain, "If work makes you hum, your whole family sings along. By contrast, if staying home makes you miserable—well, fill in the blanks."[9]

It's not necessarily a part of kids' job descriptions to be gentle with their parents, but it is a part of your job description to be gentle with yourself. Your kids will do what you do, not what you say, and if you're proud of your job, they may well grow up to be proud of you. You will also be a positive role model to your kids, your daughters who are more likely to follow in your footsteps and be professionally fulfilled and economically independent, and your sons who are likely to be supportive of their wives' careers (if they marry women).

A NOTE ON MOTHER'S DAY

In 2001, for Mother's Day, Joan asked Rachel to take a piece of paper and write, on one side, the things she had done wrong and, on the other, the things she had done right.

Dear Mom,
In the past fourteen years, you've done some things wrong and some things right. I know that it's hard to have someone's life in your hands, but I think that you have done a pretty good job with me. Nobody's perfect, but I feel lucky that you are my mom, because you have gotten close. I may not say it often, but I admire the way you have devoted your life to try and make the world a better place, and aspire to be like you in that way. You may be away from us a lot, but deep down (somewhere) I understand that it is because you want to keep other women from being in your situation.

As I enter adulthood, I find it almost shocking as I look at all the sacrifices you and Dad have made for me and Nicky, and I thank you now for them all. Being a teenager is difficult, and I may forget, sometimes, how much you love me, and how much I love you. I want to apologize now for all of the times I have been ungrateful, and all of the times I will be ungrateful. I hope you will always remember that I will love you forever.

Love,
Rachel

The letter made Joan cry. "What about the things I did wrong?" she asked Rachel. Rachel replied, "I think you know."

"There's a huge payoff at the end," said one New Girl. "When my older son was in high school, he was in the living room talking to a couple friends. As teenagers often do, they forgot that I was capable of overhearing them while I was in the adjacent room. One boy was talking about how he couldn't imagine how awful it would be if his mother worked outside the home."

The New Girl said she was moved when her son came to her defense.

"What's so awful about having a mom who likes and is good at what she is doing, is around when I need her, and not around when I don't need her? It works for me," her son replied.

Strategy 4: "Don't Leave before You Leave"

In Sheryl Sandberg's influential 2010 TED talk on why there are so few women leaders, the Facebook COO observed that many women, in anticipation of future family responsibilities, start "quietly leaning back" early in their careers.[10] As a result, they don't gun for big opportunities, and they have less of a connection with their work, meaning that it's easier for them to leave by the time they actually do have to make a choice.[11]

"I think there's a really deep irony to the fact that actions women are taking—and I see this all the time—with the objective of staying in the workforce actually lead to their eventually leaving," Sandberg said. "Here's what happens: We're all busy. Everyone's busy. A woman's busy. And she starts thinking about having a child, and from the moment she starts thinking about having a child, she starts thinking about making room for that child. 'How am I going to fit this into everything else I'm doing?' And literally from that moment, she doesn't raise her hand anymore, she doesn't look for a promotion, she doesn't take on the new project, she doesn't say, 'Me. I want to do that.' She starts leaning back."[12]

Sandberg's advice for avoiding this problem is simple: "Don't leave before you leave."[13]

It's important to start thinking about work-family balance early. As we'll discuss later, that means being clear with your partner about his or her expected contributions and being clear with your colleagues how you plan to stay involved after your baby is born. What it doesn't mean is avoiding responsibility at work before you've had a child—or even before you're pregnant at all. Several of the New Girls said they've been distressed to see that many younger women dial back on their responsibilities when they start to even think about having a family.

"I watch young women totally take themselves out of the running long before they have any children—long before they even have a date," one consultant observed.

While it's true that women sometimes lean back, often it's not women who take themselves off the fast track. Women are seen as "flight risks," which means that they may not be given the same institutional support as men are. That, in turn, makes them more likely to check out.

"We hired a woman, she was terrific and she had great credentials. We spent about two years training her and then she had a baby and left," said a woman quoted in a report on female attorneys of color. "We're not a big firm so that was a big expense. Another woman came around, we spent two and a half years training her and then she got married, had a baby, and then she left. My partner said, 'You know, it's illegal, you're not allowed to say it, but the next time a woman comes through here, don't even bring her into my office. I'm not going to interview her.'"[14]

Strategy 5: Set Clear Limits

Perhaps the most important thing, regardless of whether you choose to bring your family life into the office, is to make sure you don't turn into the woman who mistook her job for a life.[15] This can be especially difficult in the iPhone era, when it takes more effort to be away from your e-mail than to be constantly online.

"Technology is great, but on the other hand, it interferes with your ability to have a family life, because you're always on," said one New Girl.

On the other hand, the benefit of technology is that, slowly but surely, it's lessening the importance of face time. You no longer need to be in the office to be plugged into office goings-on or available in case of emergencies. One New Girl said she developed a ritual with her children that she would have lunch with them two times a week—which, in turn, made it easier when unexpected deadlines or big projects ate into her family time.

"For a long time on my calendar, every Tuesday and Thursday I had a standing meeting outside the office from 11 to 1. And I went to my kids' school, and I had lunch with them and their friends. My assistant knew where I was, and I had a cell phone. But nobody else knew I was doing that." "It just really makes it equal out, those days when I stay really late or I have to work in the evenings or I'm doing e-mails at home," she said.

Another woman this New Girl knows tells her children at the beginning of every semester to pick three events they want her to attend. They get to pick, and no matter what, she will be there. This is a common strategy: a Fortune 500 executive told us she used to sit down with her daughter at the beginning of the school year to look over the calendar. Making it clear to your family that they can count on you when you promise you'll be there can go a long way toward assuaging your own guilt and making your children feel like a priority.

"I said, 'I'm going to come to the first day of school always. I'm going to come to the Halloween party, I'm going to come to the Christmas thing, I'm going to come to blah, blah, blah, blah, blah. I promise you I will be there,'" the executive told us. "'Anything else is a special treat. So I'm not going to drive to the snake farm.' And she listened. And then I'd always make sure to pop in on her a couple times where she didn't know I was coming. And it was a special treat."

In New Girl Leslie Morgan Steiner's book *Mommy Wars*, businesswoman Ann Misiaszek Sarnoff sums up her strategy in one word: buckets. She separates family duties into three categories: things that are essential for her to do herself, like go to a child's talent show or soccer game; things that she and her husband can take turns covering, like doctor's appointments or class dinners; and things that are "completely delegable," like chores. Making sure she doesn't miss the important things means she doesn't have regrets—something that she said is important not only for her but also for her children.

"A fellow working mom told me not to ever leave the house in the morning with regret. She said that my kids would sense my conflict and be confused by it. So I've tried to follow that advice and leave and return every day with a big smile on my face. I want to show them, particularly my daughter, that you can and should enjoy work (and be successful at it) as a woman and a mom," Misiaszek Sarnoff writes.[16]

Strategy 6: Demand Change at Home

In an interview with Joan, Supreme Court justice Ruth Bader Ginsburg remembered being called into her younger son's school constantly to deal with his disciplinary problems. At the time, she was a law professor at Columbia University and finally told the school she couldn't keep leaving the office to deal with her son. "This child has two parents," she remembered telling administrators. "Please call his father next time."

Ginsburg's husband, Martin Ginsburg, was a well-known tax lawyer and professor in his own right and was also famously supportive of his wife's career. Not only did their children have two parents, they had two *involved* parents. And frankly, that's no coincidence. Ginsburg has said a supportive partner who is willing to share family work "is a must for any woman who hopes to combine marriage and a career."[17]

This strategy, of course, isn't for everyone, but in American families with a mother and a father who both work full-time, women end up doing about 28 hours of housework a week, as compared with 16 hours a week for men, according to a 2008 article by Lisa Belkin in the *New York Times Magazine*.[18] Even when men and women both work full-time, women still end up doing twice as much housework and three times as much child care.

Studies have shown that couples made up of two mothers have a more equal division of labor than heterosexual couples—but traditional gender roles are hard to shake. On average, the biological mother in lesbian couples takes on a larger share of the housework and child care than the nonbiological mother. Nonbiological mothers are also more likely to work long hours outside the home (more than 40 per week) than biological mothers.[19]

In other words, just having a partner isn't enough. The majority of couples with children are structured such that one half of the couple (usually the husband) does more paid work and less housework and the other half of the couple (usually the wife) does more of the housework and less paid work. Even when the wife does more paid work, the rest of the dynamic can be slow to change.

"Make sure your partner is a real partner," Sheryl Sandberg advised women. "I've become convinced that we've made more progress in the workforce than we have in the home."[20]

Part of the problem, one New Girl said, is that even when married women are vocal about changes in the workplace, they fail to ask their partners to make adjustments. As Meers and Strober write, "The most important career decision you make is whom you marry. (And the deals you make with him.)"[21] And it's never too early to start a conversation with a potential partner about sharing responsibility—don't wait until it comes down to the day-to-day conversations about who's going to stay home with a sick child.

One New Girl told us that she was worried that having kids would nudge her off her career, so before she got pregnant, she made her position clear. "Look," she told her husband. "If you really want children, and this is something that is really motivating you in our marriage and the most important thing you can think of to do now, then you have to be willing to make at least an equal commitment to it."

It's one thing for your partner to make a promise he'll take time off work if your hypothetical kids get sick, five years down the line. This New Girl wanted to make sure her husband was willing to walk the walk; as the first step in their coparenting relationship, she asked her husband to commit to taking paternity leave equal to her maternity leave. "The day you go back to work is the day I go back to work," she told him. They both took six weeks off, and that was in 1986. Another New Girl said she told her husband he was going to be in charge of all appointments for their children: doctor's and dentist's appointments and the like. "The perception to me was when he did those types of things, he was perceived as a great dad. And when I did those things, I was a woman who couldn't get her act together," she said. "And he actually fully bought that. It was not a question."

Note that an equal relationship doesn't actually put women on equal footing with many of the men at the top of the ladder. In an interview with the *Wall Street Journal*'s Alan Murray, PepsiCo's

---

HOW TO AVOID THE BAGEL TRAP

1. Tell your partner that men who share child care and housework more equally get more sex.[a]

2. Insist that your partner take the full amount of parental leave allowed him, preferably during a period when you are back at work. If his workplace sends strong messages that he will be penalized for doing so, keep in mind that that's illegal.[b]

3. At a minimum, set up specific times that fit into his schedule when he's responsible for the child.

4. If it's his turn and he doesn't come through, that's a big deal. Treat it like a big deal. Go to a marriage counselor and work it out—for your sake, for his, and for the sake of your kids.

CEO, Indra Nooyi, compared the dynamic she and her husband created to those of her male colleagues and their wives. "I had a very supportive spouse," she told Murray. "I had true gender equality at home. Big difference, because I look at many of the men who made it to CEOs. They had women at home who carried the burden for them disproportionately, and I think in my case I had a husband who said we're going to have true gender equality. He was working, I was working, but we juggled our schedules."[22]

Murray pointed out the asymmetry in what she was saying: a lot of the men she was competing with had wives who took on all the household duties, whereas she split them 50-50 with her husband. Nooyi just laughed. "Equal is pretty good," she said. "Equal is the best we can offer. Come on, Alan. We're not in Kansas anymore, my friend."[23]

Now, it's easy to imagine that the love of your life will be willing to make sacrifices for you and your children. But these conversations don't happen by default. One businesswoman cautioned that she had always imagined she would end up with someone willing to share family responsibilities, but she never mentioned it when she was in relationships. "That's what I wanted and that's what I assumed I would get, and I never brought it up and I never negotiated it," she told us.

She went to business school and met a man who was just as ambitious as she was. They married and had children, and that's where the problems started. They both worked full-time, but he wouldn't leave work early to pick up the kids from day care or stay home with the kids when they were sick. "When it came time to make compromises, I made all of them, and he refused to make any of them," she said. Studies have confirmed that when child care falls through, it's most often mothers who step in to fill the void.[24] "If I had been cued up early on to know how important it was going to be to negotiate with a loved one for these things, I feel like I'd be in a very different place now," she told us.

Finally, keep in mind that an equal partnership involves adjustments from everyone. An influential study on gatekeeping—when mothers take control of household work, criticize their husbands' contributions, and redo tasks that don't meet rigid standards—has found that women are often resistant to ceding control of housework to their husbands.[25] Maybe the children's clothes get a little wrinkly when your spouse folds them. Maybe he or she puts dirty dishes in the dishwasher without rinsing them first. But when women don't give their spouses autonomy in how to do household tasks, it's pretty much certain that they won't contribute equally. (Within limits: if your partner says something like, "You care about clean clothes and I don't," that's just passive aggression.)

One woman quoted in the book *Difficult Conversations* said she resented her husband for leaving her with the brunt of the "scheduling and running around" until she realized that she was actively keeping control of parts of her kids' lives—"perhaps because of my ambivalence about working full-time." Once she realized what she was doing, she was able to step back, and her relationship with her husband improved: "I both turned things over to [my husband] and shifted the way I thought about these responsibilities. They are things I've chosen to take on to stay involved, rather than things he's let slide."[26]

WANT TO SHARE THE CARE? CHECK OUT WWW.THIRDPATH.ORG

One resource you should know about is ThirdPath Institute. ThirdPath works with individual couples to help them negotiate workplace arrangements that allow them to share the care. This remains very important as long as individuals have to negotiate individually for workplace flexibility.

ThirdPath also works with institutions to help them develop best-practice workplace flexibility programs. Other organizations do this, too. The Center for WorkLife Law, which Joan runs, has an extensive list of best practices for the legal profession and academia.

Strategy 7: Present Solutions, Not Problems

Clear communication about one's professional goals becomes particularly important when adopting a part-time, balanced-hours, or flexible schedule to care for young children. It would be incredibly risky to enter a high-stakes meeting at work without solid preparation, and the same is true for negotiating an alternative schedule with an employer. An important first step is solidifying exactly what type of schedule works best for you and your family. This means thinking strategically about your goals as a parent and as a professional and developing a schedule that allows you to meet those goals.

WHAT YOU SHOULD BE ABLE TO EXPECT FROM YOUR EMPLOYER

You need to know what best-practice policies look like so you can see if your employer's policies measure up.

Best Practice: Gradual Return to Work after Maternity Leave

Some law firms allow a gradual return from work for attorneys returning from maternity, adoption, or caregiver leave. Here are best practices, derived from the PAR Research Institute, which is part of Joan's Center for WorkLife Law:

Ramp-up program models with schedules ranging from three months to one year:

1. After leave, provide for an automatic three-month graduated return on an individualized schedule (upon request).

2. Work 50 percent full-time in the first month back.

3. Work 60 percent in the second month.

4. Work 70 percent in the third month.

5. During or after this phase-in, the attorney can return to full-time or propose a more permanent flexible work arrangement.

---

6. Work 70 percent of previous schedule for six to ten months after return.

7. Offer an automatic "pace reduction option" for associates, scheduling reduced pace for up to six months without prior approval.

8. Offer a flexible return in which attorneys can propose their own return schedule, through which they gradually progress back to work over 12 months. This includes working at home, fewer days, reduced hours, or any combination.

9. There is an option to work reduced schedule for up to six months within the first year following birth or adoption.

10. There is an automatic one-year part-time option for returning attorneys.

Best-Practice Part-Time Policy

1. Offer proportional pay, benefits, and bonuses for part-time work.

2. Offer proportional training and advancement. Going part-time should not take you off the advancement track.

3. Employ a part-time policy coordinator: someone who keeps track of the schedule promised and the hours worked and intervenes with your supervisor if there's persistent "schedule creep" (when your schedule creeps back up toward full-time).

4. You should get paid for it if you work more hours than originally planned (but this is not a substitute for controlled schedule creep; if you wanted the money instead of the schedule, you would not have gone part-time).

5. Going part-time should not be irreversible. You should be able to switch back and forth between part- and full-time.

That's what your employer owes you. What you owe your employer is to figure out a schedule that's realistic given the type of work you do. If your career involves deals for which 24/7 work is inevitable, working part-time will mean fewer deals per year, not disappearing at 5:30 and leaving someone else holding the bag.

One attorney, who had a reduced-hours schedule to accommodate raising young children, determined what hours in the workday she simply couldn't miss if she wanted to succeed professionally: "Things really started to heat up at 5:00, 6:00, 7:00 in the evening, so it was important for me to be in the office then. It was really impossible to leave early. I wanted to be getting access to good cases and being seen, so what I started to do was come in later, at 10:00 or 11:00, because no one was looking for me then."[27] In a sense, this attorney was optimizing her reduced hours by being present at work during the high-impact hours and being at home when no one would miss her.

It is not only necessary to develop a business case for your new schedule, but you must also brainstorm possible objections and develop responses that will help you achieve your end goal. Take this example from Joan and coauthor Cynthia T. Calvert's *Flex Success: The Lawyer's Guide to Balanced Hours*: say an attorney wants to cut back to 60 percent (about three days per week) but anticipates pushback from her employer because of a series of upcoming trials. With that pushback in mind, the attorney prepares a response that will appease her employer's nerves, while still standing firm on her position to reduce her hours. She proposes going down to 80 percent for the first six months, with a plan to reevaluate after that time. She offers to do more hours in preparation for trial but negotiates for days off after the trial, when the "all hands on deck" approach is no longer necessary.[28] In this example, the attorney provides solutions—not problems—and illustrates a respect and understanding for the business demands of her employer. She shows herself to be a team player but does not relinquish her commitment to a part-time schedule that would benefit both her and her family.

Also keep in mind, while the importance of being clear about your intentions to your superiors is obvious, it can be just as key to signal clearly to colleagues that you still have their backs.

One New Girl said when she had young kids, she developed a

schedule in which she left the office at three o'clock every after-noon to work from home. When her colleagues (all men) started to give her pushback about her schedule, she pushed right back at them. "Look," she told them. "I work ten times stronger, ten times harder, ten times more productively at home, and I don't need you bozos at my desk and at my door trying to talk to me." "It became endearing," she said of the rapport that developed.

Consistent with common patterns of gender bias, the men she worked with would often assume she was spending time with her children when she wasn't at her desk. She anticipated this bias and defused it with a joke. "Don't expect to see me every day," she would tell them. "If I'm not here, it's because I'm out doing my job."

Strategy 8: Your Dirty Little Secret?

A generation ago, there was only one option for working mothers with regard to talking about children in the office: just don't. By far the majority of the women we spoke with said they made an effort to mention their children as little as possible.

"In my day, you just didn't say you had children," said one con-sultant. "In hindsight, what I did was kind of hide the family," mused an executive. "I didn't make a big deal of my kids or the commitment to my kids at the office," an attorney said.

This strategy remains popular in some corners. "I had some-one recently tell me that they didn't realize I had children," said one businesswoman. "I don't talk a lot about my kids with my boss because I don't want him to think that I use them to get out of work. And I want him to think that I will do whatever it takes—even though I won't."

As one academic pointed out, this is essentially what the men have been doing all along. "Men get congratulated, but they don't say much more about it, either," she said. "If a woman looks like she's too involved with her small children, it does work very much against them."

Mentioning your children as little as possible helps lessen descriptive bias, since these biases emerge as a result of assumptions about how the typical mother will behave. There is, however, an alternative. Joan was holding Rachel in her 1987 law school faculty picture, a strong political statement back then that would still be pretty bold today. Another New Girl described what she did when she moved to a new firm after having a child: "I decided to come in with guns blaring and said, 'I'm a mom. Here's my child.' I put it in the welcome bio at my new firm so that everyone would know it." "Just based on my personality, I don't think I would have survived just trying to do what I saw other women doing, which was pretending that they didn't have children—doing everything that the men did and having this dirty little secret called children," she said. "It forced people to take me on my terms." Certainly today, when many people in their 30s and 40s have business as well as personal friends on Facebook, the strategy of hiding one's little secret may be on the wane. That's a good thing.

But you should recognize the potential for pushback. Some women we spoke with said they didn't talk much about their children until the children got older and became less a symbol of distraction than a symbol of their success at raising healthy children while still advancing professionally. One executive said when her children were younger, she rarely mentioned them in the office. "I felt it was way too hard for men to have the cognitive dissonance between seeing you as a mommy and seeing you as a professional. And so why ask them to do it?"

Now that her children are older and no longer represent a threat to her attention and commitment, she said she has started to talk about them more and to bring them to work events. "It's very important for people to know that I have a successful family. Because otherwise then it's proof that I made the wrong choice, and I shouldn't have done it."

Women who reach the top can take huge steps toward eliminating Maternal Wall bias. Mary Cranston, when she became the first woman to run a major international law firm, created model part-time policies and reported to Joan that she told every incoming class of women, "If anybody tells you they won't work with you because you are on a part-time schedule, you come straight to me or to human resources." Carol Bartz, when she was CEO of Autodesk and Yahoo!, explained to Joan in an interview that she told her team, "If I ever found out that one of you came to one of my meetings and you should have been at your child's concert or your child's birthday or some special event, I'm going to be very angry with you." Both women, of course, also didn't slink around pretending they didn't have children. So other women didn't have to either.

*   *   *

A Maternal Wall Action Plan requires two related, but distinct, endeavors.

The first is to plot a strategy for handling the strongest form of gender bias, triggered by motherhood. Forewarned is forearmed. To counter the negative assumptions associated with motherhood, you need to take proactive steps to counter the stereotypes that a mother who is not in her office is home doing the hokey pokey with her kids, that mothers aren't committed, or that your family will move for your partner's job but never for yours. Even after you've done all that, you may face colleagues who, unbidden, insist you should follow their template of how to be a good mother.

Your outside-facing Action Plan is only the beginning. The next step is to look inward. Most women also have to address both the ideal-mother-in-your-head and the ideal-worker-in-your-head. The saddest aspect of work-family conflict is that all the qualities that make you a good person—your high ideals for both work and family—become your Achilles heel.

So remember: it's impossible to be both the ideal worker always available to her employer and the ideal mother always available to her children. That's the bad news.

Here's the good news: both ideals are seriously flawed. What works for most people is balance—all kinds of balance, but balance between work and family is a good place to start.

PART IV

The Tug of War

9

Spotting Tug of War Patterns

I'm not a girl at Google. I'm a geek at Google.[1]

— MARISSA MAYER

Once a year or so, a study or trend piece comes out about why women are bad to work for, about nasty female co-workers, about watercooler Queen Bees and Mean Girls at the office. And then there's popular culture: from *Working Girl* to *The Devil Wears Prada*, the evil female boss is almost as tired a trope as the prostitute with a heart of gold. For all the trendy new names, it's just a rehashing of the same old story.

"Female rivalry in the workplace may sometimes be as important as sexism in holding women back in their careers," opined an article in London's *Sunday Times*.[2] But female rivalry, in fact, is often the result of sexism. Two 2011 studies found that a common strategy for women experiencing gender discrimination in the course of their careers was to stereotype, distance themselves from, and criticize other women.[3] Joan sometimes calls this the "Why would I hang out with losers?" strategy of coping with gender bias.

An important proviso: by discussing the gender dynamics that set women against each other, we are not saying that women never support each other. Often they do. Nor are we saying that women should support each other every single millisecond: to say that would be to enforce the prescriptive stereotype that women ought to be endlessly selfless and communal. Men don't always support each other, and when they don't, we don't often suggest they have personality problems.

Instead our contention is this: that women's workplace fights over gender play a much larger role in complicating office politics for women than do men's fights over gender with men. The reasons for this are complex, and it's the bottom line that's important —gender bias against women often fuels conflict among women.

Passing

In 1766, the young botanist Jean Baret boarded the *Étoile*, a vessel captained by Louis Antoine de Bougainville and headed west from France to explore the New World. Baret worked hard onboard the ship and, when it landed in South America, proved to be a diligent and skilled explorer who, according to some sources, discovered the bougainvillea, which was subsequently named after the ship's captain. Exploring was a romantic career with extraordinary cachet, and Baret's adventure would have been enough to make him quite a successful young man.

Except that Jean was a woman. Her real name was Jeanne Baret. Although she had been a talented botanist at home in France, she would never have been able to participate in the *Étoile*'s voyage had she not bound her chest and passed as a man.[4]

It's probably safe to say that this phenomenon is relatively rare. What is considerably more common is what law professors Devon Carbado and Mitu Gulati call strategic or partial passing, which is when an outsider takes pains to assure insiders that he or she is just like them.[5] Pretending to like sports, joining in or laughing at a session of dirty jokes, or blowing off a significant other to work late are some strategies used by women to gain the acceptance of men. For some women, passing may mean acting like "one of the boys"; for others, it could mean simply not challenging masculine behaviors. In either case, it serves to defuse any potential threat

---

PASSING THROUGHOUT HISTORY

Up until not too long ago, women who wanted to do jobs traditionally reserved for men actually had to pretend to *be* men. Here are a few of the best known:

JAMES GRAY (1723–1792): After Hannah Snell's husband deserted her, she borrowed her brother-in-law's clothes and identity and joined the Royal Marines. After being sent into battle twice, she revealed her true gender to her shipmates and petitioned for a military pension. The pension was granted, and she eventually went on to open a pub called the Female Warrior.

JAMES BARRY (c. 1789–1865): Believed to have been born Margaret Ann Bulkey, Barry is thought to have adopted a male identity in order to enroll in university. After receiving certification as a military surgeon, Barry served in multiple posts in countries including India, Malta, the Crimea, and Canada. After Barry died, the woman who took care of the body discovered female genitalia. She was buried under her adopted name.

DENIS SMITH (1896–1964): A British reporter during World War II, Dorothy Lawrence went undercover as a male soldier. When her true identity was discovered, she was forced to sign an affidavit promising not to write about her experiences. She died in an insane asylum.[a]

---

to masculinity that a female might present, by reassuring men that increasing gender diversity won't require them to change their behavior or rethink their assumptions.

One New Girl said she was recently at a law firm where several of the partners went to a strip club, including one woman, Sue. "If only everyone could be like Sue!" the guys said. "'Sue's so cool, Sue's so this, she's so pretty, she's so smart, she's so athletic.' In other words, she's good because we don't need to make any adjustments for her," the New Girl said. "The women were very ambivalent about her. On the one hand, they were like, 'How can we be

mad at her? She's fantastic. She gets her work done. She's bringing all these clients in. It's completely understandable why she is
attractive to men. On the other hand, she's doing us as a group
of women a disservice, because she's so unlike most of us. They'll
want us to be her, and there's no way we can be her.'"

"The partially passing outsider employee," in distancing herself
from the stereotypes of other women, "thus becomes the exception
to otherwise valid stereotyping rules," Carbado and Gulati write.[6]
But what if a woman actually really likes football? Or a good bawdy
story? What if she's genuinely more comfortable acting in ways
that don't challenge men's prejudices? Characterizing a woman's
behavior as "passing" simply because she acts like a man is unfairly
dismissive. There are many different ways to be a woman.

The Smurfette Principle

The Smurfs, a television show popular in the 1980s, took place in
a world populated by little blue creatures, all of whom contribute
to their society in different ways. There's the leader, Papa Smurf;
Hefty Smurf, who does the heavy lifting; Jokey Smurf, who keeps
things light with jokes and tricks. There's Chef Smurf, Cobbler
Smurf, Barber Smurf. And then there's Smurfette, whose contribution is that she's a woman. The only woman.

The Smurfette Principle is a term coined by theorist Katha
Pollitt to describe an ensemble cast in which exactly one of the
members is a woman.[7] The Smurfette Principle is an example of
tokenism, which is when limited representation of a minority group
is used to provide a false sense of inclusivity and diversity. And
it's not confined to our television screens.[8] In influential studies
of tokenism, Rosabeth Moss Kanter documented that, in workplaces with few women, women face performance pressures, highly
freighted decisions about whether to assimilate into male norms
and networks, and the threat of being trapped into narrowly cabined female roles.[9]

"Frankly, I think that there is this view that opportunities for women are very zero-sum. If one woman gets a prized position or assignment, that means another woman won't. And so it breeds a sense of competition," said one attorney. The results can get brutal.

"We used to call it the 'crab pot' mentality," said a lobbyist. "Like when you're boiling a crab, and the crabs climb on top of each other to be the only ones that can get out."

Tokenism complicates relationships among women in predictable ways. "If you're used to being the one woman," said a professor, "and you've had to be that much smarter and that much better, then all of a sudden . . . it's almost like you can't work with other women because you're so used to being the 'only woman.'"[10]

"Until maybe a year ago, I had a woman who was ahead of me," said a consultant. "And when I got to her level, she would not let me through. She was very passive-aggressive. Like, she would talk behind my back, but to my face, she was my best friend. She would leave me off invitations to things, hold back information. . . . It was very clear that she was going to let me rise to a point, but there was only going to be one seat at the management table."

Sadly, the consultant said, it was true. There really *was* only one seat for women at the management table. And that's why it's important to look for the wider patterns that lead to certain workplace dynamics. There's no question that it's destructive to women as a group—and to the general health of the workplace—when women lock other women out of positions of power to secure their place at the top. But the focus should not be on the supposed personality problem of the Queen Bee. The focus should be on the gender bias that pits women against each other by sending the message that, while men will be promoted on their merits, talented and ambitious women need to undercut other women if they hope to attain the only available seat at the table.

The irony, of course, is that there's been a lot of research that's shown that as more women move into positions of power, the better it gets for *all* women.[11] When women are in the minority, sex becomes a defining characteristic, which makes all the biases we've discussed much worse. In these cases, men and women alike are more likely to see women in terms of the stereotypical characteristics that make them seem like bad fits for leadership positions.[12] Women, when in the minority, are also more likely to be acutely aware of the biases against their gender and to suffer the decreased performance that results from the stress, anxiety, and isolation of stereotype threat.[13]

As more women join the group, the salience of gender decreases. Research has pointed to the "one-quarter" rule: women are less likely to be stereotyped if they make up at least 25 percent of a group.[14] A particularly dramatic study showed that when women make up less than 20 percent of a group, their performance evaluations are significantly lower than men's.[15] When they rise to more than 50 percent of a group, their evaluations actually rise such that they exceed men's. Some New Girls said they've observed this pattern of change in their own careers.

"When you're at two women it's hard because no matter what you say, if the other woman agrees with you, people assume it's because she's a woman," one New Girl observed. "I think when you start to get to four, you start to feel a comfort."

Femmes and Tomboys

For much of history, what's considered seemly in women has been crystal clear, and it's only in the past century or so that some of the more rigid paradigms have broken down and opened up. As a result, women now have much more flexibility—but, as we saw in chapter 4, the Tightrope women walk between masculine and feminine behaviors is precarious. "Too masculine" and you're a bitch; "too feminine" and you're a doormat. It's hard enough when you're dealing with the balance on your own terms, but when another woman who has struck a different balance enters the picture, things can get very complicated.

Take, for example, two women, named Beth and Kristen. They

both work at a large consulting firm. Beth is widely recognized as brilliant, though she does not take on visible leadership roles. She rarely says no to a favor, is easy to work with, and is always willing to offer an ear when someone needs help. Kristen, on the other hand, is a no-nonsense rainmaker. She's known for working late into the night to close big deals and has little tolerance for slipups from her staff. Kristen thinks Beth is a suck-up goody-two-shoes. Beth thinks Kristen is a bitch.

The authors of *Difficult Conversations*, a book written by members of the Harvard Negotiation Project, offer some insight into this dynamic. Conversations can get difficult when the participants' identities are at stake, which is the case with Beth and Kristen. Beth has built her professional identity around gaining people's cooperation and support by making them like her, in keeping with the traditions of femininity. Kristen has built hers around demanding excellence and earning people's respect by mobilizing the traditions of masculinity. Both may end up feeling undercut, and judged, by the other.[16]

Several studies have documented that backlash against women who are seen as masculine may come from other women as much as—or more than—it comes from men.[17] A cleverly designed 2008 experiment by Elizabeth J. Parks-Stamm, Madeline E. Heilman, and Krystle A. Hearns sought to understand *why* women penalize masculine-typed women, asking subjects of both genders to review materials about a vice president of financial affairs called Andrea.[18] Half of them received evaluations describing Andrea in positive but gender-neutral ways, as "someone who is evenhanded in her treatment of others, . . . commended for her efforts to promote performance excellence, . . . [and] emphasizes the importance of having challenging work."[19] The other half received evaluations describing her in feminine, communal terms, as "someone who is understanding and concerned for others" and committed to creating "a supportive work environment."[20]

Both men and women reacted *negatively* to Andrea when she was described with gender-neutral attributes: she fell into the "respected but not liked" trap. Only when her success was couched in feminized terms did she escape the bitch label. No news so far: Andrea needed to balance the masculine with the feminine. Here comes the fascinating part. The researchers then asked subjects how they felt about themselves after reading about Andrea and found that the women participating in the experiment reported feeling fine in the gender-neutral condition: they could fault her as "too masculine." Once Andrea was described as *both* successful *and* feminine—not an easy person to find fault with—they reported feeling inadequate. Men's self-image did not suffer in the same way. When the experimenters gave a second group of women the feedback that they, themselves, had high management potential, the bias against Andrea disappeared. The experimenters theorized that the women in the first group reacted negatively to Andrea because they assumed they were unlikely to equal her success.

A similar pattern of conflict between femmes and tomboys is that women with traditional gender beliefs respond less positively to female leaders than do women with nontraditional gender beliefs.[21] A woman scientist said when she embraced the combative culture of science, she found that it strained her relationships with her female colleagues, who considered her "not nice."[22]

Tomboys, for their part, consistently reported impatience with what they perceived as more feminine women's weakness and willingness to conform to gender stereotypes. Legendary feminist Germaine Greer once famously attacked a journalist for "her hair bird's-nested all over the place, fuck-me shoes and three fat inches of cleavage."[23] In *Delusions of Gender*, author Cordelia Fine cites the Athena Factor report, a study of British women in science, technology, engineering, and mathematics (commonly abbreviated as the STEM fields). According to the report, a quarter of the women in these fields felt like their colleagues believed women had intrinsically less aptitude than men—and, the study found, the most common reaction women had in facing this bias was to adopt it.[24] The women "took up antifemale attitudes, denigrating other women as emotional, and 'heaped scorn' on women-focused programs and any work-related gatherings dominated by women," Fine notes.[25]

Another study followed women who did not consider their gender an important part of their identities at the beginning of their careers and who later encountered gender discrimination. The study found that these women were likely to display Queen Bee behavior.[26] Typically they worked longer hours than the average woman and were more likely to report behaviors commonly seen as masculine. They tended to stereotype other women, to believe that other women had less career commitment than they themselves had, and to believe that the average male has higher career commitment than the average female.

One New Girl, who identifies unreservedly as a tomboy, told us that she distanced herself from feminine women for years. "I'm going 900 miles an hour, and if you want to keep up with me, great," she remembered thinking. "If you can't keep up with me, the hell with you. The kind of woman I hated the most were the victims, the women who were saying, 'I can't do this, and I can't do that.' I was just incredibly intolerant of that. And I chose not to see bias in the workplace. I was one of those people who said, 'Ignore the walls and just climb them or go around them or break through them, but don't sit at the base of the wall whining and crying.'"

"Women want to be friends with each other," said an in-house lawyer. "And yet when someone is openly self-promoting and competitive, it is not necessarily applauded. I think it raises a disquietude amongst her women colleagues about whether or not this dynamic is friendship or a competition and raises suspicion over that person's motivations."

Finding Safety in Distance

It's not uncommon for women to respond to gender bias and resulting gender wars by distancing themselves from other women altogether. Marisa Mayer's comment "I'm not a girl at Google, I'm a geek at Google" is just one example.[27] In a study of senior women in Australia, 60 percent of participants said they didn't actively lobby for programs to advance women. (Of course, that still means that 40 percent did actively help women.)[28]

While we don't necessarily think of *women* having biases against women as a group, everyone is exposed to the same messages about masculinity and femininity, and everyone absorbs them, notes psychologist Madeline Heilman.[29] Women who internalize these messages and know or believe that *they're* different from the stereotypes may conclude that they're not like other women —instead of concluding that maybe there's something off about the stereotypes in the first place. As Heilman explains, feeling badly about oneself can lead a person to attempt to distance oneself from similar stereotypes.[30]

This strategy is not an altogether irrational one. Psychologists point out that "organizations that devalue women threaten the identity of female workers."[31] If one woman makes a mistake or acts irresponsibly, the other women around her may fall under scrutiny as well. A mother who leaves for her daughter's ballet and dumps her work on others may, in fact, reflect badly on other mothers. A diversity consultant said she noticed this fear in some of her clients. "If a woman comes in and that woman isn't successful, maybe someone will notice *they* are a woman, and then they will be painted with that same broad stroke."

It's hard to be judgmental of this distancing approach: after all, all *men* aren't burdened with having to claim an identity that will make their career progress harder. At the same time, it's worth noting one drawback: if and when women who adopt this strategy meet bumps in the road because they are women, they don't have a network of women to help them out.

The diversity consultant recalled a training she led in which one of the women spoke up to say that she didn't think the discussion of gender issues applied to her, because she didn't even think of herself as a woman. "I said to her, 'Well, you know what, you don't really have to own that identity, but I just need to let you know that

---

MALE COMPETITION

While competition between men frequently goes unremarked, the 2000 movie *American Psycho* provides a darkly funny send-up of the macho culture of the world of business. In one scene, a group of bankers sitting around a boardroom table compare business cards—paper, typeface, embossing—in an increasingly absurd contest for whose card is the best. ("Look at that subtle off-white coloring. The tasteful thickness of it. Oh my God, it even has a watermark.") Male competition is frequently cast as serious and vital—think of movies like *Glengarry Glen Ross* or *Wall Street*—while competition among women is depicted as petty and absurd. *American Psycho* provides a welcome reprieve to this Hollywood habit.

I noticed that you were a woman,'" the consultant told us. "'Your clients will notice that you are a woman. The judge will notice that you're a woman. Your partner will notice that you're a woman. So you don't have to buy that identity. But it's crazy not to notice that other people might associate that identity with you, because you won't be able to figure out sometimes what might be happening or why people are reacting the way they are.'"

Double Standards of Competition

Unlike men, who are expected to compete for the best jobs, women are expected to help and promote each other.[32] When women do compete, it's depicted as petty and ugly. In season two of the television show *Ally McBeal*, a new attorney enters the fictional firm of Cage & Fish. Nelle Porter is pretty, accomplished, and a tough negotiator. When she lets the women attorneys know she's considering an offer to join Cage & Fish, they panic.

"Are they really going to hire her?" asks Georgia Thomas, an associate already at the firm, as Nelle walks away.

"How could they possibly? She's such the bitch," replies her secretary, Elaine.

"Have you talked to her?" Georgia asks.

"No. Why?" Elaine replies.

"Sometimes it makes it easier to backstab if you've had at least one conversation."

"She's smart and she's pretty, Georgia," Elaine says. "What more do you need to know?"[33]

Sometimes other women's competence or good looks can make them as threatening as their faults. Being smart and pretty, it seems, makes Nelle the enemy. The jealousy is presented with a stunning matter-of-factness—of *course* the other women are going to hate her. She's competition. Note that she's competition only because the women are comparing themselves to one another, whereas the men are treated as individuals. No wonder gender wars happen to women but not so much to men. Men just don't have the same stake in each other's identities or job performance.

Sometimes this dynamic translates into women biased against other women. In an article titled "You've Come Which Way, Baby?," cultural critic Elayne Rapping describes showing a clip from *Ally McBeal* to her "Gender and the Media" class. The men in the class were all horrified by the stereotypes of women: "These women are so competitive and catty," said one student.

The women were scornful of the male students' chagrin: " 'That's how women really are,' they insisted, or, 'That's what you have to do to be successful.' "[34]

The men on *Ally McBeal*, of course, also have conflicts, but theirs are presented largely without comment. They argue, they posture, they get over it, and the work gets done. With the women, conflict is interpreted to reflect a deep-seated insecurity that deflects their energy from the work at hand. Stereotypes like this one are self-reinforcing—people come to expect such motivations from women and read them into situations that would go unremarked for men. Further, women are well aware that they are being judged on what they look like no matter how many accomplishments they rack up. (How many stories have been written about Hillary Clinton's clothes?) As with so many gender stereotypes, women are not only the victims of this double standard—sometimes they help perpetrate it. Women may react more negatively to aggression from another woman, seeing it as unnatural, than they would to aggression from a man, which is simply expected.[35]

"Why Secretaries Hate Working for Women Partners"

In an episode in the fourth season of the AMC television show *Mad Men*, Joan, the head secretary at advertising company Sterling Cooper Draper Pryce, begins to have problems with a young cartoonist, Joey. Joey refuses to respect her authority in the office, making lewd jokes whenever possible. His harassing behavior culminates in his taping in her window a cartoon of her in a compromising position.

When copywriter Peggy—one of the few women in the office in a nonsupport role—finds the cartoon, she fires Joey. But when she tells Joan what she's done, she doesn't get the thanks she expected.

"Now everybody in the office will know that you solved my problem and that you must be really important, I guess," Joan says witheringly.

Peggy is taken aback by her anger. "What's wrong with you? I defended you!"

"You want to be a big shot," Joan tells her. "But no matter how powerful you get around here, they can still just draw a cartoon. So all you've done is proved I'm a meaningless secretary, and you're another humorless bitch."[36]

Mad Men is set in the 1960s but frequently pinpoints modern-day tensions with laser precision; in 2010, law professor Felice Batlan published the results of a study she conducted on legal secretaries working at large law firms. Among other topics, the study —titled "If You Become His Second Wife, You Are a Fool"—looked at the changing role of legal secretaries, their responsibilities and career mobility, and the relationship between secretaries and female attorneys.[37] Perhaps unsurprisingly, the last issue was the one that received press coverage. While almost half had no preference, not a single legal secretary preferred working with female attorneys over their male counterparts.

There is an understandably complex relationship between legal secretaries (some 95 percent of whom are female, the study found) and female attorneys. The article quoted several legal secretaries whose observations were right out of the Tug of War playbook. "It would seem as if female associates/partners feel they have something to prove to everyone," noted one secretary.[38] "Females are harder on their female assistants, more detail oriented, and they have to try harder to prove themselves, so they put that on you," said another.[39] In other words, the women lawyers feel they can't afford mistakes because they have to "prove it again." Yet again, bias against women fuels conflicts among women.

In addition to the increased pressure and scrutiny that drives some women lawyers to require more from their support staff, Batlan observed, the relationship between legal secretaries and women lawyers also reflects the Tightrope. Women lawyers fill a traditionally masculine role, while their secretaries fill a traditionally feminine one. "Secretaries are expected to engage in traditionally feminine behavior such as care giving and nurture, where women attorneys are supposed to engage in what is stereotypically more masculine behavior. Given these very different expectations and performances of gender that occur in the same space, the potential for conflict is enormous," Batlan concludes.[40]

The study was careful to emphasize that "we must continually recognize that these survey results cannot simplistically be understood to mean that women just cannot get along with other women or that they are about individual personality traits. Rather we must understand them in the context of complex, powerful and institutionalized gender constructs."[41]

That message was lost in translation. When the *ABA Journal* published an article on the study, it was titled "Why Secretaries Hate Working for Women Partners." The headline garnered such a backlash that it was quickly changed to "Not One Legal Secretary Surveyed Preferred Working with Women Partners," but even so, the American Bar Association's Commission on Women in the Profession (chaired by New Girl Mary Cranston) wrote a letter to the editor of the journal demanding an apology.[42]

Then Joan and Rachel wrote a blog post on the issue, titled "The Bitchy Boss and Other Fables: How Bias against Women Becomes Conflict between Women." The editors at the *Huffington Post* changed the title to "Are Female Bosses Harder on Female Employees?": an attention-grabbing line that fed into the very same stereotypes the article itself called into question. When we complained about the mischaracterization, the title was quickly changed again to "Hate Your Boss? Ask Yourself If Gender Bias Is to Blame."[43]

The whole debacle sheds some light on the dynamics behind gender wars. First, conflict among women makes a vivid story, something the press, understandably, is very interested in providing. The pull of this traditional story line means that any discussion about conflict between women is more than likely to be flattened out into a catfight narrative, which in turn perpetuates the negative stereotypes of women.

Second, this particular Tug of War played out along predictable boundaries. Female attorneys are in a traditionally masculine role; legal secretaries are in a traditionally feminine role. As is always the case with gender wars, both groups of women are disadvantaged by gender. Secretarial jobs are undervalued and underpaid and have little or no career track—the classic ways women are disadvantaged when they do "women's work." Secretaries are disadvantaged by the devaluation of femininity. Women lawyers are disadvantaged by the glass ceiling patterns we've identified. Each group is disadvantaged by gender in different ways, which triggers conflict among women.

It's controversial to discuss these kinds of conflicts among women. The more common strategy is to deny that they exist, because of the risk (amply illustrated in the *Huffington Post* incident) that discussion of gender wars will be misinterpreted as confirmation that women are prone to catfights. But the solution is not to sweep this problem under the rug.

Gen(d)erational Conflict

One Christmas vacation while Rachel was in college, she was in an airport with the rest of the family, waiting for a flight. A good old boy—white hair, navy blazer—came up to her and asked if she went to Yale. Rachel looked down, realized she was wearing a college sweatshirt, and said yes, in fact, she did go to Yale. Joan, sitting next to her, got visibly nervous.

"Good for you!" the man said. "I was class of '62. Go Bulldogs!"

Joan waited until the man walked away and then said, "I can't believe that just happened."

Rachel didn't understand. "That happens all the time when I wear college gear."

"It happened to me, too," Joan said. "But when I was your age, men who looked like that would come up and tell me I was ruining a hallowed institution."

It's an oft-repeated truism of contemporary gender issues: a lot has changed in the last generation. When Joan went to Yale, in 1970, she was in the second class of entering women, and the idea that they should even be allowed to attend the institution was controversial. When Rachel went, in 2005, the gender ratio was approximately 50-50, and no one would have dreamed of questioning her right to be there. We may have gone to the same university, but it's fair to say that our experiences were completely different.

A similar divide exists between young women just entering the workforce and those women who were on the front lines of the gender revolution. Because of the rapid pace of change, the older generation of women faced a very different set of obstacles from today's young go-getters, and sometimes it feels as though the two belong to different universes.

"For my generation of women, our strategy has been to make it invisible and make it appear easy. And I think that's coming back to bite us in a number of ways," one New Girl said. "Young women say, 'You're full of shit, and it's not that easy, and we all know it, and you're not being honest. So, therefore, we're really not going to use you as role models.'"

For many of the women who pioneered a gender-integrated workplace, the strategy of choice was to minimize gender as much as possible. In the 1960s and '70s and even into the '80s, the women who climbed to the top often felt more comfortable with masculinity—because, if they hadn't been, they wouldn't have made it all that far. A lawyer in her 50s recalled noticing as she started her legal career that women who had made it to the top "replicated traditional male roles and, to a large degree, male mannerisms." Said a former CEO of Joan's generation, "I've always got along with the guys." In fact, she said, "I was frankly less comfortable with women—I never had tons of girlfriends. I had special girlfriends. So I think I was more comfortable with my masculine self, and so therefore I fit in." As Joan often points out to Rachel, Joan never would have entered what was then an intensively masculine profession if she hadn't felt comfortable with lots of masculine behaviors and traditions. Even women who were comfortable with acting more femininely tended to downplay visible differences between the sexes in order to fit more comfortably into a man's world (as it was openly called in those days).

This gen(d)erational dimension of the femmes/tomboys dynamic can lead older, more masculine women to take a dim view of younger femmes. A study of scientists in The Netherlands and Italy found that, although female doctoral students reported the same level of career commitment as their male colleagues, women professors were more likely than male professors to see female graduate students as lacking career commitment.[44] A prior study

NEW GIRL FASHION TIPS

There are none. It is impossible to give fashion tips without setting off serious gen(d)erational conflict and other gender wars. Older women often get into trouble advising younger women to "dress vanilla," avoid cleavage, don't show so much leg, and so on, with the message that dressing in too feminine a way jeopardizes their chances of being taken seriously. Younger women often feel fervently that they should be able to dress however they want and do not want to mimic men.

Here's the fact: Some women do just fine with dress that's downright masculine. Others do just fine with dress that's very feminine. Just make sure that you want to fight the battles you're choosing. If you dress in a very masculine way and start getting backlash problems, consider either dressing more femininely or choosing a different way of femming it up a bit. If you dress in a very feminine way and start noticing you're not being taken seriously, consider dressing differently or choosing a different way to Man Up.

of full professors reported that they described themselves as more masculine, and less feminine, than other women.[45]

As people have gotten more used to women in positions of power, a much wider range of behavior has emerged as acceptable. Said a lawyer in her 50s, "I do sense, looking at women who are younger than I am, that they feel much more free with their femininity in the workplace than even my generation does." Recall the woman professor who was on a "backlash mission" to act feminine in professional contexts—to wear dresses, to bake cookies for students, to bring her child to class.[46]

Younger women may see their older counterparts' attitudes as rigid, humorless, and out of touch. Older women see younger women engaging in behaviors that would have ended their careers in ten minutes flat and assume that the younger women just don't know what it takes to succeed. "I'm always careful when I talk to the younger generation, because I've just seen so many instances where they don't like to be told that things might be a certain way, or 'here are some things to keep in mind,'" said an older executive. "And they think that their style is their style and they shouldn't have to make modifications in the workplace."

Objectively, of course, women *shouldn't* have to make modifications in the workplace in order to conform to the narrow range of acceptable female behavior. But many women we spoke with said they've chosen to save their political capital by not fighting that particular fight so they can use it on things that are more important to them. When they try to explain their strategy to younger women, often they get pushback. What feels like realistic advice for the person giving it can seem like judgment for the person on the receiving end.

A New Girl who works at a major consulting firm said she had done a series of focus groups with the younger women at the company, and what she heard them say "time and time again" was that

---

**GEN(D)ERATION GAP: RACHEL VERSUS JOAN ON
WHAT TO WEAR TO AN INTERVIEW**

RACHEL: I can't stand it when people tell me how to dress. I have a modicum of common sense, and I know it's inappropriate to show up to the office in a bikini. Beyond that, it's up to me the extent to which I'm willing to sacrifice my personality to my career. Say I don't get a job because I'm wearing a pantsuit and flats instead of a skirt and heels or because my outfit lets out the dirty secret that I'm a woman. In that case, everyone learned something: the company learned they didn't want me as an employee, and I learned I didn't want them as an employer.

JOAN: I've definitely told Rachel to tone down the cleavage before. She just doesn't notice it and doesn't think anyone else will. I mean, it's her choice, but it's not a battle I would fight. If young women do choose to fight that battle, it's important they make a self-conscious decision that that's how they want to spend those points.

there were no female role models. There were some senior women, but the younger women dismissed them as "really just men in disguise." "I know a lot of the women in the senior positions—besides myself—and I know that they're not like that," the New Girl said, "but I can see how they would be perceived that way. Because they've had to create a hard shell to deal with all the guys in those senior positions to make their way to where they are."

A second type of gen(d)erational conflict arises when younger women fault older women for failing to help them. Sometimes, of course, the younger women have a point. But sometimes more senior women feel so embattled that they feel unable to help women junior to them. "I never felt like I had the power to be in a position to mentor somebody else. Like I couldn't use my influence because I didn't have enough," a New Girl said wistfully. Younger women may not see that the older women are struggling, too, and have fewer political chips than one might think from the outside. They may be fighting their own battles, having to prove themselves over and over, or having to do damage control because they are seen as bitchy. This is yet another way that gender bias against women fuels conflict among women.

Mommy Wars

Motherhood is the most powerful trigger of gender bias, as we discussed in chapter 7. Maybe it's not surprising, then, that the Tug of War emerges when women have opposing aspirations for motherhood as well as differing ideals about the correct way to mother. Women who don't have children are often treated like they're defective women, while women who do have children can be made to feel like defective workers, defective mothers, or both. "Either you have kids or you don't have kids," said one consultant. "And it becomes this difficult sort of noninclusive conversation when it could just be about how do we help navigate the day-to-day demands of our personal and professional lives."

A 2010 study by Stephen Benard and Shelley Correll found that, while both men and women saw mothers as less competent and committed than fathers, women but not men penalized mothers who were unambiguously competent and committed to work. The college women who participated in the study rated highly successful mothers as significantly less likable and warm than highly successful fathers. The go-getter moms were also less likely to be recommended for promotion than equivalent fathers or nonmothers.[47] In the eyes of these college women, successful moms were both defective parents and defective workers.

One New Girl said she spent years being unapologetically judgmental of women with children: "I was probably one of those women who thought, if you're going to be a girl and come in here and have a bunch of babies, you're not going to bill enough hours to make partner, and that's life," she admitted. Another woman

---

IDENTITIES AT RISK

Conversations become explosive when they present a threat to our sense of who we are in the world. Mommy Wars are a classic example of a difficult conversation, because of what's at stake: "Am I a good mother?"

In order to navigate these identity conversations better, the book *Difficult Conversations* suggests moving from this framework:

ASSUMPTION: I'm competent or incompetent, good or bad, lovable or unlovable. There is no in-between.

GOAL: Protect my all-or-nothing self-image.

. . . to this framework:

ASSUMPTION: There may be a lot at stake psychologically for both of us. Each of us is complex, neither of us is perfect.

GOAL: Understand the identity issues on the line for each of us. Build a more complex self-image to maintain my balance better.[b]

said that before she had her own children, she often viewed women with children as a liability.

"I'm sad to say that I can remember feeling resentment sometimes for people who couldn't put in the time or effort on a project because they just really were constrained. It definitely took me getting a little older and wiser or nicer or something to realize it shouldn't be that way." But if women who have children face judgments from women who don't, the reverse is also true. Said one woman, a lesbian who did not yet have children but planned to, "Numerous colleagues have perceived me as someone who doesn't want kids just because I've been committed to my career for so long." She explained that it was not only her work ethic but also her sexuality that contributed to this assumption: "Their perception is obviously I'm not in a traditional relationship, so why would I have a traditional family?"

There's also a gen(d)erational component to Mommy Wars. Older women who felt that they had to miss out on parts of their kids' childhoods may have a lot invested in convincing themselves that that's just what it takes to succeed in their careers. One New Girl described the perspective of these older women: "'I've made these sacrifices, and so I have the right to make you miserable.' It makes you feel guilty if you want something different."

One New Girl told us that when she returned from maternity leave, her older female boss started to micromanage her schedule, refusing her requests for flexible work arrangements and even going so far as to schedule meetings at difficult times just to see if the New Girl would attend. "I think there was a lot of sort of personal guilt going on," the New Girl said. "Her daughter was grown up at the time, but she would tell me, 'I came back to work when my baby was four weeks old, and I didn't have the luxury of some of these things that are in place now.'"

Despite the name, no women—whether they are mothers, childless, or child-free—are exempt from Mommy Wars. They erupt between women who have children and women who don't, between women who take time off to spend with their children and women who go back to work immediately after birth, between women who have children but disagree about the right way to raise them. What all these conflicts have in common is that they translate personal hurt into hostility against other women. With something as personal and sensitive as the decisions we make about when and how to have a family, the potential for disagreement and hurt feelings is huge. Once again, it's important to recognize that these conflicts stem not from the defects or shortcomings of individual women but rather from a system that presents women with two mutually exclusive ideals and then punishes them for failing to live up to both.

Who Has the Perfect Balance?

Conflicts between generations about work-life balance are a particularly controversial corollary to the Mommy Wars—whether kids are involved or not.

"As a young woman today, you might look at that and say, 'What were you, crazy?'" said one New Girl, who remembers trying to get a new company off the ground—while still working in corporate America—when her children were young. "And, yeah, if there's a way to do it now where you don't have to run as fast as I did, then maybe it does make some sense."

"I've heard associates say, 'I'm not going to go part-time. I'm going to quit rather than go part-time because if you go part-time, you're a loser,'" said a law firm partner.

"I'm not prepared to contract out my life like people like you have," another partner reported hearing.

One New Girl described a meeting where an older woman gave some "very practical advice" about priorities, which she illustrated with the example of bathing her children. She just didn't like giving her kids baths—"You know, our bathroom floors are made out of tile and it hurts my knees to be down there for the half an hour it takes to scrub and wash and whatever. So, if my husband wants to do it, if our babysitter wants to do it, great."

Many of the women in her audience were horrified by her comment, as though delegating bath time were akin to child neglect. This goes back to the discussion in the Maternal Wall chapter about helicopter parenting—current mores dictate a near-impossible level of involvement in parenting and childrearing, which of course places additional pressure on working mothers who already feel insecure about both their commitment to their families and their jobs.

As we discussed in chapter 7, the norm of the ideal worker available 24/7 was until recently taken for granted, a persistent relic of a semimythic era in which male breadwinners were responsible for all the work outside the home and female homemakers took care of all the domestic labor. Children who grew up in families in which mothers tried to fill both roles are now entering the workforce with a very real sense of how unrealistic that model is. And yet there are very few role models for how to successfully balance work and a personal life.

"Nobody was really making it work and going, 'Yes, I have work-life balance,'" said one younger attorney, who said that when she worked at a law firm, she found the lack of successful female partners to emulate discouraging. "Work-life balance tended to mean, 'I have a partner who has sacrificed something so that I can do what I want to do,' or 'I have sacrificed my own goals in order to have other things besides my job,' or something like that. You never got the feeling of balance."

Women who are now at the top of their chosen fields often felt they had no choice but to conform to the systems already in place. When younger women enter the workforce and question those decisions, it can be hard not to get defensive.

"We certainly get a lot of younger women saying, 'Why would I want to be a partner? Your life looks miserable,'" said a partner at a professional services firm. Another New Girl had even harsher experiences. Younger women, she said, say, "Your life sucks. Why would I dream of trying to be what you are?"

"I had a couple of younger women say to me, on their way out, that part of why they were leaving is because they didn't want to be me," one New Girl said. "Which, after a while, takes a toll on you, because you may or may not ever be somebody's role model, but you certainly don't want to be somebody's *negative* role model."

"It's hard," said another woman. "The senior women lawyers, when they hear the younger women talk like that, feel like they're being disrespected—basically, that they're being trashed for having given so much of their lives to the law firm. And that's tremendously damaging to their egos, because they *did* give so much."

The part that makes the younger generation's reaction sting so much, this woman said, is that women of her generation did have to make so many hard trade-offs. "In their heart of hearts, they may be questioning whether that was a smart thing to do or not."

It can also be hard, several New Girls said, to see younger women reject the opportunities they worked so hard for. "Younger women decide that they're just going to opt out, which is frustrating," one woman said. "I don't think they fully appreciate what they're giving up. They've worked so hard to develop skills so they can have this professional life. They jettison it so easily, by my judgmental way of thinking." "I do think the work world needs to change, but it's not going to change if the people who want it to change just leave," she said. "I think the job that I have and the work I have and the way I do it—it's all available to me, and it would never have been available to me when I graduated from law school 25 years ago. It exists because I made it happen."

Women need to work hard to ensure that their different experiences of gender don't pit them against each other. The following chapter is designed to help.

* * *

The good news is that only 55 percent of the women we interviewed reported Tug of War problems. So if you encounter them, rest assured that you could probably find another environment where you won't.

Two distinct and apparently contradictory forces lie at the heart of the Tug of War. One is that conflicts among women are often dismissed or belittled as catfights. Out of fear that acknowledging these conflicts would reinforce the stereotype that women are inherently petty and prone to undermine each other, many feminists simply choose not to discuss them at all. What that strategy elides is the fact that gender pressures actually *do* sometimes make it more difficult for women to support each other. We need to talk more about these issues—but we need to talk about them sensitively, without slipping into judgmental moralizing or easy stereotypes.

Understanding the role that gender bias plays in the Tug of War makes two things clear: one, ignoring the fact that underlying problems exist is not going to solve them, and two, the ways in which the issues often emerge make these problems worse, not better.

The strategies in the following chapter provide ways to address gender wars without making them worse. The key is that gender wars are not "catfights." That characterization is inherently insulting, a carryover from an era when belittling women and treating them as irrational was accepted behavior. Deep conflicts arise when people's identities are at risk. Professional women face unique challenges to identity, in all the ways we've discussed so far in this book. Women fight in this situation not because they are catty but because they are human.

10

Tug of War Action Plan

Any woman who chooses to behave like a full human being
should be warned that the armies of the status quo will treat
her as something of a dirty joke; that's their natural and first
weapon. She will need sisterhood. —GLORIA STEINEM

Gender wars can get very ugly. Often, during Joan's interviews, women who described gender wars often swore her to silence. They felt embarrassed and vulnerable discussing conflicts with other women. One reason was that these conflicts were particularly recognizable, and they didn't want to be outed. But the reasons went deeper. Somehow these conflicts were just deeply troubling.

The issues that spark Tug of War are deeply personal. Controversy about the "right way to be a woman" gets to the heart of the most personal decisions we've made in constructing our identities and our lives, and it's almost impossible not to react negatively when we're told, explicitly or by implication, that we've made the wrong decisions. After all, we all worry, sometimes, that the choices we've made have been the wrong ones. What if we *didn't* have to pull 80-hour weeks to secure that promotion? What if we *could* have worn our favorite biker jacket or sundress in the office? What if we *hadn't* taken such a long maternity leave?

Tug of War was reported in just over half our interviews (55 percent). While it was slightly more common in the NSF interviews (57 percent) than The New Girls' Network interviews (54 percent), it appears to cut across race and profession. There were some differences in the types of Tug of War problems: women interviewed for The New Girls' Network were much more likely to report conflicts among women over motherhood (39 percent versus 12 percent). The scientists in the NSF interviews were slightly more likely to report conflict with colleagues (56 percent versus 53 percent) and conflict with women administrative assistants (32 percent versus 8 percent)—although this number should be used with caution because the NSF interviews specifically asked about that, whereas The New Girls' Network interviews did not. More than the other types of bias we've discussed, Tug of War bias appeared to depend largely on working environment—some workplaces had huge conflicts between women, and some none at all.

In order to get over the Tug of War, we all need to recognize that the questions it raises are real and frightening—and stop working through that fear by criticizing women who chose our own roads not taken. What this means is that the simplest step in overcoming Tug of War problems may be the hardest to take. Other women are powerful allies who understand what it's like to be a woman in the workplace in a way that male friends and mentors just can't share. The most important thing we as individuals can do to combat the Tug of War is to recognize that all women have had to make difficult trade-offs, and they have responded in very different ways. None of us have made perfect choices because none of us had perfect options.

"This is not about the choices you have made," one New Girl sad. "This is about creating a better array of choices for our kids. In order for them to have a better array of choices, we need to get to work now."

Strategy 1: Recognize the Limits of the Sisterhood

While other women *can* be valuable allies, it's important to recognize that the abiding belief that women should always support each other simply because they share a biological sex isn't how real life works—and there's no reason it should be.

Once again, Tina Fey and Amy Poehler nail the pretense behind our unexamined assumptions in the Clinton-Palin *Saturday Night Live* skit. Tina Fey's Sarah Palin character is talking about how regardless of party affiliation, women everywhere can agree that it's time for a woman in the White House, when Poehler's Clinton interrupts. "I'm sorry," Poehler says. "I need to say something. I didn't want a woman to be president! *I* wanted to be president, and I just *happen* to be a woman! And I don't want to hear you compare *your* road to the White House to *my* road to the White House. I scratched and clawed through mud and barbed wire, and you just glided in on a dog sled wearing your pageant sash and your Tina Fey glasses!"[1]

The underlying assumption, prevalent in the media back in 2008, was that Sarah Palin's nomination as John McCain's vice president should be a good consolation prize to Clinton (and her supporters). This assumption takes for granted that the salient part of female candidates isn't their substance—not their political party or their policy platforms or the interests of their constituency—but rather their lady parts, to use a Tina Feyism. Just imagine similar logic applied to any two male politicians. ("Well, Mr. Gore, it's really too bad you didn't win the election—but at least another *man* will be president!")

Frankly, it's hard to criticize women who don't go out of their way to reach out to other women. After all, we wouldn't call a man a traitor for failing to privilege his relationships with other men simply because they share the same biological sex. In fact, we'd call him a sexist if he did. One important strategy in defusing gender wars is simply to recognize that you will meet some women over the course of your career with whom you have very little in common, and that's fine.

"Sometimes there are individuals who just happen to be women who are just apples and oranges in personality," said one New Girl. "If you have that issue with men, it's not a big deal, not a gender issue. It should be the same with women."

When you're dealing with an apple to your orange, try to be

conscious of the biases that might be at work and actively avoid exacerbating them. One New Girl remembered a co-worker who would constantly make disparaging comments about her in meetings and on calls. "There's a person in my group, a tomboy, who finds it so difficult to work with the femmes that she's visibly very objectively rude and mean and nasty to those women, whom she finds to be a threat," explained the New Girl.

Finally, after a particularly public takedown on a big conference call, the New Girl decided to talk to the other woman in private. "I sent her a message and just said, 'I recognize that you're very good at what you do, and I value you as part of our team. I would never let anybody talk to you the way you are talking to me. And if I've done something that is upsetting or offensive to you, it was unintentional and please let me know so I can correct it. But the way you're treating me is unacceptable.'"

The other woman backed off.

The strategies for controlling your anger that we listed in the Tightrope section all apply here as well. Don't let your anger control you, and if you feel you need to draw a line in the sand, make sure you name the business goal that makes it important to do so. Women don't need to be your allies—but that's no reason to make them your enemies. There are always going to be other allies eager to seek out female colleagues for mutual support.

"I never try to convince somebody that the choices that they're making are not good," one New Girl said. "I would so much rather help the women who are champing at the bit and dying to move forward but are being held back."

Strategy 2: Senior Women: Remember That the Younger Women's Experience Is Different

People know Joan's a feminist, of course, and some respond by complaining to her about younger women: "That cleavage! How can she expect to be taken seriously?" "*Four* children: she's going nowhere fast." "*Girls*! After all our hard work, they call themselves *girls*?" Even sober voices complain that younger women don't recognize the blood, sweat, and humiliations experienced again and again by professional women now in their 50s and 60s.

As one New Girl pointed out, the point that all this complaining misses is that the struggles keep changing—but that doesn't mean one set is more valuable than another. "Everybody has a different on-ramp, and we forget that," she said. "So when folks say, for example, 'Oh, you didn't live through the '60s and '70s when the Equal Rights Amendment was on the agenda and we had all these marches and birth control became available,' I want to say, 'Yes, and there were many who didn't live when the Model T was here either.' You have to accept people where they get on because they're taking advantage of their particular situation, their place in time, which is exactly what you're supposed to do."

Joan entered college in 1970 and became a law professor in 1980. The "Yale girls" who entered college with her were, by all accounts (including their own), weirdos. The joke was that they had either built a nuclear reactor in their basement, published a novel, or completed a career in architecture. They had to be comfortable with an eight-to-one ratio of men to women, with being the only woman in the room, with people getting angry with them for desecrating a temple of learning. They had to be pioneers.

Most also felt comfortable assimilating into a broad range of masculine behaviors. If Joan had not felt comfortable with masculine assertiveness and one-upmanship, she would never have ventured into territory that, at that time, was intensely, unapologetically, and unremittingly masculine. Her generation also had to be willing and able to tune out social cues that told them they were treading where they didn't belong and doing what they should not do. They needed to be comfortable crossing boundaries.

Today, a much broader range of women become professionals. While the world Rachel grew up in was by no means free of gender bias, most of the overt discrimination was gone. No one, through-out the course of her education and her career, has had any doubts because of her gender that she belongs there.

This is *success*. Women no longer have to be at the far end of the continuum to enter traditionally male arenas. But that also means that the older generations of women differ from the women who followed them. And this creates a culture gap. Gender wars bubble up between older women and their younger colleagues, who are often more comfortable with the traditions of femininity and less interested in fighting big battles.

Over and over, the older women look at younger women who want to take longer parental leave or go part-time or take a career break or just act like girls, and they say, "You just don't understand what it takes to make it in this field." And the younger women say to the older, "We don't want your sorry-ass lives. You just turned into men." Again, this culture gap reflects *success*. It means that the battles the older women fought have borne fruit and made room for a much broader range of women. It's time for older women to accept younger women for who they are.

Strategy 3: Younger Women: Senior Women May Not Have as Much Power as You Think

For younger women, it's helpful to remember that older women have had—and continue to have—their own struggles. Several of the New Girls told us they found it frustrating when younger women faulted them for not being supportive, when they simply felt they didn't have enough power themselves to throw around.

When Rachel was working in an office, she was acutely aware that some of the female attorneys were skeptical of her, for two reasons. One, as a paralegal, she was in a service role, meaning that she had more leeway on the Tightrope than the lawyers. Certain behaviors rankled: she could wear sneakers or low-cut dresses to work and make jokes over e-mail, simply because the standards for professionalism were lower for her. The men were more likely to think these behaviors were cute and goofy; the women may have felt she was being unprofessional or taking unnecessary risks. The second reason women may have hesitated is that because Rachel was low on the totem pole, associating too closely with her meant losing rank—no one wants to go to lunch with a paralegal when they could be going to lunch with a managing partner.

As a result of these tensions, it was in many ways easier for Rachel to find mentors in the male attorneys than the female attorneys. Rachel's impulse was to find someone whose life looked how she wanted her life to look and to learn from that person—but the female associates made it pretty clear that their relationships were to remain strictly professional. In part because she saw some of these gendered forces at work, Rachel respected that desire. The women she worked with were supportive and excellent colleagues. They just didn't have the resources it would have taken to actively advocate for and ally themselves with her.

Unless they were doing it behind the scenes. The more senior women we spoke with said much of their advocacy is invisible to the very women they're helping, which may mean it goes unnoticed and unappreciated. A New Girl who worked in finance remembered speaking at a mentoring lunch for female vice presidents at her organization, along with two other female managing directors. In the middle of her talk, one of the women in the audience stood up and asked, "Well, how much do senior women at this firm really fight for junior women?"

The answer, the New Girl said, was that the three managing directors all spent "a lot of personal capital" looking out for junior women. But they were never particularly obvious about it. "What I realized in that exchange is that you cannot be public about fighting for women," the New Girl told us.

The generational divides between professional women don't have to drive a wedge between us. But in order to bridge that gap, it's important to understand that the world has changed significantly since the first women entered the workforce. For older women, that means accepting that women today can take advantage of a flexibility that stems from the hard-won battles of their foremothers. For younger women, it means understanding just how difficult these battles were and are.

Strategy 4: Managing Down Is Just as Important as Managing Up

If you're having trouble with someone who is lower on the totem pole, the first step is to take a hard look at yourself: recall the wise advice of the New Girl who, when she was called a bitch, first took the time to ask herself, "Am I being a bitch? Am I being difficult to work with?"

The second step, as always, is information gathering. Are other people having similar kinds of problems with the same person? You can ask around to people in your inner circle without going into grim detail about your own difficulties.

Once you've done your homework and can be confident that there's a problem, the next question is how to raise it. A useful working assumption is that the person in question does not recognize she is treating men differently from women. You need to come armed with specific examples of unfair treatment and with good tone control. But remember that people call it unconscious bias because it's often unconscious. It's particularly important in this kind of situation to be attuned to Tightrope issues; women who give negative feedback tend to be viewed negatively.[2] The "feedback sandwich"—criticism sandwiched by praise—is one good way to get your point across with softeners.[3] As is often true with this type of confrontation, backing off the gender angle may be your best bet.

One way to avoid these problems is to proactively bond with administrative personnel around you. Several New Girls said they do this by sharing personal information or taking the time to express interest and concern about the lives of those who work for them.

Note that this is the kind of "nice work" expected of women but not of men; if you decide not to do it, no judgment here. Joan spent years refusing to do this kind of emotion work, most notably mothering of students, on the grounds that she "gave at home."

But she does it now, and things do flow a lot more smoothly. In the context of relationships with administrative personnel, it helps to keep in mind that, although you may have to pedal harder because you're a woman, the fact remains that you're still at the top of the heap. It's not fair for women, but not men, to have to take that into account. But you're a person, making moral choices as an individual.

HOW TO BE A GREAT BOSS

1. Now that you know the patterns of gender bias, be self-conscious about whether you are correcting for them in your everyday workplace interactions. Remember, those patterns influence women as well as men.

2. Show the people you supervise that you care about their career development.

3. Praise early and often. Compliments build morale, cost you nothing, and help make you a good person. Besides, if you've done a good job of hiring, you have fabulous people around you; make sure they know you know it.

4. Have the courage, and take the time, to give negative feedback in real time—don't wait until months later, during the performance review.

5. Communicate to the people around you that you will be loyal to them if they are loyal to you. They need to know you have their back.

6. If someone is just not right for the job and you have to let them go, remember: the message is not that they are a failure, it's that this is not the job for them. Help them think through what kind of job you think might better fit their strengths.

Your choice—and no doubt there are limits, for sure. If someone expects you to take lots and lots of time on her personal issues, then she probably needs a resource who is not you. At the same time, the women who work for you can be important allies. They can either cover for you or call you out when you are taking care of business at home. They can make you look highly professional or highly unprofessional. They can speak of you with respect or fuel gossip that you're a witch.

One law firm managing partner said she's always looking for ways to reach out to other women around her. "Sometimes I'll tell people things just to hear what people's reactions are or make me seem more real, especially to the women," she told us. "You know, I'll walk by, and the receptionist will say, 'Your hair looks nice today.' And I'll say, 'Oh, I got hair extensions last week' or something." Such personal tidbits, she said, improve her relationship with all the women in the office, which helps contribute to a mutually supportive environment.

Strategy 5: Make an Enemy into an Ally

Once you recognize that a lot (not all, of course, but a lot) of the tension between professional women stems from shared pressure, it may become easier to avoid it. This means not only understanding other women's behavior as motivated by bias rather than by spite but sometimes stepping back on your own competitiveness as well.

"There was a woman at my office who was quite competitive with me," said one New Girl. "And there arose a situation where I could do something or she could—something really high profile. It was really in my bailiwick. But I let her do it, and it really eased tensions between us."

Sometimes a generous gesture can turn an enemy into a friend. Sometimes you need to take a more direct approach and, in the nicest possible way, call out the person who is undermining you. "I think it's hard if you feel that someone doesn't respect you or is trying to belittle you or undermine you," said one New Girl. "No matter how tempting, it's not a good idea to start going after them the same way."

Instead, this New Girl recommended going to the root of the problem. "In my experience, the most common situation is they're insecure," she said. If—and only if—the person is really inhibiting your effectiveness, you need to take them on in private: "I perceive —and I may not be correct in this—that you view me not in the best light always. I'd really like to have a good relationship with you." She continued, "If there's something that I've inadvertently done, I'd love your feedback because my intent is always to be respectful of you and try to have a good relationship with you. So just help me understand if there's somehow we've gotten off on the wrong foot."

Strategy 6: Get Women Working Together

One thing we heard over and over again from the women we spoke with is that being female in a male-dominated world can be very isolating. "The whole experience, both while I was experiencing it and looking back at it, was very lonely," said a former attorney. "That, to me, was the biggest issue of all. It was very lonely."

"There's so much loneliness in this field," said another New Girl in a male-dominated industry. "And after being in the field for a very long time and becoming more and more isolated, I realized that everything I would try to do that I thought would make a difference wasn't working."

One particularly effective way to counter isolation is to become involved in a women's group or initiative at your office or in your industry. When there are no organic ways for a community of women to come together, a women's group can serve as a remedy for isolation, as well as a place to address some of the problems women confront. For example, women often report struggling to develop their own client base. Several of the New Girls said they

---

FIVE WAYS TO SUPPORT OTHER WOMEN

1. If you hear a man steal an idea previously brought up by a woman, say, "You know, that's an excellent point. I have been thinking about it ever since LaShawn brought it up, and . . ."

2. If a woman is faulted for being outspoken or pushy or whatever, recharacterize her behavior like this: "Gee, I noticed just the same thing, but I think about it a bit differently. I don't see her as aggressive; I see her as assertive, and I think that's just what we need to get this kind of deal done."

3. If you see a woman taking on the office housework again and again, go talk with her. Tell her you've noticed she's being given more than her fair share, and ask if she'd like to brainstorm with you about how to turn that around.

4. If you hear people assuming that someone will not want a challenging assignment because of her children, go to her and say, "This is what I am hearing, and I just wanted you to know, because some women see this as welcome considerateness and others see it as depriving them of opportunities. If you see it as kindness, great. If you see it as something different, I'd love to brainstorm about how we can turn this around."

5. If you hear women trash-talking another woman, say, "You know, I don't always agree with her either, but I can see where she's coming from." Try to highlight how all women are struggling with the same problem, and come up with a continuum of solutions.

---

had made connections during women's group meetings with people in their company or industry that had helped them land important business later on.

Another New Girl said she was organizing some women's programming at her firm and realized she would have to invite one woman in particular who was notoriously uninterested in women's issues. She was worried, she told us, because the woman was outspoken about her belief that discussing gender was a waste of time —"I made it, and so can others." But the New Girl couldn't *not* include her.

To everyone's surprise, the woman ended up getting a lot out of the program, and the New Girl ended up with an unexpected ally. "Her sitting through the program and hearing young women talk about their issues for two days actually had quite a profound effect on her, because I don't think she'd ever listened to that before."

Keep in mind that, in order to not alienate potential allies, you have to make your women's initiative inclusive. One New Girl told of a women's initiative founded by two women in her firm; they "wanted it to be solely focused just on work-life issues rather than related to women's path to partnership, into leadership roles, or any number of other things." A younger attorney who had no children came to her and said, "This initiative is driving me nuts. These people are just focused on the work-life balance situation. I really want to be working on business development. This isn't inclusive of our entire group." So the senior attorney talked to a wide range of stakeholders and began looking at the agenda beforehand, to make sure it included topics of interest to a wide range of women, including those without children. It's the basic Tug of War message: remember that there are a lot of different ways to be a woman.

A women's initiative won't work as a way to get women working together when key women won't participate because they don't identify with women's issues. An alternative is to organize a way for women to work together that does not stress women's issues. What it is will depend on the culture of your office: having all the women do a public-service day together might be a good choice. So might a spa day, but beware: sometimes the key people you're seeking to attract may find that too girly.

*   *   *

Gender wars are another reason why women need to be politically more adept than men to thrive in business and the professions.

Most of the strategies in this chapter boil down to one central insight: women have to make difficult choices about how to fit in an office environment that is often still a man's world. Some women choose to assimilate, to the maximum extent possible, into male norms and networks. Other women stay closer to the traditions of femininity.

But you know what? Most of us do both—as we have seen in the discussion of the Tightrope, most successful women mix masculinity and femininity, assimilation and resistance. This means that if women start judging each other on the right way to be a woman, they will be dividing by the infinite gradations between tomboy and femme, with each one judging the other for being one notch too much in one direction or the other.

Don't go there. Not every woman has to be your friend, but think once, twice, and thrice before undermining another woman in public—for selfish reasons: it looks bad; and strategic ones: what goes around comes around, and at some point in your career, you will probably need the help and support of other women.

PART V

Double Jeopardy?

11

The Experience of Gender Bias Differs by Race

The image conjured up by the label "scientist" remains that of a white male hovering over test tubes in a darkened laboratory.

— KENNETH MANNING,
PROFESSOR AND EDITOR OF
MIT: SHAPING THE FUTURE

Our First Lady is an incredibly accomplished woman.[1] Michelle Obama went to Princeton as an undergraduate and then on to Harvard Law School. After earning her JD, she worked for several years at law firm Sidley Austin as an associate specializing in intellectual property, where she was assigned to mentor a summer associate who was to become her husband—and later the 44th president of the United States. Michelle eventually left Sidley Austin to start a youth mentorship program for urban children; after her first child, Malia, was born, she began working as a vice president for the University of Chicago Hospitals and served on the board of food supplier Treehouse Foods. As First Lady, she has become an undisputed style icon and has spearheaded an initiative to reduce childhood obesity.

In other words, Michelle Obama is a consummate New Girl. And yet, both during the 2008 presidential campaign and again after the publication of a 2012 book that depicted her arguing with her husband's staff, she's had to defend herself against a very specific set of stereotypes. "That's been an image that people have tried to paint of me since the day Barack announced, that I'm some angry black woman," she said in an interview with CBS's Gayle King.[2]

In the book *Sister Citizen*, author Melissa Harris-Perry observes that Michelle Obama took a sharp turn toward domesticity partway through her husband's campaign. The woman who had met her husband when she was his professional superior, who earned more than he did at several points in their life together, and who had, early in his campaign, told humanizing anecdotes about how he never picked up his dirty socks suddenly recast herself as maternal and supportive, clad in J. Crew cardigans and pursuing a campaign for childhood obesity.[3] No Hillary Clinton–esqe health-care gamble for her.

Some feminists felt betrayed at the transformation from hard-charging lawyer to high-profile homemaker. But, Harris-Perry points out, what one commentator called the "momification" of Michelle Obama was radical in its own right.[4] White American feminists from Betty Friedan on have depicted the homemaker role as stifling, but for many professional black women, it represents a cultural ideal that has long been the province of whites.[5]

This is a book about gender, not about race. But it is not a book just about white women. Women of color have been incorporated into the first ten chapters, which contain quotes from women of many races. (For reasons of confidentiality, they typically are not identified by race.) This chapter aims to explore the extent to which the everyday experience of gender bias differs by race. It examines in detail the hypothesis, forwarded in the 1960s by Frances Beale, that black women are in "double jeopardy": that they (and perhaps other women of color?) are doubly disadvantaged by race and gender.[6]

Far fewer experimental studies have studied this issue than the issue of "gender" alone. One important study, by Isis H. Settles, found that black women identified more as "black women" than as either "women" or "blacks."[7] In a response to this insight, Joan got a National Science Foundation (NSF) grant to fund interviews of 60 women scientists of color about their experience of gender bias.

FROM TERRORIST TO FASHION ICON

During the early stages of Barack Obama's first national campaign, Michelle Obama just acted like herself. She said that when her husband was nominated, she was proud of her country for the first time. She told *Good Morning America* that one of the reasons her husband was qualified for president is that "he is very able to deal with a strong woman" and can handle her "loud mouth."[a] She playfully fist-bumped her husband.

She ended up on the cover of the *New Yorker* as a terrorist and faced widespread criticism as an "angry black woman."[b] So after Obama was elected, she did a sharp right turn. She proclaimed herself "mom in chief" and spent a lot of time talking with fashion magazines.

Within a few years, she was extremely popular. She was considered a fashion icon and regularly compared to Jackie Kennedy. Did she sell out?

No, actually. She was doing important political work — reshaping standards of beauty, for one thing. She might not have "the bluest eye," to quote Toni Morrison, but she convinced America that a black woman could epitomize elegance.

And she claimed for black women an ideal long denied many of them: that of the stay-at-home mother. During Reconstruction, freed women were ridiculed for "playing the lady" and refusing to join the men in the fields.[c] Today, black women are about half as likely as white women to be stay-at-home mothers — often because financially, that's just not an option.[d] The meaning of even the most conventional of gender roles — the elegant women, the stay-at-home mom — differs by race. What would have been conventional for a white First Lady was downright revolutionary for Michelle Obama.

(Most are academics.) This chapter combines material from those interviews with material from the New Girls of color.

Women of color were more likely to report each of the four patterns of bias than white women were. The biggest gap concerned Tug of War bias, reported by 59 percent of women of color but only

50 percent of white women. Next came the Tightrope, reported by 77 percent of women of color and 68 percent of white women. The Maternal Wall came third, reported by 63 percent of mothers of color and 56 percent of white mothers. Prove-It-Again! bias showed the smallest gap: 64 percent of white women reported it, as compared with 70 percent of women of color. Remember, though, that most of the women of color were scientists; we cannot tell to what extent these differences stem from race and to what extend they stem from science.

At the Intersection of Race and Gender Bias

Women of color experience not only gender but also racial bias: the experiences they share with men of color. A black woman recalled being deeply offended when a college professor joked that she must know all about rats because she came from the inner city. An Asian American born in the United States has a "forever foreign" experience commonplace among Asian Americans: she keeps being asked what country she grew up in and complimented on her English. A Latina commented, "There seems to be this stereotype that, if you are from Mexico, you are lazy, and you only like to either sleep by a cactus or party. And I have battled extremely hard [against] all of these stereotypes." Another Latina recalled raising her voice only to have a colleague joke, "Oh, be careful, she's Puerto Rican, and she may be carrying a knife in her purse."

Again and again, women of color described their interactions as "demeaning" or "disrespectful," words that didn't come up in the interviews with white women. One woman recounted hearing that a white male senior professor threw a board eraser at a colleague of color and said, "Hey, you, why don't you write this down?" She heard from students that other professors in her department did not believe she would make tenure. "It was just like somewhere somebody sitting in the back and making armchair comments like that to a student. And it just—it felt so wrong."

Another distinctive theme that emerged strongly was that many women of color reported feeling a sense of bleak isolation. "This has been a very lonely life," said a black woman.[8] Another reported "feeling inadequate, some depression" because "you really don't have the support you need." The most striking story was of an Asian American whose department chair put up on the blackboard a diagram with three circles depicting the interrelations within the department. She was way out, isolated, on the extreme edge. "I said, 'You know, if I was a little bit to the right, I'd be out of the department,'" she quipped. But, she admitted, "It gets to me. It's hurtful." A black woman explained why she avoided socializing with her colleagues: "If it's too social, then I think there's a great risk of you being put in that subservient position and being looked at that way."

Racism is an important factor in the lives of women of color, but our focus here is on the experiences women of color share with white women. The interviews show they share a lot. Said an African American, upon hearing the description of the four types of gender bias, "I can identify with each of the four buckets. I can identify with each." All informants identified with one or more patterns of gender bias. One woman, upon hearing the four patterns described, simply burst into tears.

Some provisos: The analysis that follows is very preliminary. It simplifies the experience of women of color in many ways. First, it lumps them into three groups—Latinas, Asian Americans, and black women—that erase many important differences within each group. This is easiest to see with Asian Americans, a group that includes descendants of people from China, Japan, Korea, and India, to name just a few of the highly different Asian countries that have sent many immigrants to the United States. Latinas include women from a wide range of racial and ethnic identities, ranging from Americans from Puerto Rico to Portuguese-speaking Brazilians; the group of black women includes everyone from recent immigrants to women whose ancestors were brought to the United States in the 17th century. The grouping of minorities into categories like Asian American, Latina, and black does more to describe stereotypes of people of color than it does to describe identities experienced by individual people—although, of course, it's complicated, because the experience of stereotypes can play a role in the shaping of identity. Nonetheless, these categories are widely used in the study of race bias, and we will be using them here.

Black Women

PROVE-IT-AGAIN! AND AGAIN AND AGAIN AND AGAIN

Black women trigger two sets of negative competence assumptions: one because they are women and another because they are black. Many studies document that black people have to provide more evidence of their competence than whites do in order to be seen as equally competent. The most striking study examined job applications and found that someone with a black-sounding name had to have *eight* additional years of experience in order to get the same number of callbacks as someone with an identical resume but a white-sounding name.[9]

Hence the African American aphorism "We have to try twice as hard to get half as far." Black women are well aware that they have to provide more evidence of competence in order to be seen as equally competent.[10] However, unlike the Latina and Asian American scientists we interviewed, the black women tended to assume that their Prove-It-Again! problems stem from race rather than gender.[11]

"I absolutely agree with the statement that for African American women it is prove it again and again and again and again. It's interesting—I have to say, I've always thought about it more just as being African American as opposed to being a woman," said a lawyer. A scientist noted that at the two yearly conferences in her field, "when I go to give presentations, it's not that I feel like the audience doesn't necessarily believe my results, but I do feel as though I have to, at times, defend it before I can even present it. I

DEALING WITH DIFFERENCE FROM A YOUNG AGE

As we've discussed, bias against white women often doesn't become noticeable until they are well into their careers. Not so for women of color, many of whom reported childhood experiences of racism. Women of color are more likely to report that gender discrimination is a problem than are white women; one theory is that this is because bias in general is such a major force in their lives that it's just harder to overlook.[e] Many reported learning early how to stand up for themselves.

One lawyer recalled moving from a diverse neighborhood in New York to a "pretty much all-white" neighborhood out West. One day, while she was riding her bike in the street, another kid called her a "brownie." She went home to her mother and cried.

"My mom said, 'Guess what? You are different. You will always be different in every context for the rest of your life for one reason or another, and you just need to be comfortable,'" this New Girl remembered. "She was like, 'You're special. You're wonderful. You're different. And it's okay to be different, but everybody doesn't always understand that. Go back out there. Get on your bike. If you want to ride your bike down the street, you ride your bike down the street and ignore these people.'"

The New Girl took her mother's words to heart. "I still remember that story, and I was six years old," she told us.

---

really don't think it's just because I'm a female. I think that that's secondary to my race." Another agreed: "I think people expect that I got here by some fluke, by some series of affirmative action things and set-aside programs and that I may not be as strong a scientist as others."

A black doctor who originally had been an engineer contested the "race, not gender" interpretation. She highlighted the importance of context. As a doctor, she felt that people's initial reluctance to take her seriously was more because of her race than her gender. She attributed this to the fact that, in medicine, women are common but black people are rare. When she was in engineering, though, where women are rare, she felt her Prove-It-Again! problems stemmed from gender. Studies confirm the importance of context; perhaps the conviction that race, not gender, explains black women's Prove-It-Again! problems reflects that professional workplaces often have more women than black people.[12]

Black women's experience of Prove-It-Again! differs significantly from both white women's and from black men's. A study by social psychologists Ashleigh Shelby Rosette and Robert W. Livingston found that black women are rated more harshly when things go awry than either black men or white women are.[13] The double-jeopardy hypothesis appears to be true on the Prove-It-Again! axis of gender.[14]

"There's just no room for error," said a highly respected and accomplished lawyer. "It's just so deeply ingrained in you that I don't even think about it anymore. To the extent that other folks might feel that they can have a bad day, . . . I never feel I have that luxury. You're just always on, and if you're not on, you'd better make people think you're on."

"It sounds unbelievably exhausting," Joan said.

"It is. It absolutely is," the lawyer replied.

A black woman lawyer echoed similar sentiments in the outstanding report *Visible Invisibility: Women of Color in Law Firms*: "White associates are not expected to be perfect. Black associates . . . have one chance and if you mess up that chance, look out. There is no room for error."[15]

A vice president at a major company felt the same way. "You need to be on your A game," she said, "and when you are, you can turn the liability of stereotyping into an advantage. Frequently enough, some white men do not expect someone who looks like me —or so visibly different from them—to speak the way I speak or show up the way that I do. They seem initially disarmed by the common ground that we may share. Frankly, I just don't observe the same reaction with women or people of color for the most part. If they [the white men] can see a common history or experience, you get extra brownie points. But if you're not showing up with your A game, the consequences seem more severe given the scrutiny and presumptive challenge of your intellect, vocabulary, and background."

"I don't have that margin for error," she continued. "And, on the other hand, to be frank, I recognize that I'm probably given more kudos than your average male or, perhaps, white woman because I am relatively eloquent, presentable, and articulate. Regardless," she concluded, "the stakes are big." This pattern is documented, too: social scientists call it "shifting standards" when we perceive that someone does well *for a woman* or *for a person of color*—most women of any race have heard some variation of "You climb [or throw or negotiate] well for a girl."[16]

Because success is so precarious for women of color, performance pressure becomes "a self-fulfilling negative prophecy," to quote a company vice president. This is called stereotype threat: when "over-efforting" on the part of a stereotyped group member leads to decreased performance.[17] Another black woman said, "In my more cynical moments, it's an unrealistic expectation to think that one can consistently be as good as you feel you need to be."

"I've been doing this now for almost 20 years. You never feel as though you have a comfort level where you're not on your toes because you have to prove it and prove it," said a lawyer. Said a vice president, "The Prove-It-Again! is, I think, exponentially increased when you have double minority status. I certainly feel like that is the reality of my experience. Notwithstanding the 'halo' effect, you're as good as your last . . . trial, deal, or novel. Women and people of color may face the additional obstacle of a presumption of less-than-competency. More precisely, white men may have an unwarranted presumption of legitimacy. For many of our well-intentioned 'white' brothers, this presumption is not promoted or self-created. It's deeply embedded within our culture."

She recounted her experience with the Stolen Idea. "Typically, in my experience, it tends to be a male who will speak over the point, rather than allowing for the question to be addressed and attributed to you. Someone may bring up the same issue later in the conversation and restate precisely (or close enough) what you offered up to the audience, without attribution or acknowledgment that . . . they were parroting you or adding on to your thesis."

"My instinctive internal reaction to these events is—'Was I not clear? Was there something deficient in my communication? Was I not forceful or authoritative enough? Did I not speak with sufficient authority? Was it me? Or was it them?'" She said it gets easier to be more forceful and commanding if you work with enough men and whites "to realize they're as much of a nincompoop as you are."

The scientists reported Prove-It-Again! problems both with colleagues and with students. Said one, "I have always had the impression when I start a class, a course, it is always an uphill kind of battle. I get the impression that students don't believe that I know what I'm supposed to know." Another scientist recalled that, back when she was a student and assigned to work in a group, her contributions fell on deaf ears. "And it wasn't until the professor came around and said, 'Are you guys listening to what [she] is saying?' where it hit home to me that, you know, it didn't matter what I was saying. But it was just the fact that it was coming from my mouth."

Colleagues, too, often assumed the worst. One scientist recalled that, when a student called to complain about a professor, an administrator automatically assumed that the problem professor was her. (It wasn't.) She also reported a classic Prove-It-Again! pattern: "even when I get really good evaluations, then the next thing that follows is, 'Well, you're an easy grader, and so that must be why.'" Note how casually her success was discounted and written off.

ARE YOU AN ANGRY BLACK WOMAN?

The bad news is that black women are in double jeopardy on the Prove-It-Again! axis. The good news is that black women may have fewer Tightrope problems than white women and other women of color do.

Black women may have more leeway to behave in masculine ways because black people, as a group, are seen as more masculine than whites—so masculine-type behavior may seem less jarring in a black woman.[18] Black women also may be less threatening to the power structure simply because they are so marginalized in many professional contexts. "When a black woman speaks up and asserts herself—that's cute," noted an academic.

A black woman in medicine described the Tightrope in classic terms: "I've learned how to speak my mind without pissing people off," she chuckled. "I don't come across as too masculine, that bitch with the chip on her shoulder. I've just figured out how to hold my ground and not be pushed over but, at the same time, not be considered a witch."

When Joan asked a focus group of black women scientists if they had felt they had to choose between being liked-but-not-respected or respected-but-not-liked, several women looked at her pityingly. The option of being liked but not respected, they said, was never open to them. Their only choice was to be respected-but-not-liked. Blacks in general seek to be respected more than whites, who are more likely to seek to be liked, according to one study.[19]

However, this isn't to say that black women do not face any Tightrope problems. Like white women, the scientists of color we spoke with felt under tremendous pressure to do committee work —a classic example of office housework. Such committees play an important role in academic governance, but service on them is severely undervalued. What gets professors tenure and accolades is research, not service.

The most poignant story was of a black scientist whose mentors were "very adamant" that she didn't "need to sit on every blasted committee." So, in a meeting with the provost, she pointed out that whites as well as people of color could be tapped to serve on diversity committees. The provost cluelessly responded by inviting her to serve on another committee. "Of course I'm not going to say no to the provost. This is the man who basically has my tenure in his hands."

Office housework aside, black women were less likely than white women to report feeling that they could not be their authentic selves because of their loyalty to feminine traditions, with two exceptions. One was self-promotion, which may present an even bigger hurdle for black than white women. A lawyer pointed out that black people are taught as children to be humble. "You do not boast because it's not humble. And it's important to be humble." She continued, "You hear over and over again, nobody is better than anyone else." A scientist agreed: "Even those who do it eventually, it takes a very long time to learn that. And you pay a price for it," she said.

The second "too feminine" problem black women faced concerned clothes. If "you come from a culture—Latino, black southerner— where your grandmother wore a hat every Sunday and/or like a lot of loud, flashy colors and big bling jewelry, there can be a dilemma about how to fit in and yet be your most authentic self," noted a black professional in San Francisco.

Black women also reported fewer problems on the "too masculine" end of the spectrum. This is not surprising, given a truly fascinating study by Robert Livingston, Ashleigh Shelby Rosette, and Ella F. Washington, which found that black women are allowed to behave in more assertive and dominant ways than white women are. Their study found that assertive black women were not evaluated more negatively when they expressed dominance, although both white women and black men were.[20] This finding has been confirmed by other studies.[21]

Our interviews included many examples in which black women used an assertive, nondeferential style at work. A black woman professor recalled her response when students tried to beg off work—there's only so many times your grandmother can die. "I'm like, I do keep count of how many grandmothers people have. You can't do it three times." A woman lawyer noted that black women at her firm "are actually lauded for that sort of assertiveness, aggressiveness" but said she's "sure it isn't the same for some of the Caucasian female associates." A scientist agreed. "I've never really dealt with being thought of as a bitch, but I kind of aspire to that a little bit because I see, at this university at least, that actually it's a very effective perception" to create. Noting that she is "very outspoken in meetings," she said she felt she was rewarded for assertive behavior.

A black doctor said she was confrontational when a male doctor of color attempted to take over a room she needed for patients. "I was using three rooms. He had two. He basically walked up to me and he said, 'I need three, so I'm going to take room three. You can use two.' I basically turned around and said, 'No, you're not. I'm using three rooms.' He goes, 'I can't have the third room?' I said, 'No, I'm using it.' I just turned around and kept working." Two nurses nearby said, "You should have seen the look on his face."

Said a lawyer, "I think there's a certain amount of sassiness, if you will, that is oddly enough even expected." She continued, "I've certainly never been accused of being too feminine." "I've been rewarded and praised for dominance," said another lawyer. "It's something people admire about me." Still another explained in *Visible Invisibility* that her white co-workers "expect a Black woman to be extremely aggressive and to do really well on trial."[22]

Black women's room to be more assertive has limits. One black scientist told a truly hair-raising story that occurred after she had suffered a traumatic brain injury. The people at the hospital observed one interaction she had with people who worked for her and said that she was "unnecessarily brusque, undeferential": "Let's remember that these people worked for me. They were white males." The hospital staff said "it was obvious that I needed to stay in rehabilitation longer until I started acting like a woman." She recalled wryly, "This was in [the South]. I don't know how to be the southern belle. I'm from [the Midwest]." She had little choice but to play along. "I dropped my IQ by several points and started looking for little things to decorate myself with."

Many women of color noted their awareness of the need to avoid being seen as an "angry black woman." Said a black woman in medicine, "African American women sometimes have the stereotype that if you're aggressive, then you're definitely the B word."

A lawyer also noted the risks of anger. "I am allowed to be passionate, even to demonstrate some level of anger, but it better not be personal. It better not be about me. If I become angry about anything personal, then that is perceived as being an angry black woman." This quote perfectly illustrates the findings of a still-unpublished follow-up study by Robert Livingston, which found that African American women are allowed more "get it done" agency—but not more "get ahead" agency.[23] Our interviews confirm this. Black women can use a direct, assertive style, but not to act in ambitious, self-promoting, or power-seeking ways. Black women have license to be assertive in achieving the goals of the group—but not in seeking power for themselves.

NO ONE TO LEAN ON

Black women definitely face the Maternal Wall. A 2006 survey by the American Bar Association found that the same proportion of both women of color and white women—nearly three-quarters—felt like their career commitment was questioned after they gave birth to or adopted a child.[24]

Women we spoke with reported both hostile and benevolent prescriptive bias. A black scientist recalled an incident in which a colleague was told to go home and have more babies. It's hard to get more hostile and prescriptive than that. Another black scientist recalled her boss saying, "Wow, why are you here so early? You should be home with the baby." He meant well, she recognized, but still it troubled her.

One black lawyer told us her boss was telling other people he wasn't sure she was going to come back after she had her baby. "I finally had to talk to him about that. I had to tell him, 'Please stop telling people that you're not sure I'm coming back. I'm coming back. I want to come back. I like to do the work. I need to work, and having a child really puts more pressure on me to be successful at work so that he can have the opportunities I want him to have.'"

She concluded, "He was creating problems for me that he probably wasn't aware of."

At the same time, the contours of Maternal Wall bias are slightly different for black women than they are for white women. If white women's work-family conflicts typically stem from motherhood in two-parent families, black women's conflicts may reflect that they find it harder than white women to find a partner. "I think it's easier for people to understand work-life balance issues in the context of kids, right? As opposed to 'I'm single and I want to find a mate, so that's the balance I'm trying to achieve,'" said a lawyer. Among those who were surveyed for *Visible Invisibility*, women of color were more than four times more likely to be single than were white women: 35 percent of women of color reported being "single, never married," as compared to 8 percent of white women. And only 56 percent of women of color reported being married, as compared with 81 percent of white women.[25]

Family structures of black women are often different from those of white women. *Visible Invisibility* found that three-fourths of women lawyers of color were the chief or sole breadwinners in their families.[26] "A lot of women of color don't have husbands or partners, or their husbands could be in a different kind of career with less flexibility," one New Girl said. Another observed that at her workplace there's a significant difference between a man with three kids and a single black woman with three kids. "The man will be treated like a breadwinner and the woman like shit," she said bluntly.

The bright side is that wider circles of care offer some women of color resources unheard of in white families. A black woman in medicine met a family through her church. "They said, 'We'll be your family away from home,' and they were very true to their word. They kind of adopted themselves as my surrogate mother and father. . . . When my daughter was born, they were like, 'Oh, we have another grandchild.' I can say really that, for me, I've been really blessed."

Historically, women of color have not had nannies, which led to a distinctive form of prescriptive bias: some women felt criticized for their reluctance to take this path. "We haven't done the nanny thing a lot. That's kind of new for black folks," a New Girl said. One black woman scientist told us that when colleagues have asked questions about why she doesn't get a nanny so she can work more, she felt her parenting style was being questioned.

TUGS WITH A RACIAL DIMENSION

African American scientists reported a wide variety of classic gender wars. "I have seen females trying to be very accommodating and playing a certain role that made them more likable. I tended to be very professional, straightforward, and not stroking people's egos or whatnot," said a black woman. She recalled "woman wars" where someone strives to prove "she is better: she can give more, she can do more, and there were games played along those lines." "That happened over and over again," she said.

Another black scientist noted that, at a monthly meeting, the only other woman in her group "pretty much focuses attention on the men," and she added, "rarely she'll look at me. I'm thinking she might be one of those type of women where, okay, there's only room for one."

The classic tokenism effect is also in evidence. Said a black scientist, "I have been in an organization where there was room for one woman, but one woman decided that she was it and would simply sabotage her colleagues, which unfortunately included me."

Sometimes Tugs of War arise between black and white women based on different understandings of womanly behavior. One scientist noted strain with white administrative assistants because, she felt, black women don't share white women's habit of bonding by sharing personal information. She expressed relief that black assistants "just do not expect [her] to want to know anything about their personal business." The same was not true of their white counterparts. "I think white women share a lot of personal business, and it's a bonding with them," she said. What Deborah Tannen calls "troubles talk" may lead to conflict between black and white women.[27]

In addition to this race-specific tension, a few women we interviewed reported other kinds of pushback from administrative assistants that sounded very similar to what happens to white women. One noted that administrative staff took longer to complete work given by women than men. Another agreed: "My stuff won't get done first."

An African American scientist reflected on the femmes-and-tomboys dynamic as she mused about her treatment of a younger woman. "I would always tell her, 'You need to man up, stop all that crying, because they are going to keep walking over you and keep criticizing your research and your papers if you don't stand up and take charge.'" "Probably I could have told her in a different way," she added.

Sometimes these tensions take on a disquieting racial dimension. "I went to my first job, and it was fine. I never got any feedback on my personality," remarked a lawyer. "When I came to my current company, the culture was so completely different. I immediately got feedback about being a more empathetic person and being a person who would be easier to relate to." She continued, "I certainly think that if I was a white man, I would never have been given so much feedback about being an empathetic person and how important it would be to try to make people more comfortable with me. I also think that part of what has been interpreted as my hard edges are attributable to me being a black woman." She said, "The feedback I've gotten about being nicer, more empathetic, all come from white women. No black woman has ever told me that, and no white man has ever told me that."

Sometimes racial conflict is less subtle and less forgivable. One lawyer recounted a white female supervisor who, when a white colleague said she was leaving early one Friday, cordially told the colleague to go get a pedicure and enjoy herself. But when the lawyer, who is black, said she was leaving too, her supervisor bristled and started cross-examining her about whether she had gotten all her work done. This was one of many instances of hyperscrutiny and hostility by her supervisor. The lawyer ended up leaving the firm. It's hard to know whether the supervisor's behavior reflected racial hostility, but that's a key point about racism—it's often hard to tell exactly why someone is acting negatively toward you. That in itself is draining.

At the same time, several of the women interviewed described a cultural tradition of respecting elders that they said eased some of the Tug of War conflicts they faced. "They didn't mean any harm," said one. "They were trying to protect me from grief."

Latinas

PROVE-IT-AGAIN AND AGAIN?

Recall the scientist who had "battled extremely hard" against the stereotype that Mexicans are lazy and "only like to either sleep by a cactus or party." The same scientist listed the possibilities: "the friendly Mexican or the passive Mexican or the disorganized Mexican." The Latinas we interviewed expressed no opinion about whether their Prove-It-Again! problems stemmed from race, gender, or both. But there was no question that the problems were there.

Latinas, as for blacks, probably trigger two sets of negative competence assumptions, although there's a lot less research to document this with regard to Latinas. A study by Denise A. Segura quotes a Chicano professional saying, 'I think you have to prove yourself more just because you are—number one—a woman, and then [because] you are Latino. So, it's like you have two forces that I think people subconsciously or consciously judge."[28] The interviews confirmed this sentiment.

"Some people have these knee-jerk reactions that people of color or women of color aren't as competent," said one Latina scientist. She recalled coming upon a group of her colleagues discussing her

---

HOW BEING A LATINA VARIES FROM EAST TO WEST

Joan grew up partly in Venezuela, speaking Spanish. When she lived in Washington, D.C., she would often ask, "¿Habla usted español?" when she met native Spanish speakers. People generally appreciated her efforts to communicate in a way that felt comfortable to them.

Not so in California, where she quickly learned that asking the question was considered an insult. This makes sense, given the quite different history of Latinos in the East and West. In the West, Mexicans were a major racial group. They were exploited, and many families were evicted from lands they had held for generations by the Mexican "Repatriation" Program of the 1930s.[f] And, because so many immigrants from Mexico live in the West, all Latinos there live under the "immigration shadow": they are assumed to be recent immigrants, with the accompanying set of negative stereotypes, even if their families have long since been citizens.[g]

This gap between East and West also reflects that Latinos in different parts of the country typically whose heritage is from different countries with quite different cultures. While westerners are more likely from Mexico, easterners are more likely from the Caribbean, Cuba, or Central America. The research (including this chapter) that aggregates these geographically and culturally diverse groups together elides these differences — which can have a huge impact on the forms of bias women experience. It's important to keep in mind that the discussion here is only the beginning.

---

own experiment—without her. "Guys, are you talking about my project? Then I should probably be involved," she said to them. She observed, "And it was a surprise to them that I should be involved in the discussions of my project because I was not considered to be able or capable of offering any useful information."

Another scientist had her success in an experiment discounted by male colleagues who attributed her success to the fact she was using their protocol, as if the precision with which she had carried out the protocol was of no consequence. The examples go on and on. A Latina scientist remembered when audience members actually interrupted her while she was in the middle of a presentation. A Latina lawyer recalled that she wrote a brief for a supervisor who gave her a bad review and never gave her a second chance, although he championed a male associate "who time and time again completely annoyed him and produced substandard work product. He didn't write that person off." The same woman recalled with rueful amusement a somewhat soused colleague telling her she had given a really good presentation at a meeting: "He said, 'Yeah, but I mean you were just so authoritative, and like you really knew your stuff,' and went on and on, probably four times. . . . And then he said, 'You were just really articulate.' . . . It was the funniest thing, and I mean funny in a sad, sad way."

FIERY LATINAS AND OFFICE HOUSEWORK

In some ways, Latinas get the worst of both worlds. They face enhanced Prove-It-Again! bias (similar to black women), but they also (unlike black women) face major Tightrope problems. "How do you portray yourself?" asked a Latina doctor. "I mean, you are a woman, you don't have to be a man. But at the same time, if you want to fit in, do you have to behave like the men?"

Latinas' Tightrope problems cluster on the "too feminine" side. Clothing is a particularly charged issue, said one scientist, who "toned down" her style so that people would take her more seriously. "I don't want them to be distracted by my earrings or by the loud print in my shirt or by my hair or whatever. I want them to concentrate on what I am saying," she said.

Another scientist found this downright confusing. "So if you dress well, sometimes you get less respect," she lamented.

By far the most common "too feminine" problem is the pressure Latinas feel to play the office housewife. One scientist described herself as "the mother of our research group." Another Latina scientist found herself in a similar role: "On the too feminine side of things, I think there are times when I am asked to be kind of the mother of the group. I'm the one who has to make sure that everybody fills out their paperwork, and I'm the one who takes care of things, sets up the meetings and things like that. I mean, I play many roles that could be done by a competent administrative assistant if we happen to have had a competent administrative assistant, which we don't. . . . It's assumed that I'll take care of it because nobody else will."

One of the women who found herself doing administrative work tried to get out of this role. "I'm like, 'I told you I'm not going to be doing that for everybody anymore.' And everybody just kind of throws up their hands, and simple things like scheduling a conference room become my problem." She blamed herself, saying that she had trouble delegating. But she didn't appear to have much choice. "I mean, these kind of administrative duties eat into my time," she said poignantly.

Not only colleagues but also students "treat you like their mother," said one Latina scientist, "like they can get whatever they can from you and there's no limit." She mused, "It's natural to go ask for help to mom." But, she explained, "I have noticed that if I act like too much of a mommy, I get a lot of kids." She suggests they go ask someone else, often to little effect. Of one student, she commented, "I think he is embarrassed, sometimes, by showing lack of knowledge to a guy but not to a girl." Said another Latina, "Students may think they could get away with not doing certain things because you're a woman."

"Too masculine" problems appear less common among Latinas than "too feminine" problems. One attorney reported losing her temper with a colleague—just once. "I basically chewed him out at work and, unfortunately, lost all respect of my colleagues. After that, I've been very, very careful about that." She said, "I just feel like you're never going to get ahead by getting angry." Men could get angry, she said, but women could not. "I have one partner who is known to scream and yell at his assistant, and everyone just says, 'Oh well, that's him.' They've replaced assistant after assistant after assistant for him." One assistant filed a complaint, and instead of addressing the problem, people around the office just said, "Well, that's too bad she couldn't cut it because he's very high maintenance." A female partner at the same firm would "get really irritated with her assistant and yell at her, and the interesting thing is that she was perceived as a bitch. . . . There was less tolerance for her behavior."

A Latina professor agreed. "I got angry because there was something being done that I thought was inappropriate, and I was called to the principal's office, to use a metaphor. And I am absolutely sure that none of my [male] colleagues that get angry at faculty meetings get called." It may be that the stereotype of the fiery Latina means that anger is even more perilous for Latinas than it is for women in general. This woman certainly thought so: "I'm Latin, so I'm passionate and I could go there. I do rein that in and make sure that I'm more placid with my responses. I usually, if someone says something inflammatory to me, will take a few seconds before I respond, or if it's via e-mail, I will wait a couple of hours before I respond—just because that is such a feminine stereotype to have this emotional response to something. . . . For those that know my specific background, they'll make comments about that. 'Oooh, she's a fiery Latina.'"

"EVERY GOOD MEXICAN WOMAN HAS KIDS IN HER 20S"

Latinas not only face high levels of Prove-It-Again! and Tightrope concerns; they also reported lots of Maternal Wall problems. "Usually people take over the country with wars, but you Mexicans are doing it by having lots of babies," one woman quoted in a study of middle-class Latinas reported hearing.[29] Maternal Wall bias may well be built into the racial stereotype of a Latina because of the assumption that all Latinas will have lots of children.

A Latina lawyer said she sensed, after she had triplets, "fixed expectations that I would not resume my career and not return to work." That assumption simply struck her as odd. "My career was not as disposable as other people might have seen it," she said. "Ironically, I worked at the time for a woman who was a Latina, and it was she who made the most disturbing comments about, 'Oh, honey, I know you're not coming back, are you?' I think she genuinely intended to be supportive, but as my supervisor, it came across as an out-of-hand dismissal of what I knew I was capable of."

Commented a Latina lawyer, "We know the workplace will have evolved when instead we hear, 'Wow, your professional accomplishments are being achieved *in addition to* all the additional personal responsibilities you have. Incredible leadership skills at work there! We are going to nurture your career, because if you can do all this now, you are going to be a rock star around here in the future.'"

Latinas also reported intense family pressures to have children, to have them early, and to play traditional family roles. "You're supposed to have kids in your 20s. Every good Mexican woman has kids in their 20s," said a Latina scientist. "We have a very firm and entrenched culture of family, of big family, and everyone's connected to everyone's last cousin and grandma and whatever."

"I think a lot of it is self-imposed," said another scientist. "Hispanic women are mothers—we take care of our families. Women are considered the matriarchs." "I feel like I have a very specific role in keeping the family running," she said. "And here's another complication," she continued, "for many women of color I know, particularly those in immigrant families, the cultural expectations that define family can extend to a caring for extended family members, such as elderly parents or grandchildren. At least one reason for that may be that our values are informed by cultural expectations, and this is even more true in immigrant families like mine. On one hand, it's a beautiful thing to live out our strong family ties; on the other hand, what does this imply for women of color advancing to leadership in the workplace, especially when the period for serious career advancement tends to overlap with the 'sandwich generation' years? Whether it's an issue of feminism or not, I think you see more women of color juggling additional cultural expectations. Do we embrace them all and exhaust ourselves in the process, or distance ourselves from these multifaceted roles while risking a loss of important cultural values?"

The assumption that professionals do not have family obligations beyond the nuclear family can lead to particularly negative reactions because of the sense that these obligations aren't important enough to miss work for. A Latina attorney quoted in a Catalyst report described having to go to the funeral of a cousin's baby. "One partner was like, 'Who was this?'" the attorney remembered. "I don't think she understood."[30]

WILL YOU BE MY MOTHER?

Some Latina scientists spoke warmly of the relations among women in their department. "We bond together. We support each other a lot. . . . And we're always rooting for each other. We're always hoping there's more of us. So the 'room for one' I definitely have not experienced," said one. "We have quite a large number of women in my department, and we try to have a good collegiality among us," said another.

Others weren't so positive. "I would say that there's definitely a kind of divide or separation between the female faculty members, young and old. Those older ones feeling that 'I worked to make this happen,' whereas the younger ones are reaping the benefits, if that makes sense," said a Latina scientist. She continued, "And there is a change, at least in my field, where women are very comfortable with being mothers as well as go-getters and being great scientists and starting out their labs."

One woman reflected on the interpersonal dynamics that fuel competition among women as she worried about being compared to another woman in her department. "She's funded, she's publishing in high-impact journals. I'm not right now. And I'm jealous and I'm fearful that if we were compared on the same scale, that I'll come up way short."

"I was probably mad at the women who had children," said another, "thinking, 'Why should I, who does not have children, pick up the slack for the women who do have children? It's a choice.' And then, of course, you think about this for ten minutes and you realize that it's not the women you need to be pissed off at. It's the men who make the assignments."

The scientists were asked specifically about conflict between support staff and scientists. Latina scientists in particular reported a lot of it. "Female bosses have a lot more resistance from the other females in the group, from everybody, but it happens especially if there's a difference in race," said one. "They say the bosses are too demanding," said another, recalling a conversation with administrative assistants who worked with her. She said to them, "Well, the boss that you had before was equally demanding. The guy that you were working under was equally demanding." The assistants' reaction: "Yeah, but that's different." Mused another woman, "If a male boss asks, 'Can you bring me a copy?' they will, and if you ask the same thing, they will say, 'Well, why am I going to bring you the copy?'"

Some women just laughed it off. "The staff call the females by their first names, but they talk about 'Doctor Such-and-Such' and 'Professor Such-and-Such' when they refer to the men, which I find very funny," said another Latina scientist.

"I am absolutely sure that my male colleagues don't get this type of treatment," said a scientist who reported pushback from administrative staff about how files should be kept. She attributed the problem both to gender and race. "It may be an overall issue of respect. For them, having female bosses, it's a whole new thing." But she felt there was a racial component as well. "Here they have this Mexican woman telling them what to do."

The Latinas we interviewed were particularly thoughtful about the advantages of being a Latina, pointing out how their heritage helped them negotiate the complexities of being women in traditionally male careers. "I think I have a huge advantage in having a very refined cultural radar," said a Latina scientist. A Latina lawyer agreed: "I can read the cultural landscape pretty quickly and automatically discern the dynamic that's going on and what I need to address." She felt her cross-cultural background had sharpened her political radar. "Just reading the dynamics of a room and how you, and others, are being perceived is very helpful," she said.

Said another scientist, reflecting on her close cultural ties to another country, "You have to be like context switchers, . . . reading the context and then doing what's appropriate for that context at any point in time." She mused, "It's the same thing switching between masculine and feminine roles."

Asian American Women

AN ASIAN OR A WOMAN?

Whereas African American and Latina women face double jeopardy because they trigger two different sets of unflattering assumptions, Asians are in the very different situation of being seen as a "model minority" group. The model minority stereotype may seem to be complimentary, but Asian Americans are "seen as too competent, too ambitious, too hardworking, and, simultaneously, not sociable."[31] The model minority stereotype means that Asian Americans may be considered competent and envied but considered lacking in social skills and leadership qualities.[32]

There's some evidence that the model minority stereotype may mean that Asian American women need to give *less* evidence of competence than white women do. "In some sense, I'm more acceptable, if you will, as an Asian woman scientist rather than a woman scientist," one woman observed.

Yet women who felt they had been helped by the model minority stereotype were rare. Many more reported Prove-It-Again! problems. An Asian American lawyer recalled a situation in which a white man and woman both got promotions in a context where the rules didn't allow them. "You know that the rule only applies to the people it applies to," she observed. "Generally speaking,

THE COMPLEXITY OF ASIAN AMERICAN STEREOTYPES

American stereotypes of Asian Americans have changed dramatically over time. Nineteenth-century stereotypes were unambiguously ugly. Asians and Asian Americans were seen as devious, untrustworthy, and clannish. The stereotype of the "Oriental despot" was sometimes seen as evidence that Asians were incapable of participating in a democracy.[h] The "Yellow Peril" mentality led to lynching, murders, and the burning down of Chinese businesses.[i] Infamously, during World War II, these stereotypes led to roughly 50,000 people being put into internment camps in the United States.[j]

The "model minority" stereotypes arose during the last half of the 20th century. This stereotype depicts Asian Americans as competent, hardworking, and ambitious — but this stereotype is limited to technical and rote roles and does not apply to leadership or social skills.[k] Asian also stereotype one another. Koreans are sometimes referred to as the "Irish of Asia": "emotional and entertaining and unruly."[l] Japanese are stereotyped as rigid and proper: "We have a stiff upper lip — like you British," read a headline after Japan's posttsunami nuclear meltdown.[m] Chinese people may be referred to as the "Jews of Asia."[n]

Which of these stereotypes is triggered — if any — depends on individuals and social context. Several different ones may be triggered at once, or different ones can be triggered during different periods of a woman's life. Navigating all this makes office politics trickier for Asian American women than for most other groups.

women—and women of color—would be strictly held to rules and then some."

Other Asian Americans reported that their successes were discounted, in a variant of the "he's skilled, she's lucky" pattern. One described her department chair saying that she got grants not due to merit but to politics. "You have to be ten times better than everyone else; you always have to be more prepared," said an Asian American lawyer. "My mentors, those practicing lawyers who have observed my growth in the profession, often say to me, 'One day hopefully you're going to just trust your gut.'" She continued, "I feel men are raised to just basically go with instinct and not even question it. As an Asian American woman growing up in my household, I had to validate everything, unlike my brother, and this experience has transferred to my practice of always explaining my decisions and actions before diving in. I feel women often feel that they have to validate their actions before taking them."

"I don't know if it's an Asian thing or a woman thing, but it was definitely a combination where I felt like I had to get [approval] on different things. I was definitely less comfortable about going rogue," said another woman.

THE "LITTLE ASIAN DOLL" OR THE DRAGON LADY?

An attorney quoted in the ABA's *Visible Invisibility* report articulated the very specific Tightrope that Asian American women walk: "I am frequently perceived as being very demure and passive and quiet, even though I rarely fit any of those categories. When I successfully overcome those misperceptions, I am often thrown into the 'dragon lady' category. It is almost impossible to be perceived as a balanced and appropriately aggressive lawyer."[33] Asians are seen as "quiet, obedient, and courteous."[34]

While black women are seen as more masculine than white women, Asian Americans tend to be seen as more feminine—so it is not surprising that Asian American women reported many "too feminine" problems.[35] An Asian American lawyer noted, "There's a mystique about the Asian woman: we're so cute and so delicate. . . . You get to the point where you try to 'mannify' yourself."[36] This is the stereotype of the little China Doll—the demure, petite, deferential, passive Asian woman. An Asian attorney remarked to the authors of *Visible Invisibility*, "I've had opposing parties, opposing counsel, treat me like a little girl. Part of that is the Asian thing, because they see a little Asian doll. . . . It's really annoying and I'm tired of it."[37]

Asian American women reported a wide range of "too feminine" problems. Some problems stemmed from expectations that they would do the office housework, like the consistent reports we heard from Asian women that they were treated like perennial lab assistants as postdocs. As with Latinas, expectations about office housework have a particular flavor: women of color are expected to perform ministerial tasks in a subservient manner.

Asian American women reported particular difficulty with self-promotion. "You're taught to be humble and not boast about your achievements and give credit to others," said one scientist. This Asian cultural norm can feed the perception that Asian American women are too passive. "All my mentors have told me, 'You have to be more aggressive because they're not going to respect you if you're not aggressive,'" said an Asian American scientist. "But I don't like to be aggressive. I like to get along with everybody." Said another, "I'm not particularly assertive. . . . I might be a more assertive version of a stereotypical Asian woman but a less assertive version of a generic woman."

One "dark-complected," shy Indian graduate student was undercut when a fellow student made negative comments about her work. The head of the lab "never bothered to actually address that with her or talk to her about it or actually watch her in the lab. He just took the word of the male grad student in that lab." The grad student ended up leaving without getting her PhD.

"In our culture, we're raised with the idea of respecting culture and seniority," said an Asian American lawyer. "How it plays out at work, for me, is that I always felt that if I was rendering an opinion, it had to be clearly supported." That often showed up, she felt, as a lack of self-confidence. "Self-confidence just seems so second nature to some people, while it is always something I have to build and maintain consistently."

Asian American women reported far fewer "too masculine" problems, which is not surprising, given that whites code Asians in general as more feminine. Yet it is clear that Asian Americans who do not conform with China Doll submission often encounter pushback. "I was never part of the in group," said an Asian American scientist. "I'm very candid and I do not hesitate to open my mouth, and that was probably not the submissive female" they were expecting. "I immediately started, I guess, having the reputation of being a dragon lady."

A 2012 study found that all Asian Americans, men as well as women, tend to trigger workplace harassment if they act dominant.[38] This, of course, reinforces the stereotype of Asian Americans as passive by discouraging them from acting dominant. Interestingly enough, Asian Americans also tend to trigger workplace harassment if they act warm, the study found—a classic double bind.[39] Asian American women face this double bind along both a race and a gender axis, which may make it particularly difficult for them to find the right balance.

ARE HARDWORKING MOTHERS GOOD MOTHERS?

Asian American mothers, like other mothers, hit the Maternal Wall. "If you had a full-blown career, that's inconsistent with being a mother. I certainly feel that sentiment," said an Asian American scientist. One scientist commented, "I feel like people think that Asian women, they are caring and then they will give up their professions for their children."

Yet the model minority stereotype can help shield some Asian American mothers from negative assumptions about their work commitment. Said one lawyer quoted in the ABA study, "They have a very positive stereotype of Asians, and especially Asian women. They see us as hard-working—we'll work seven days a week, 24 hours a day; we're very smart, very dedicated. One of the Asian women who recently made partner just had twins, and they're sure she'll keep working, while they think other women would quit."[40] Although Asian Americans are stereotyped as being family oriented, the stereotype that they are devoted to work may trump that stereotype.[41]

The assumption that Asian American mothers will continue to

be dedicated to their jobs does not always work in their favor.[42] A lawyer said, "The problem I see is that they really don't understand what you're doing here. They may prize you as a lawyer, they may think you're a heck of a litigator, but deep down they're wondering, 'What's she doing here? Why isn't she home with the kids like my wife is?' It's a real problem when people just don't get what you do."

Several scientists who are immigrants from Asia had their parents come from abroad to help take care of their children so they could work full-time. Said one, "I think Asian parents [are] more willing to come over to really provide this kind of day-to-day help. So, right now, like in [my university], we really have quite a lot of Chinese faculty. And I saw many of them do have their parents come over to help them, much, much higher frequency than the Caucasian faculty." First one parent will come and stay the six months his or her visa permits. Then the other parent will come, she explained.

Again, assumptions that families of color conform to the nuclear pattern common in white professional families sometimes disadvantages women of color. An Asian woman lawyer said she hesitated to ask for time off to care for her mother's cousin: "I don't know if they'd understand that context, which I know is normal within the Asian community, or at least the South Asian community—to always support extended family."[43]

NO TUG OF WAR?

Asian Americans reported few Tug of War experiences. "No, no, this is not a pattern I can relate to," commented an Asian American scientist. She had always been in groups with very few women, but, she said, "we've stuck together to fight—not to fight [each other] but to actually share and be a cohort of peers with my female friends."

Another woman's comment may help explain why Tug of War experiences may be rare for Asian American women. She had defused conflict with an older female faculty member by communicating the importance of the efforts of the older generation: "[Without them] I wouldn't be here. I wouldn't have made it. So I'm continuously humble." "It's the same in general when you express respect and gratitude to your grandparents or even your great-grandparents if they are still alive," she commented.

Sexual Harassment of Women of Color

Though inconclusive, studies suggest that women of color are sexually harassed more than white women are. One study found that 16.6 percent of white women indicated that they had been sexually harassed, in comparison to 48.6 percent of black women.[44] Another found minority women in double jeopardy: when racial and sexual harassment are combined, minority women face significantly more harassment than do minority men, majority women, and majority men.[45] When women of color are targeted for sexual harassment, what we see is not only a gendered power dynamic but also a racial power dynamic. The interplay not only influences the instance(s) of harassment (often called the "first injury") but also the likelihood that women of color will be met with resistance when they attempt to seek outside help to stop the harassment (the "second injury").[46]

THE FIRST INJURY

Racial stereotypes taint not only the language and style of sexual harassment but also the harasser's perception of the victim's willingness to submit to harassment. In general, women of color are seen as both sexually available and likely to submit, stereotypes dating back to the 17th century for blacks and Latinas and the 19th century for Asian Americans. Women of color also are underrepresented in the workforce—particularly in positions of leadership —and are more likely to be in economically precarious positions or solely responsible for children and family. Combined, these factors put many women of color in a vulnerable position, fueling images of women of color as ideal victims for a harasser hoping to avoid any consequences in the workplace.[47] Further, given their position at the bottom of both the gender and racial hierarchy, women of color may be victimized by both white men and other men of color, while "a man of color is not likely to feel that he has the prerogative to harass a white woman."[48]

Despite some similarities, women of color—as individuals but also as members of different racial groups—face unique obstacles and stereotypes.

The Lotus Blossom stereotype of Asian American women as submissive fuels a misconception that they are "desirous of sexual domination," are "easy to have sex with," and will likely "not fight back."[49] A lawyer noted that the delicate Lotus Blossom image combined with the image that Asian American women are "sexual vixens in bed."[50] Indeed, one Asian scientist overheard a group of white men discussing her sexuality at an airport restaurant: "There were some men in another table. They were looking me up and down. And they were talking. And they probably thought that I couldn't understand English or something. But they had comments like, 'Oh, she would be a submissive one' or something like that. . . . Boy, I was mad. I almost went up to them and slapped them."

Like Asian American women, Latinas also are stereotyped as sexually available; they are seen as "naturally sexual," fiery, passionate, "hot blooded."[51] One Latina professor speculated why she, a married woman, was routinely receiving sexual advances from single men at work: "They tend to think Brazilians are very friendly and approachable, even, I don't know, party animals. . . . The only image that they show about Brazil most of the time on TV internationally is Carnival."

Sexual harassment against African American women often incorporates images and stereotypes that are shockingly clear legacies of the era of slavery. In the case *Continental Can Co. v. Minnesota*, the harasser told his black victim that "he wished slavery days would return so that he could sexually train her and she

---

WHERE ARE THE WOMEN-OF-COLOR DIRECTORS?

It's almost too obvious to be stated, but one of the key ways that harmful stereotypes of women of color, like those described in this chapter, are perpetuated is through the media, particularly television and film.

As in many prestigious fields, women of color are underrepresented in entertainment, especially in the roles with the most creative control.

The Directors Guild of America analyzed over 2,000 prime-time television episodes produced between 2010 and 2011. It found that white women directed 11 percent of all episodes, and women of color directed less than 1 percent. White men, on the other hand, dominated by directing 77 percent of the episodes listed.[o]

In 2008, only one black woman directed one of the top 100 grossing films. The year before, not one black woman made the list.[p]

---

would be his bitch."[52] The Jezebel stereotype, which portrays black women as promiscuous, naturally sexual, and sexually available, is particularly apparent.[53] One black scientist felt that her confidence and comfort were often read as sexually inviting by white men: "It's hard work being a black woman, because you are kind of a forbidden-fruit thing from a white man's point of view. . . . If you simply relax in your own skin because you happen to be comfortable in it and exude any confidence, all the sudden [the men think], 'She's hitting on me. She's being too sexy. I don't know about this.'"

THE SECOND INJURY

Women of color face a series of barriers when they seek help to stop sexual harassment, whether they attempt to do so internally through human resources or externally through the courts.

For one thing, the series of stereotypes we discussed earlier help promote a belief that women of color are not likely to be victims, because they either are seen to invite sexual attention or are seen as too asexual to warrant it. Beauty norms that highlight physical attributes coded as white don't help the matter, particularly when the accused harasser himself is white. When male sexual desire is expected to follow certain racialized norms, onlookers may be less likely to believe a woman of color who says she is experiencing sexual harassment. If she is targeted, the logic may follow, it was because she acted in such a way to elicit the harassment—or, to invoke another stereotype, she might just be lying.[54]

When the harasser is a person of color, another set of predicaments arise. The so-called cultural defense argument—that certain behavior is acceptable when enacted between members of a racial group—has been used to justify harassment of women of color by men of their own race. The Anita Hill–Clarence Thomas controversy illustrates this dynamic. During the confirmation hearings for Clarence Thomas, a black man and the second African American to serve on the U.S. Supreme Court, Anita Hill, a black woman and successful attorney, accused Thomas of sexually harassing her; afterward, she received a wave of media backlash.

Some people argued that Thomas's behavior was not harassment but instead "down home courtin'," a style of innocent banter common between black men and women.[55] Others were less concerned with the character of the relationship between Thomas and Hill and more concerned with what they believed to be Hill's selfish disregard for her community. "By accusing a Black man of such a heinous sexual act she was violating an understood racial agreement—that Black people should not place their personal concerns, no matter how grave, serious or destructive, above or ahead of the goals of the larger community or group," many suggested at the time.[56] Not only do black women fear community backlash, but they also fear that "speaking about sexual abuse will reinforce negative racial stereotypes about Black men in particular."[57]

Most women of color face workplaces, as well as human resource departments and courts, that are largely dominated by white men and women. Both white and nonwhite women fear what may happen if they report harassment: perhaps someone will think that if they were wearing a tight skirt (or talking to a male colleague or having a drink with a supervisor), they were asking for it; maybe someone will think they just slept their way to the top (because, come on, how else would they have gotten there?); or someone will think there's no way it could have happened, because he's such a nice guy and she's—well—sort of mannish. These are fears that

---

OBSERVATIONS I MADE WHILE CODING THE INTERVIEWS

Past a certain point, there are so few women that the Tug of War disappears. Some scientists didn't recognize the pattern at all because there were so few women in their environments.

Physical appearance was mentioned far more often in the NSF interviews, whether it was along the lines of "I wear a T-shirt and jeans because that's what all the guys around here do" or "No one really dresses up here, but I make a conscious effort to." The New Girls rarely mentioned how they dress.

The NSF interviews discussed bias outside as well as inside the workplace. Despite being prompted by similar questions about the same four patterns, the New Girls tended to look at the patterns just in the context of careers, whereas almost all the women of color interviewed for the NSF project had at least one or two anecdotes about how they had encountered the patterns in their education and in their everyday lives.

The scientists, especially Latinas, often reported intense family pressures to have children. They seemed caught between pressures from work/school environment to delay starting a family and cultural/family/friend pressures to get married and have kids. It was really interesting to read about how these women have encountered and dealt with such conflicting messages/pressures.

—Meghan Guptill, Center for WorkLife Law intern

white women and women of color share. But added to these experiences for women of color is a legacy of racialized stereotypes in an environment designed not just for men but for white men.

* * *

Sometimes women of color face double jeopardy, but the intersection of race and gender is a lot more complicated than that. It's well-established that women of color experience challenges that stem from both race and gender. Other conclusions must remain tentative. Black and Latina women may well have to provide even more evidence of competence than white (and Asian American) women do. Latinas and Asian Americans appear to have more "too feminine" problems than do white (or black) women. To this extent, the double jeopardy hypothesis appears partly true.

But the hypothesis does not fully capture the complexities at the intersection of race and gender. Most notably, black women are less likely than white women to be penalized for having a direct, no-nonsense, don't-suffer-fools-lightly style. That comes at a cost, of course: black women are not eligible for the cherished status that is reserved solely for white women. And God forbid they use an authoritative style to advocate for themselves; it's accepted only when they are furthering the goals of the company or institution. Asian American women may face fewer negative competence and commitment assumptions based on motherhood—but then run smack into backlash against hard-driving mothers.

In other words, it's complicated.

Complicated, but important. Exploring how gender bias differs by race is crucial for several reasons. The first is that women's initiatives too often are called "white women's initiatives" behind closed doors. The experiences of women of color differ from those of white women. Not only do women of color face racial as well as gender bias; their experience of gender bias differs from that of white women. Women's initiatives need to take these factors into account if they expect to engage women of color.

The second reason an advice book like this one needs to explore how gender bias differs by race is that the styles and traditions of different groups of women can offer important resources. One example is that women of color offer important insights into how to defuse gender wars. These women, by and large, showed a greater sensitivity in the interviews to social inequality and to the travails faced by women who came before. In part, this may reflect cultural traditions of respect for elders. And while women of color, to some extent, may face more bias in the workplace than white women do, those we interviewed said there were many benefits as well. A study by Isis H. Settles found that some of her black women subjects felt that their identities as black women gave them a sense of personal self-esteem.[58] "I feel that I am stronger emotionally and consciously," said one woman quoted in the study. Another said, "Black women have usually been portrayed as strong and independent. This gives me a lot of confidence in my ability"—although, she acknowledged, it also sometimes felt like a burden: "I'm not a superwoman."[59] The image of women as strong and self-confident is something other groups of women could benefit from.

The takeaway here should, by this point, be familiar: there's no right way to be a woman. What this chapter shares with the others is that it seeks to describe highly individualized experiences in general terms. The tension between the general and the unique comes to a head in the analysis of how gender bias differs by race. Women of color face different challenges from those faced by white women, and on the flip side, they have advantages that are unavailable to whites. The challenge is to keep the conversation open to the things that make our experiences different as well as the things that make our experiences the same.

PART VI

Leave or Stay?

12

Leave or Stay?
Reading the
Tea Leaves

A woman is like a tea bag—you can't tell how strong she is until
you put her in hot water. —ELEANOR ROOSEVELT

One of the biggest mistakes you can make is soldiering on in a job that's not going well long after you should have left. In chapter 3, we discussed ways to get credit for your work in the face of stereotypes that men are better professionals than women. In chapters 5 and 6, we discussed strategies to avoid getting pegged as a doormat or labeled a bitch. In chapter 8, we discussed how mothers can overcome or avoid stereotypes that they are less competent and committed than their peers. In chapter 10, we discussed what to do to defuse potentially career-destroying conflict between women.

Sometimes, none of these strategies work.

The nature of organizations is that sometimes you make a misstep that there's no recovering from. The nature of hierarchies is that there are always some people at the bottom. And the nature of bias is that sometimes you're not what's wrong—there's just not a fit between you and the organization you're in. Sometimes, in other words, it's time to leave. This is not a decision to be taken lightly. This chapter and the next are designed to help. Here's how to figure out if the office you're in is right for you.

Sign #1: You're Undervalued

One of the most common patterns of gender bias is that women get stuck in a few tightly cabined roles: a gofer, called on to service other people's clients but not develop their own or to do a never-ending stream of "nice work" that, while important, leads nowhere. We've already discussed ways you can try to turn this pattern around. But if none of them are working, it may be time to move on.

One consultant found that, after she had children, she hit the Maternal Wall. "I knew I was undervalued," she said. "I knew it was because I was a mother and I wasn't willing to do everything that my male counterpart was willing to do. So I took myself out of contention. But the salary was just unacceptable." Knowing she wouldn't be able to rise any higher at her current company, she started searching for jobs elsewhere—and found another position where she was paid twice as much.

Another New Girl said she left her job after being sent messages that she would be the next promotion, but only because the company needed to promote a woman. What her business head said was, "The next person I need to take in this job is a woman. And if I take a woman, you're the one I want. But I don't need one right now." What she heard was, "We need to take a woman, and you're the girl we want. But if we didn't have to take a girl, we wouldn't want one." It was a strong signal that she could find a place to spend her career that would be more supportive of women—as individuals rather than as boxes to check.

Whether it's that you're not getting good assignments, not getting promotions that you deserve, or not getting paid as much as your peers, there comes a point when you need to ask yourself if your loyalty is being rewarded or just taken for granted.

"Getting passed over once, I don't think you need to get all freaked out," said an employment lawyer. "I think when you've been passed over twice, you really need to start doing something or thinking things through. You get passed over three times, it's a big problem."

Sign #2: There Aren't Many Women at the Senior Levels of the Company

When Rachel was a paralegal, she would often conduct intake interviews with potential clients for employment discrimination cases. Some of the claims were funny, like the man who wanted to sue his employer for discriminating against him because of his beard. She had to explain that "bearded men" are not a legally protected category.

Some of the calls, however, hit close to home, like one woman who called for a gender discrimination intake. She had been working at the same company for several years, she said, and her progress had stalled. There were almost no women at the top of the organization, and she had mostly given up on promotion. "You look around at the people above you and kind of know what your life is going to look like, you know?" she said.

Several of the New Girls said the same thing. If you don't see anyone who looks like you, there's probably a reason for that.

A FOCUS ON DIVERSITY MAKES A REAL DIFFERENCE

A 2010 study by McKinsey & Company came to what should be an obvious conclusion: companies that place gender diversity as a higher priority have more women in the C-suite. Eighty-seven percent of companies where gender diversity was a top-three agenda item had more than 15 percent women at the C-level, compared with 55 percent of all respondents. In other words, if your company is a place that's open to women's advancement, chances are you'll know. The bad news is that only in 28 percent of companies studied did gender diversity break the top ten. This is a problem not only for women but for the bottom line: other research from McKinsey has found that companies with higher levels of gender diversity also have higher equity, operating results, and stock-price growth.[a]

Think twice about staying at a company where the highest ranks are devoid of women.

"You have to look at where you're going. Really study the structural characteristics of your firm. If there are no women in top management, the chances of you actually succeeding there are pretty low," one New Girl said.

"I was doing very well on Wall Street, but the firm I was at didn't have any women partners," said an investment banker. "I thought, 'Well, if anyone should be made partner, it would probably be—if not me, then someone very much like me.' But I was also very aware that the further you got up in organizations, the more politics there were. I just decided I didn't want to take a five-year risk and lose the gamble. So I thought, 'Well, let me just forge out on my own.'"

These women knew instinctively what social scientists are now documenting: when women are at the top of organizations, women below them tend to fare better. One study found that companies with a higher share of women on their boards also had higher numbers of top executive women.[1] Another found that companies with female CEOs or chairs are more likely to have a greater number of women executives—and better-paid ones, at that.[2]

When there are no women in the top ranks of a company, one has to wonder why. As we've discussed, there are literally dozens of ways women get shut out of positions of power. Perhaps time norms bar people with family responsibilities from success. Perhaps the organization sees itself as a meritocracy and insists that women prove themselves repeatedly while promoting men on potential. Perhaps the environment is just unpleasant for women. Perhaps it's a self-reinforcing cycle: it's hard to envision yourself at the top when there's no one there who looks like you.

You don't have to figure out all on your own whether women have advancement opportunities at your company. It may be helpful to talk with senior women—or, if there are no senior women, other women at your level—to see what their experience has been. For example, many women face bias when they get pregnant or come back from maternity leave, which you wouldn't necessarily know when kids still seem like they're in the distant future.

One major sign that there may be a problem is if, as sometimes happens, a large group of women leaves the company all at once. (Joan was once at an employer where four senior women left in a single year.) If this happens at your company, try to find out why. Employees who have already announced that they're leaving may be more likely to be honest with you about their situation than women trying to hold on to their jobs.

"If you go to three or four of those women and they just tell you, 'I tried everything there is. There's just no way,' that gives you the opportunity to leave before you get to that point," said an employment lawyer.

Someone always has to be the first woman at the top. Maybe it will be you. But diverse companies have been shown to perform better than homogeneous ones, so finding companies with women and minorities in the top ranks may not only be good for your mental health—it may be good for your wallet as well.[3]

Sign #3: You Can Move Up Elsewhere

Even when there's nothing immediately wrong with your professional situation, several New Girls advocated keeping an eye out for opportunities for advancement outside your current company.

"I think it's important to change jobs fairly frequently," one New Girl said. "Not every six months, not every year and a half, because then you'll get a reputation as flighty. But I think it's important to move up whenever you possibly can, to increase your leverage and your position and your salary. All of that offers you protection. When you just stay in the same position, you become a sitting duck."

An attorney said, "I leave law firms easily and frequently to get promoted. I started doing that at an early age. And years ago, people used to ask the question, 'Why do you move so much?' They don't really ask that anymore."

"I knew I had to leave where I was born, so to speak," said a consultant. "If I stayed where I grew up, they would always see me as the child."

One study found that for highly educated men, the return on tenure in the same job is about 50 percent higher than for women; for highly educated women, the return on experience brought from prior jobs is about 40 percent higher than it is for men.[4] This is not to say that you can't make it to the top of the company where you started your career. There are several examples of high-powered women who rose to the top of companies after decades of service: Virginia Rometty had been at IBM for 30 years when she became CEO in 2011, and Xerox CEO Ursula Burns famously started working at that company as an intern.[5] A report by Catalyst indicates that women much more than men may face a wage penalty for moving too frequently—while there was no difference found in the wages of businesswomen at their first and second post-MBA jobs, wages for those who had worked at three or more jobs showed a sharp decrease.[6]

There are two key takeaways. The first is, don't move too often. If it looks like you can't keep a job, this can have a serious negative impact on your career. A New Girl who works in finance had a simple rule of thumb: "It can't be too hard to explain your resume," she said. "You have to have a resume that makes sense."

Moving too frequently is a problem because not only might you end up looking like a flight risk or disloyal, but it also stunts the kind of close professional relationships that are so important in creating a solid network.

"I carried my skills around in a backpack on my back. I just sold them to whoever would offer me the package that I was shopping for," one New Girl said. "The downside of it, which I'm confronting now, is that I didn't really build long-term client relationships over years and years. I didn't do those things that you do over a decade of establishing a reputation in your field. Those kinds of things that are really important for business development, I wasn't really paying attention to."

The second takeaway is that you should only move up, never sideways or down. This is a particular problem for women, who may be more likely than men to follow a partner to a new city, another New Girl said. "It's important to leave when you're in a position of strength. It can be deadly to make lateral moves because the spouse is making a move. Quitting work and leaving your geographical base can be the kiss of death."

A 2009 study by Thomas J. Cooke and colleagues demonstrated that a woman's earnings significantly decline following a move.[7] Just one year after relocation, women on average saw a $1,153 decline in salary, and it took three more years of working for them to return to the salary levels they had before the move.[8]

Sign #4: You've Exhausted Your Options (or Yourself)

Gender bias comes in lots of different flavors. Some are harder to swallow than others. We've already listed a wide variety of strategies for confronting a wide variety of biases, but there's no magic bullet. If you're facing severe gender bias at work, sometimes the best solution may be to start over at a place where you haven't already been cast in a gendered role.

For instance, one major source of potentially career-stunting bias is the Maternal Wall. Taking time off for family responsibilities or using flexible work arrangements may lead to stigma that could be hard to shake. A study of women who had taken advantage of work-family accommodations found that those women often faced limited opportunities when they returned to work full-time, which they could escape only if they moved to a different job altogether. However, the study also warned, "job changing itself carried a hefty wage penalty."[9]

As we mentioned earlier, women who make lateral moves—who move to a new job without an accompanying promotion—usually take a financial hit. Before you get to a point where you feel you

WHAT IF YOU'VE TRIED TO BE "ONE OF THE BOYS" AND ARE SICK OF IT?

As we've noted before, women often have to navigate a fine line between fitting in and protesting male banter, flirting, or worse. What if you've tried the "one of the boys" strategy and have come to the end of your rope?

Several New Girls suggested ways to opt out gracefully: "I love hanging out with you guys, but I'm just realizing I'm not so comfortable when you go to the strip club. If you want to go there, I need to leave," one New Girl suggested. Another idea: "Find the friendliest guy, tell him that you feel uncomfortable. Add that 'I'm not the only woman who feels this way,' and ask him whether he would be willing to tell the other guys. You might well find out that he feels as uncomfortable as you do."

What happens if you do speak up, and the guys say, "I didn't know you were a prude." Here are some options:

- "I've talked to others and they're uncomfortable too."

- "I thought about it, and it just doesn't work for me."

- "It appears so."

- "At work, yes I am."

have to leave, there are several internal options you can pursue to reverse or interrupt patterns of gender bias. Kathy Dickson, a plaintiffs'-side employment lawyer, tells the women who come to her to start looking for simple solutions and elevate as necessary. Here are the most important things to take into account:

1. *Whom can I talk to who may be able to help?* If your problem is that you've been passed over for a promotion you felt you deserved or that you're not making as much money as Joe down the hall, step one is simply to ask for what you want.

If you haven't done this yet, get up, walk down the hallway, and do it right now. Asking doesn't always help, but it often does. If you get what you want, problem solved. If you don't, you now know you've tried. Another option may be to ask a supervisor what you need to do to get ready for the next round of promotions. This helps you set some concrete goals —and get a sense of what is being expected of you. It also lets them know you are interested: "Maybe you lose this one, but at least you put down a marker," advised an audience member at one of Joan's panels.[10]

2. *Will things get better on their own?* This is a hard one because the line between taking the long view and remaining passive in a tough situation can be hard to see. But everyone has rough patches at work. You may choose to give yourself a time line ("If I'm still unhappy in three months, I'll start looking for another job") or a goal to meet ("I'll see if I'm recognized for my work on this project"). The worst problems sometimes fix themselves. But if you reach the end of the trial period and things aren't looking any brighter, it may well be time to get your resume out there.

3. *Can I transfer to a different department?* If you're having problems with a particular person or the dynamics within a particular group, you can ask to be transferred to a different department or assignment within your company, provided that it's big enough. It's common practice for big organizations to transfer employees to resolve internal conflicts. This strategy works well if you want to maintain the clout and position you've developed at a particular job but need to get away from, say, a manager's constant commentary on his sex life or the expectation that you'll keep the coffeepot full.

4. *What are the formal processes you can use to fight back?* If your problem is particularly severe, you may decide to file an internal complaint or even take legal action. This route is definitely not for everyone, but regardless of whether it's for you, it's important to know how to protect your legal rights.

PROTECT YOUR RIGHTS

Whether or not you choose to sue for discrimination or harassment, here are some basic steps all women can take to make sure you're keeping your options open:

Don't write about your situation on your company's servers: whether you're writing to a friend or your attorney, anything you write on your company's servers is their property and could easily be used against you in an investigation.

Do keep copies of important documents, including contracts, performance reviews, and even old e-mails or voice mails that may be relevant to a potential complaint. Print these out or put them on a personal flash drive and keep them at home.

Don't record conversations without the other participants' knowledge and consent. This is illegal in many states.

Don't sign anything without first speaking with a lawyer.

Do know your EEOC deadlines: before you file a discrimination lawsuit, you need to first submit a complaint to the Equal Employment Opportunity Commission (EEOC), the federal agency responsible for workplace discrimination claims. Generally, if you don't file an EEOC charge within 180 days of the alleged discrimination, you may be barred from pursuing your claim. The specific rules vary from state to state; consult a lawyer to find out the laws where you live.

If you decide to take on the fight, step one is often to file an internal complaint. Public employees may be legally required to exhaust internal remedies before seeking outside help. Even if it's not required, it may be helpful to have on record that you brought up the problem and your company failed to address it. Make sure you understand how your company's system for dealing with these complaints works: you can ask Human Resources if you can't find this out in the employee handbook, but know that often HR will go to your supervisors with the information that you spoke with them.

It's also a good idea to consult a lawyer before you proceed —not necessarily because you're going to sue but because a good employment lawyer does a lot of work behind the scenes. "Jobs could be saved actually if people did talk to a lawyer earlier," Dickson said. Many lawyers will help you out on an hourly basis: treat this as an investment in your career.

A lawyer who represents employers agreed. "Be comfortable hiring a lawyer to work behind the scenes," she said. Her advice to employees: "Use the lawyer as a coach to plot strategy; you're the mouthpiece. The lawyer can tell you, 'This is how you write it.'" She continued, "It's just less toxic." Ultimately your lawyer may have to come out of the shadows, but you'll know if that's necessary after you've exhausted the possibilities of what a lawyer can do for you working behind the scenes.

Both lawyers agreed on the need to take care in hiring a lawyer. Beware of the lawyers you keep reading about in the papers. They are people who like to get their name in the papers, when the most effective approach is often for the lawyer to stay behind the scenes or to seek mediation or arbitration. Do your homework—and network. "People know who are the good plaintiffs' employment lawyers," said a lawyer who represents management. If you have a lawyer who's respected, it will affect how people react to your case.

If you do file a complaint, you need to know that it's probably going to get back to whomever you've complained about and that you are legally required to cooperate with an internal investigation. And be careful whom you talk to: for certain complaints, like sexual harassment, anyone above you, including managers and supervisors as well as Human Resources, is legally required to investigate once you've made an allegation, even if you thought you were just sounding off in their office.

Sign #5: You Hate Your Job

Finally, even if you can't put your finger on what's wrong, the ultimate sign that you may want to look for a new job is if you just don't like the one you have. You deserve to have a job you enjoy. It's as simple as that.

One attorney said she left the law firm world after she realized it was literally making her sick. Everyone assumed she was looking to start a family, but the reality was that she just didn't want that lifestyle any longer. "Migraines, back pain, skin peeling, insomnia, chills. You name it, whatever thing you could have—it just got to that point. And you just really can't do it anymore," she said. "I'm physically making myself ill, and I don't see any way up from here. I don't see anyone doing this in a way that I want to do it. I have people telling me they don't want my life, and I don't see anyone whose life I want."

So she left. Early in her new position, the New Girl met with her boss and had a conversation about the expectations for her position, including benchmarks and timetables. "It was such a revelation, you know? I could see a link between what I do and how I'm compensated and how my contribution is valued," she said.

Now, it's relatively rare that you hate your job so much you're getting physical symptoms. If you're unhappy, you should definitely leave before it starts affecting your health. But long before that, there are reasons to leave a comfortable job simply because you aren't doing what you want to do—particularly if you're young. One New Girl said that shortly after graduating from college, she was working in criminal justice and planning to go to law school when she realized that she just didn't like the work that much. "I quit my job, which was a very good job for a recent college graduate, and took time off and thought about it and elected to go a different path," she said. Instead of going to law school, she took a job in public policy, where she's been working ever since.

Remember, though, that early in your career, every assignment isn't going to be thrilling, and the ratio of hard, boring work to rewarding work may be discouragingly high. Most organizations are set up so that junior employees are expected to pay their dues before getting to work independently on substantive projects. Which is to say that everyone is miserable at work some of the time.

So how unhappy is unhappy enough? One New Girl said she follows the 80 percent rule: "I'm generally a happy person. And if I don't enjoy what I'm doing 80 percent of the time or more, then it's time to make a change." If you're really stuck, the New Girl recommends putting both of your options—stay and go—into a hat. "If I pull out stay and I feel nauseated, then the right answer is to go," she said.

* * *

There are a lot of reasons women persuade themselves to stay in jobs they don't like. They feel loyalty to their company, even if the company doesn't treat them well. They're too scared to leave. The money is great. They need to stay in a certain area so they don't uproot their family. These reasons may feel convincing, but they're not insurmountable obstacles.

This isn't to say that there *aren't* good reasons to stay at a job you don't love. But women are often expected to make sacrifices for the community that men wouldn't even consider. Women, for instance, may be more likely to uproot for their spouse's jobs than men are and more likely to stay at a company where they're mistreated, out of fear of leaving their co-workers or their company in the lurch. Don't get caught in this trap. It's not good for yourself *or* your family.

13

Leave or Stay?
Don't Dismay

I love to see a young girl go out and grab the world by the lapels.
Life's a bitch. You've got to go out and kick ass.

— MAYA ANGELOU

Leaving isn't always the right option. Bouncing from job to job can have serious consequences: it may make you look fickle to potential future employers, keep you from developing long-term working relationships, or stunt your development of the in-depth skills and knowledge expected of senior employees. There are certain points when you may be particularly vulnerable—right before or after having a baby or in response to a particularly time-consuming project, for instance—and it's important to maintain some perspective on whether the situation will improve with time.

One New Girl remembered a talented lawyer who had worked at her law firm. When she had her second child, the head of the practice group approached the litigator and suggested she take on a narrower role with less responsibility, which would have more defined hours. The New Girl counseled her against it. "You're going to make your own decision, but let's talk about what might go into that decision," she said. "So you just had your second baby. You're feeling overwhelmed. But let's talk about what your work would be like."

The New Girl suggested that instead of taking on this new role, the lawyer approach the firm with a five-year plan for how she intended to remain on track despite a reduced schedule. She didn't take the New Girl's advice and ended up taking the dead-end position her supervisor had offered. "They hit them up when they're vulnerable," the New Girl told us in frustration. "She loved her work, so it wasn't that she didn't want to go back. Maybe if she had been asked that question a year or two later when things were less overwhelming, the answer would have been different."

Making the decision to wait out a rough patch, one New Girl said, means you also have to make a decision to get something out of it. "If you choose to stay for a period of time, because you're getting some valuable experience or you don't want to look like you've got a rotating door on your resume, then stay. But just say, 'Hey, I'm staying. Yes, there's a lot of stuff I don't like, but I'm getting XYZ out of it, and I'm going to revisit it in three months, six months, and when the timing's right, I'll probably leave,'" she said.

HOW DO I GET GOOD ASSIGNMENTS?

- Be the first to volunteer.

- If you want to do a certain kind of work, ask for it.

- Project confidence but show humility.

- Be willing to stretch—volunteer even if you have never done it before.

- No project is "beneath" you, but you also need stretch assignments that allow you to grow.

- Expect to excel and do the very best work you can do.

- Show commitment to the positive outcome of all projects.

- If you are not getting work, consider the possibility that your performance on prior projects wasn't up to standards—go looking for feedback.

- Develop a strategy for turning your reputation around—get help.

        —New Girl Vernā Myers, nationally recognized diversity consultant

Several New Girls who had become champions for women at their organizations said it was actually the obstacles they faced that kept them going. "I got to a point where I had decided what I was going to tolerate and what I wasn't," said an executive. "Then I had to decide, did I want to stay and be somebody who worked on change in the culture, or was I going to leave?" This New Girl decided to stay and got some really incredible things done under her tenure. "You can take it on directly, you can leave, you can do nothing, but you're making a choice," she said. "So don't rehash old tapes when there's nothing new to learn, because it just drains your energy and it's not worth it. My biggest advice overall would be don't let yourself become a victim. Vote with your feet, change it, but try to stay positive and constructive and make choices that are right for you."

As a caveat to this advice, it's important not to become so caught up in a sense of duty that you sacrifice yourself in the process. "A lot of women have an identity as being part of a larger group, and consequently your actions are not your own. That's a whole lot of burden people who think of themselves as individuals don't have to deal with," said one woman of color. "I remember when I left my first white law firm, I felt like I was letting down my race."

Either Act on It or Let It Go

Here is one of the most important pieces of advice in the entire book. If there's something that's frustrating you, an executive suggested, think it through and "make a choice to either change it, live with it, manage it, whatever—but make a choice." Ask yourself, "Am I having any breakthroughs? Is anything different from the last time I thought about this and got frustrated?"

Don't allow yourself to obsess about the things that are making you think about leaving. Think them through, for sure. But stop thinking about them when there's no new learning.

Don't Go Out of the Frying Pan into the Fire

Remember the wise woman who, when someone called her a bitch, thought hard about whether she was acting bitchy? Self-awareness is not easy, but it's not impossible. If things get rough, talk over your impressions with your inner circle. Ask for constructive criticism. "Listen to it and shut your mouth; process it without being defensive. As soon as you open your mouth, the advice stops," warns one New Girl.

Particularly if the problem stems from your dealings with a difficult person, you need to find out whether others are having the same difficulties. Diplomatically find out if other people have had problems with that person. "If someone is a bully," remarked another New Girl, "you are not going to be the only one who knows that."

The larger point is that it takes two to tango. If things have gone south, you need to know what you might have done to contribute. Otherwise, you lose the opportunity to correct something you might carry over to the next job—and the next and the next.

To figure this out, feedback is crucial. "Do you have an idea about how you are perceived by others?" one of the New Girls asked Joan.

"Not really," she replied. "Do you? How do you get that kind of information?"

"You ask people," the New Girl said. "Go to your network, which should be eclectic and should include both peers and more senior people. Ask them, 'What do people say about me when I'm not in the room?' If their eyes dart, say, 'Don't you go there. I want you to be honest with me. I'm trying to get better.'"

Maintain good tone control. Don't be defensive. You are not trying to file a lawsuit. You are making it safe for people to give you honest feedback.

"How could I have done this differently? How could I have done it better? You need to invite people to be critical: remember, it's a lot easier to say, 'Good job,'" the New Girl noted. Joan does much the same thing in a different context. After a speech or a press interview, she asks, "What is one thing I could have done better?" If the person compliments her, she thanks them and says, "But surely there's one thing I could have done better?"

Another good question is "What are three adjectives that define me?" suggested the same New Girl. "Do all this when you're not in trouble," she advised, "and it will help guide you if you ever are in trouble." For example, if you are perceived poorly in your department but well outside, that suggests a transfer. But if you are perceived poorly throughout the organization, whether deservedly or not, transferring may well not be in the cards.

Should You Leave to Spend Time with Kids?

Women executives leave their jobs at nearly two times the rate of men.[1] No doubt a whole series of factors contribute to this imbalance, including glass-ceiling patterns like having your mistakes given disproportionate weight or getting the job but not the title. Senior women may simply be exhausted from decades of proving it again.

But the single biggest reason women leave their jobs is the Maternal Wall. One study of professionals with graduate degrees found that 43 percent of women with children take time off during their careers, while only 24 percent of men do.[2] Every year, some one-third of married mothers in the workforce leave to take care of their children.[3] Work-family issues are a huge factor for almost every working mother, and as we've discussed, the high commitment expected from top professionals can place tremendous pressures on family life.

"The reason I left was because I felt like I was subcontracting my life because I traveled so much," said the then institutional broker, now hedge fund manager, who took several years off when her children were young. "I remember when I went to the preschool, they checked my ID, and I cried."

This is a personal decision and a wedge issue in the Mommy Wars. One New Girl said when she announced her departure, everyone around her was mystified by why she would do such a thing: "How could you possibly leave? You're doing so well. You're like the best woman that's ever been here. You're making more money than God."

She, along with the other New Girls who took time off when their children were young, ultimately went back to the workforce. About two-thirds of mothers who leave to take care of children have the same plan, and 87 percent of women who didn't intend to return when they left either did return or were looking to return.[4]

It's impossible to talk about the decision to take a break from the workforce without also talking about how hard it can be to reenter it. The hedge fund manager just quoted had a relatively easy transition back, but it doesn't always work that way. One study, conducted by professors at Wharton, found that women who take a break from the workplace are often out for longer than expected and find the process of trying to reenter "negative and depressing."[5] It may be difficult to compete with recent graduates, who are also looking for jobs but who come with a lower price tag than a more experienced worker.[6] Resume gaps may be hard to explain.

As a result, about one-fourth of women who try to return to the workforce after a prolonged career break fail to find jobs, and the majority of those women who do find new jobs don't return full-time.[7]

Several New Girls either left the workforce or went part-time temporarily to take care of their children and were able to come back to very successful careers. It's by no means impossible, and for many women, the risk is worth it. This particular decision is much too personal to give any real advice on without knowing all the details, but it's important to make it armed with all the necessary information about its possible outcomes. The sad fact is that, according to one study, women who take a single year off work lose 32 percent of their annual earnings, and those who take two to

---

HOW TO LEAVE—BUT NOT LEAVE YOURSELF HANGING

STRATEGY 1: Negotiate

STRATEGY 2: Have a New Job Lined Up

STRATEGY 3: Keep Your Network Intact

STRATEGY 4: Money Matters

---

three years off lose at least 40 percent of their annual earnings, as compared to women who take no time off.[8]

Most of us have probably had fantasies of quitting our jobs after a particularly late night or discouraging meeting. Actually taking the steps to quit is a different story. Every woman's situation is different, but there are several things you can do to try and ensure your transition is as smooth as possible.

Strategy 1: Negotiate

Several New Girls mentioned that their complaints about bias or unfair treatment weren't taken seriously until they announced their intention to leave. Once good workers are ready to quit, companies may scramble to find ways to get them to stay. This can actually be a good negotiation strategy—as long as you're not bluffing. Threatening to leave with the expectation that you'll get what you ask for can backfire in a big way.

"I started asking for my title three years ago, and I asked and asked and asked," one New Girl said. "And finally, I just said, 'Well, I'm going to leave if I can't get that title.'"

She got the title.

Another New Girl said she was considered the best negotiator in her company, which generated respect but not compensation. She waited until her children were old enough that she could leave her

---

STRATEGIES TO FIND OUT IF YOU'RE UNDERPAID

Recruiters

If you work for a private employer, the best thing to do is to befriend a recruiter. Many people receive recruiter calls when they aren't looking for a job and just blow them off—but that's passing up an important opportunity to build your network. Recruiting firms have a wealth of information regarding job qualifications, salaries, and benefits. Talk with them, and if you are not interested in changing jobs, try to think of someone who might be. As always, the best way to build your network is through reciprocal favors. Your recruiter friend can provide resumes, salaries, and benefits for positions comparable to yours.

If You Work for the Government

If you work for the government, typically salaries are public information. If you work for a federal contractor (and one in five American workers do), pay is publicly available under the Office of Federal Contract Compliance.[a]

Other Strategies

Ask a guy who's a friend how much he's making. Ask human resources, if people think they can be trusted to keep the inquiry confidential, about your job grade and the range of salaries in that grade. Or ask questions that give you information that allows you to figure out where you stand. For example, if your firm has tiers tied to rainmaking, you can ask whether there is anyone in your tier who brings in more money —and whether you should be in a higher tier, based on your numbers alone. Be careful: some employers have rules prohibiting employees from discussing compensation with each other, although such rules are illegal in some states (notably California).

---

current company without having to negotiate a flexible schedule at a new company and then stated her demands. "I held back until I was finished needing the accommodation, so then they knew that it would be easy for me to leave," she said. The company tried to offer her a promotion in title without a corresponding increase in salary, but she was in a strong enough position at that point to be able to demand that they provide her with both.

One lawyer remembered a colleague who decided to retire early after the men who started when she did went up "markedly" in compensation. "She had a financial situation with her spouse and her own income that she could just stop doing this. She wasn't even 50 yet. She had no interest in going to another firm. She was just quitting," the lawyer remembered.

The colleague's supervisor assumed she was retiring because she wanted to spend time with her family. The New Girl set him straight. "It is absolutely about the money," she told him.

The firm ended up reviewing the attorney's book of business and adjusting her compensation, and she stayed. This is a great

---

HOW TO NEGOTIATE A PAY RAISE

Follow Mika Brzezinski's good advice in *Knowing Your Value*.

- Put together a brag sheet with objective facts that show why you deserve a raise.

- Don't be afraid to leave.

- Before you make an issue of salary, it's best to put out some feelers and know what kind of options you have out there. (Another reason to befriend a good recruiter or two.)

Brzezinski also gives some great advice about how to frame the actual question, based on a conversation with financial guru and TV personality Suze Orman:

"You should never, ever, ever ask a yes or no question. If you ask for a ten percent raise and the boss says no, what are you going to say?" Instead, she suggests giving your boss two options: slightly more than what you want and then a lower number that you actually expect to get. "So you would say, 'I really think I deserve a ten percent or twelve percent raise. Which one would you like to give me?' "[b]

example of how a network can come in handy to speak up for you when you're not comfortable speaking up for yourself.

The flip side of this strategy is if you aren't in a position where you have the freedom to change jobs, it may be hard to negotiate. "I really feel like no one at all is worried I'm going to leave, and I can't do false drama. I just can't," said one New Girl. "If I leave, that means I'm going to have another job in my pocket with an offer letter. And then, if they tell me then that I can be a VP, it'll just break my heart. It's like you break up with a boyfriend, and then he wants to marry you."

Sometimes it's more effective to have someone else negotiate for you. "Have an ally or sponsor go behind the scenes and say, 'You're going to lose this person,'" said a New Girl. Sometimes having other people with a lot of credibility or clout vouch for you is more effective than doing it yourself. That's why we keep stressing the importance of building and keeping up your network.

Strategy 2: Have a New Job Lined Up

Sometimes, things get bad enough that women choose to leave their current job without a new one lined up—and some women have enough money to weather the storm. For the rest of us, it's a good idea to start looking for a new position before you've given notice at your old one. It's almost always easier to get a job when you have a job. We know that job searching can be stressful, time-consuming, and sometimes demoralizing. If you're not entirely sure you're ready to leave your current company, it's easier just to avoid the process altogether. But just *looking* for a new job may also help improve your situation at your old one.

"I've been encouraging women to see what's out there," said one woman at a New Girls meeting. "Going on the market alone starts building confidence."

"I did just that," another said. "I just went out and started interviewing, and it made me realize that people want me."

Again, it's important to keep in mind that you should be looking for a chance not just to move but to move up. Not only is moving for a promotion a good strategy in the short term; it's also easier to explain on a resume.

If you do have a resume that's difficult to explain, "you really have to understand how your resume can be misinterpreted and be proactive about it," one New Girl said.

A Fortune 500 executive said she knew a woman who started work at a new company, only to realize very quickly she wouldn't be happy there. When she started interviewing again, she was careful to state her reasons for leaving in politically neutral terms: "It's a really good company in a lot of ways. The group I was in just didn't reflect my values."

Going on the job market may have one of two effects. You may realize that your current job actually is a pretty good fit. Or you may realize that you have marketable skills that can take you to a company that better fits your needs. Don't let anxiety leave you tethered to a job that's going nowhere.

Strategy 3: Keep Your Network Intact

Networking becomes particularly important when you're thinking about leaving. When it comes to announcing your departure, it may be tempting to pull an *Office Space* and make your exit memorable. It's probably not necessary to clarify that this is not a good idea. The people you work with will continue to be valuable connections for the rest of your career (50 to 70 percent of professionals get jobs through "weak ties"—acquaintances).[9] Give proper notice, make sure all projects are finished or handed off, help train your replacement, and don't start bad-mouthing the company or your colleagues. Even if management is terrible, consider the effect that speaking out against them could have on your future career or on the co-workers you leave behind.

One New Girl stressed the importance of maintaining connections, particularly as a tool to help others in need. She said she had received countless phone calls from women who are unhappy at their current jobs but didn't know where to turn. "I don't know how many people have called me and said, 'I don't know what to do. I don't know anybody. I don't know anything about this!'" she said. "I've helped a lot of people that way. They tell me what they want to do. I think of my network," she said. "It's really important that people have a network. Because your peer group is going to go a bunch of different directions, so maybe they can hire you, maybe they can't. Maybe their spouse can hire you one day."

Again, what goes around comes around. If you give someone access to your well-developed network in their time of need, they are likely to return the favor.

LinkedIn is a great resource for maintaining connections and keeping up with former co-workers. Connect with them, if you haven't already, and make sure to send a personal note. Clueless about LinkedIn? Here are some basics: Upload a clear, professional picture. Link to any relevant accomplishments (articles, blog posts, professional videos, or portfolios), and use key words in your profile that are common to your industry; this will lead recruiters to you during searches. Connect with as many people as you can —again, the more personal the invitation, the better. Join groups relevant to your industry or alumni groups that may give you a leg up on exciting new opportunities. Follow companies of interest. Lastly, participate! Update your status, link to interesting articles, and comment in forums and discussion. If you are still lost, do some research; LinkedIn is a relatively new tool, so there are many resources online to help you navigate it.[10]

Facebook may also be helpful in keeping professional networks intact, but proceed with caution; unlike LinkedIn, Facebook is a more personal platform, and that presents some complications. What you might want to show to your mother or best friend may not be what you want a future employer or old co-worker to see.

If you left on good terms, staying connected with colleagues from your old company or organization through social media is a smart move. Sometimes, though, things just get messy. If you've been in a bad situation long enough, or if you've tried to raise issues of inequality only to be faced with a harsh backlash, there may well be some simmering resentment. You need to consider seriously the effect that this will have not only on your future career but also on how you're leaving the people who stay at your office.

One New Girl left her job after she tried confronting her colleagues on the unfair compensation system, which consistently left women in the bottom tier of earners. She landed on her feet, but she said she did regret leaving the other women at the firm in a tricky situation. "The part that I didn't fully anticipate was how it put some of the women in such difficult positions. They weren't prepared to leave, and they weren't prepared to risk punishment for supporting me."

When it hits the fan and a graceful exit seems elusive, just remember one thing. You can get another job, but you can't get another life. Keep your dignity.

Strategy 4: Money Matters

Personal issues aside, money may be the number-one reason why people stay at jobs they don't like. The New Girls recommended thinking ahead to make sure that if you have to leave your job, you have the resources to do so.

One New Girl said she had a professor in business school who told his students to always have a "F**k you fund"—some money set aside that gives you the flexibility to leave your job without having a new one lined up. (Humphrey Bogart famously had a "F**k you fund" saved up so he could walk away if he wasn't happy with the way a movie was going.)[11]

Other New Girls advised women to time their departure so that they have the maximum possible leverage. One marketing executive said she stayed in a bad situation for longer than she otherwise would have because of advice she received from a former co-worker.

She called him after a terrible day and said, "Tell me again why I'm doing this?"

"You're waiting until they pay you to go," he reminded her.

That, the New Girl said, hadn't even occurred to her until that moment. "I think I wouldn't have figured that out if he hadn't given me that advice: 'Wait until they offer you a really nice package to leave.' It's not like I was incompetent or anything like that. They weren't firing me for cause. They needed to offer me a package to leave, to just move on."

She ended up with an excellent severance package that eased her transition to her next job. Companies often offer severance for employees who are laid off and sometimes also for employees who resign or are fired, said Kathy Dickson. If you're offered a severance package, it's often possible to negotiate a higher one. Keep in mind that severance agreements usually include a release of claims (meaning you lose the right to sue), so be sure you're comfortable with that before you sign. "Should [you] try to negotiate for more severance?" Dickson said. "Yes, about 100 percent of the time."

It's also important to note that, while money does matter, it's important not to languish in a job you hate. "You have to leave before you don't have the juice to do it anymore," one New Girl observed.

*   *   *

Leaving your job is not a decision to be taken lightly. But—equally important—it is not a decision to be avoided at all costs, either. The most basic point is to figure out, if you hate your job, whether the problem is inside you or outside you. Sometimes, of course, it is both. But leaving a job you hate without thinking hard about how you may have contributed to a bad situation risks leaving you to repeat your mistakes at the next job you land. So it's worthwhile thinking very carefully about where things went south and whether you could have handled differently any or all of the steps down that path.

The other important, overarching point is that some workplaces that are great for some women are pretty awful for others. Sometimes this is a Tug of War issue. But sometimes it's just an issue of fit. "Being mean to me was a social bonding activity," said one New Girl of a job she ultimately left. "People were socialized into it when they came, and the savvy ones soon came to realize that there was a strong in-group out-group dynamic, and the way to ensure you were in the in-group was to rag on me."

In that situation, the choice is easy: leave. Many situations are subtler. But in most if not all cases, it takes two to tango. You need to figure out what it is about you that got you into that mess—if only to assess whether there were warning signs you could have seen. The problems may all be outside you. But don't assume that. And remember, if it doesn't kill you, it makes you stronger.

PART VII

20
Lessons

14

The Science of Savvy in 20 Lessons

This book is based on hundreds of experimental studies and nearly 150 hours of interviews. We felt pretty good that we were able to boil them down into just 13 short chapters until someone handed us a challenge: if you really want to change things, she said, give them 20 takeaways. Just 20. So here they are.

1

Women often have to provide more evidence of competence than men in order to be seen as equally competent. You may have to prove it again, but *don't* prove it so often you burn out.

2

If you have a trust fund and enjoy conflict, call this bias out every time you see it. Otherwise, fuhgeddaboudit, unless dwelling on unfairness is giving you new insights or helping you solve a specific problem.

3

Building and maintaining a network is an integral part of being a successful professional—particularly if you're a woman. Remember two important rules. One: no random acts of lunch.[1] If you take the time to reach out to somebody, take the time to follow up. Two: networking involves the reciprocal exchange of favors—although the favors (particularly for young women) can be as simple as giving someone else a sense of accomplishment in your success.

4

Take real-time notes of your accomplishments and report them matter-of-factly in performance reviews and other appropriate contexts. Remember, men's bragging is an established part of their "mine's bigger than yours" give-and-take. Toot your own horn by using the facts.

5

Form a posse that includes both men and women and celebrate each other's accomplishments in a good-citizen way. If you lead a team, celebrate the successes of your team in a way that subtly reminds people that you led them.

6

Just say no to office housework like taking notes, answering the conference-room phone, planning parties, and serving on four billion committees—or figure out a way to get something in return for your contributions.

7

Balance the masculine with the feminine. Women need to act masculine enough so they are seen as competent at their jobs but feminine enough so they are seen as competent at being women.

8

Don't serve your anger hot. Many successful women decide that showing anger at all is just too tricky for them, but if you feel you need to stand up for yourself, link your anger to the way the recipient's actions have jeopardized a shared business goal.

9

If you get pregnant, and when you return from each maternity leave, make sure the people around you know you remain committed to your career. This means both your supervisors and your co-workers—make a plan so that the work that comes up while you're on leave doesn't just add to everyone else's load.

10

There's no such thing as a perfect mother—especially when the expectation is that good professionals commit 24/7 to their jobs and that good mothers commit 24/7 to their children. Shoot for good *enough*, and remember, the research shows that what matters is whether you are happy with the trade-offs you've made.

11

Make a plan: decide which of your kids' school and other activities you will participate in for the next six months. Put them on your calendar as meetings and let your kids know they can count on you being there. Then don't second-guess yourself.

12

If you're thinking of getting pregnant, make sure you talk over caregiving expectations with your partner. You shouldn't be the only one making accommodations. If you already have kids and your partner isn't pulling his or her weight, that's a big problem. Go to a marriage counselor and treat it like one.

13

If anyone tells you they don't know how you can work, or work full-time, tell them Tolstoy was wrong: happy families are *not* all alike. Different things work for different families, and you are doing what works for yours.

14

Bias against women fuels conflict among women. Stop judging other women on the right way to be a woman, and keep in mind that we're all fighting our own battles.

15

Gen X and Millennials, remember that older women are just trying to help you when they tell you to suck it up and beat the boys at their own game. Baby boomers, remember that insisting that younger women take your path is not helpful. It makes many of them feel demoralized and undermined.

16

If you are in an environment where the message comes through loud and clear that there's only room for one woman, then leave—unless you are that one woman, in which case do what you need to, and then use your position at the top to change that sorry situation.

17

Remember fuhgeddaboudit? There's no reason every woman has to feel a moral duty to spend her political points trying to make the world a better place for women. Feel free to decide that's not your battle—just make sure you don't go too far in the other direction and undermine the women who are.

18

If you decide to become a vocal advocate for women, remember to use up only as many points as you can afford to spend—and no more. You need to preserve your effectiveness and your serenity. If you drive yourself nuts, younger women will just look up at you and feel discouraged—which defeats the purpose of fighting for them in the first place.

19

Gender bias differs by race. While it's tempting to focus only on the things we share, this often translates into removing women of color from the conversation altogether. There's room in women's initiatives to take differences into account and to make sure no one is left out and left behind.

20

Don't waste your energy trying to work through an unworkable situation, or your time in a job where your talents aren't valued. If you're facing a poisonous working environment or a dead-end job and there's nothing new to learn, vote with your feet and find a job where you can shine.

* * *

Those are the takeaways from 35 years of study of experimental social psychology and 127 interviews of successful career women. It's not easy; don't hesitate to get help. And good luck!

15

Conclusion: Jump-Starting the Stalled Gender Revolution

At the current rate of change, equal numbers of men and women won't be CEOs of Fortune 500 companies for 276 years, and Congress won't reach gender parity for nearly a century.[1]

Equality won't be on offer until organizations change—and they aren't changing fast. Gender bias remains a common experience.

One reason the gender revolution has stalled is because of implicit bias. The typical implicit association training sends a simple message: we are all biased. True, but not very useful. In order to help people spot and correct for bias, what they need is to understand how bias plays out in everyday workplace interactions. That's what this book does.

We now have some concrete answers about why women don't reach the highest levels in proportionate numbers. Men get promoted based on fewer accomplishments than women would need to reach the same level. Women are more likely than men to be penalized if they make a mistake. And when women have children, they need to start proving themselves all over again—and to cope with disapproval from colleagues who believe, explicitly or unconsciously, that a mother who is still highly committed to her career is failing as a mother.

If women need to accomplish twice as much to get half as far and accomplishments are distributed evenly among men and women, it stands to reason women don't reach the top. But that's not all. Even highly accomplished women face office politics that are far trickier than office politics faced by men.

Men are allowed a wide range of behaviors: the socially clueless geek, the gentle soul, the slick politician, the office screamer, the bull in the china shop—in many environments, men can progress without being particularly savvy. For men, political savvy helps, but much is forgiven.

Savvy is a threshold requirement for women. We have to be astute enough to tack back and forth, navigating between the Scylla of being "too feminine" (and so liked but not respected) and the Charybdis of being "too masculine" (and so respected but not liked). Unlike men, women face gender wars. Men don't have other men undercutting them for a coveted position because there's only room for one man. Men don't have to navigate the tight space between being "too tied up with women's issues" and being "queen bees" who do not help other women enough. And those are just two of the way gender bias against women complicates office politics for women. Assuming savvy is equally distributed between men and women, it's hardly surprising that women don't reach the top as often as men do.

"Let's call the book 'Dealing with the Crap While Waiting for Change,'" said a friend of Joan's. Women need tools *now* to help them navigate office politics deeply shaped by gender. That's what this book has tried to bottle.

But providing women with individual strategies to navigate through gender bias is not the ultimate answer. Individual strategies do not erase the pressing need for institutional change. Many people are earnestly committed to changing institutions to retain and promote more women—but are going about it the wrong way. What's required are two startlingly simple steps.

The first is to change what Arlie Hochschild long ago called "the clockwork of male careers."[2] In high-level professional jobs today, the ideal worker must be ready, willing, and able to work 50 hours a week or more—sometimes much more.³ The last time Joan looked, less than 10 percent of working mothers aged 25–44 worked more than 50 hours a week. The percentage of college-educated mothers is a little higher but not much: only 13.9 percent of college-educated mothers work more than 50 hours a week.⁴ Most people stoutly refuse to believe this statistic. But it's true. And it means that, *even if employers do everything else absolutely perfectly*, they will never attract a proportionate number of women, given that over 80 percent of women have children.⁵

Changing time norms involves not the marginalized part-time schedules and flexible work arrangements that are commonplace (though by no means universal). What's needed instead are careers in which *men as well as women* can, without stigma, take a family leave or a career break or reduce their hours *without* falling off the career track or, as one young father allegedly was told so vividly, "cutting [his] own throat."⁶

The second step is to control for implicit bias in basic business systems: hiring, assignments, evaluations, promotions, and compensation. A single implicit bias training is not the answer and may, in some circumstances, do more harm than good.⁷ Important work by Alexandra Kalev, Frank Dobbin, and Erin Kelly shows that organizations with structures that imbed accountability, like a diversity officer position, a diversity committee, and an affirmative action program, show the greatest increases in both race and gender diversity over time.⁸

So while networking programs, mentoring and sponsorship initiatives, and bias trainings may be the easiest to implement, they alone cannot solve the problem. Business processes need to be redesigned so as not to artificially advantage one group. We will end with a single example of how to do so. It returns us to the "women don't ask" problem we have discussed before.

Most organizations have responded with programs designed to teach women how to negotiate better. But if you've read this book, you have a good idea of *why* women don't ask. They're walking the

Tightrope: women who *do* negotiate tend to be seen as not nice and too demanding, a 2007 study found. Both men and women were less likely to hire or to want to work with them.[9]

The solution is not to scold women for not negotiating. It's to change a salary system that's artificially advantaging men. A 2012 study found that if women are told that they are expected to negotiate their salaries, the gender gap in negotiation disappears.[10] That's not a hard change to make.

This book has focused on what women can do for themselves because Joan decided that, after working on institutional solutions for 15 years, organizations are changing so slowly that women need tools now to navigate the world as they find it. But the real solution is to level the playing field.

In the meantime, women need not only stand and wait. We have provided some savvy to help you play the hand you are dealt or to go find a different game. Better yet, become the dealer or invent your own game. Then you can make your own rules—and make them fair.

Acknowledgments

Rachel's acknowledgments: Thank you, as always, to Dad and Nicky, for their infallible good humor and support. Thanks to Molly Coyne, Peter Petroff, Erin York, and Josh Weiss, for listening to my ideas and my frustrations and for providing me with brilliant insights of their own, and to Jenni Romanek and Anna Dorn for reading over early drafts. Thank you to the Wise Women, who believed in me and provided me with their wisdom and support. Thank you to Katherine Ullman for her truly invaluable insight, her painstaking edits, and her incredible patience. And most of all, thank you to Joan, for giving me this opportunity and raising me to believe I could take it. I know you don't believe in the perfect mother, but you've come pretty close.

Joan's acknowledgments: Thanks, as always, to my family: To Nick, for showing me how to look at life in a very different way. To Jim, for sharing my life for 35 years. And to Rachel, for her astonishing and generous decision to write this with me. I can't get over that she agreed to do this with her mother. The opportunity to work with her has been one of the high points of my life.

All books are the product of a team. This one is, even more than others. The anonymous readers who read the manuscript for NYU Press offered incredibly helpful insights. Our editor, Ilene Kalish, has improved the book tremendously in a wide variety of ways.

Our agent, Roger Williams of New England Publishing Associates, worked incredibly hard on our behalf. Meghan Guptill, Mount Holyoke College '14, did a yeowoman's job with the coding: I thank her for going over the interviews again and again and again and for loving them as much as I do. Special thanks for Jennifer Berdahl, who went over the entire manuscript very closely and gave extensive and incredibly helpful feedback. Thanks to Michele Coleman Mayes, without whose comments I would never have felt comfortable with chapters 12 and 13, and to Kathy Phillips, for giving me comments on chapter 11, for introducing me to Erika Hall, and for working with me on the Double Jeopardy? Project. Thanks to Erika, without whose interviewing skills chapter 11 could not have been written, and to Alison Gemmill, a PhD student in the Department of Demography at UC Berkeley, who helped me crunch some very important numbers, and my friend Ron Lee, who found her for me. As always, I could not do anything I do without my library liaison, Hilary Hardcastle. Thanks, too, to Linda Marks, Cynthia Thomas Calvert, and Robin Devaux of the Center for WorkLife Law, for putting up with the highly pressured process of producing this book in the midst of all our other projects.

I also want to thank all the social psychologists who have participated over the years in my working groups: the Cognitive Bias Working Group (2001–2003), the Caregiver Bias Working Group (2003–2005), and the Flexibility Stigma Working Group (2006–2008). They have been infinitely patient with me. Without them, I could never have become comfortable reading the experimental studies that form the backbone of this book.

Rachel and I both owe a profound debt to Katherine Ullman. Without her, this book would have come out in 2025. Katherine has a truly unusual combination of very precise text-production skills, analytical rigor and precision, creativity, and unbelievably good judgment. And she worked incredibly hard to get this out on time. I look forward with excitement to following her future career.

I want to end with a final note thanking, once again, the Wise Women. Several years ago, I decided to begin this project and did not want to wait for the agonizingly slow process of foundation funding. The Wise Women's contributions allowed me to start when I needed to start. Their networks allowed me to start the snowball that ultimately yielded 67 interviews. Their savvy gave me something to say. But, most of all, their belief in me, in Rachel, and in this project is something I will always treasure. Thank you, ladies, for your wisdom and your generosity of spirit.

Notes

Notes to content in the boxes are lettered rather than numbered and follow the notes to the text within each chapter section here.

Notes to the Preface

1. Catalyst, "Catalyst Quick Take: Sex Discrimination and Sexual Harassment," July 1, 2012, http://www.catalyst.org/publication/213/sex-discrimination-and-sexual-harassment.
2. Amy Tennery, "Studies Show 63% of Female Architects Say They've Experienced Gender Bias," *Jane Dough*, March 20, 2012, http://www.thejanedough.com/discrimination-women-architecture/; Deborah Rhode, *The Unfinished Agenda: Women and the Legal Profession* (Chicago: American Bar Association Commission on the Status of Women, 2001), 8.
3. Brian McGill, Fawn Johnson, and Ryan Morris, "Washington Women Report Gender Discrimination," *National Journal*, July 11, 2012, http://www.nationaljournal.com/washington-women-report-gender-discrimination-20120711.
4. Marilynn B. Brewer, "Research Design and Issues of Validity," in *Handbook of Research Methods in Social and Personality Psychology*, ed. H. T. Reis and C. M. Judd (New York: Cambridge University Press, 2000), 3–16; Craig Anderson and Brad Bushman, "External Validity of 'Trivial' Experiments: The Case of Laboratory Aggression," *Review of General Psychology* 1, no. 1 (1997): 19–41.
5. Diana Burgess and Eugene Borgida, "Who Women Are, Who Women Should Be: Descriptive and Prescriptive Stereotyping in Sex Discrimination," *Psychology, Public Policy, and Law* 5, no. 3 (1999): 665–692.
6. Ibid.
7. Jennifer L. Berdahl, e-mail to author Joan C. Williams, November 21, 2012.

8. Jennifer L. Berdahl and Celia Moore, "Workplace Harassment: Double Jeopardy for Minority Women," *Journal of Applied Psychology* 91, no. 2 (2006): 426–436 (citing other studies).

9. Alice H. Eagly and Linda L. Carli, *Through the Labyrinth: The Truth about How Women Become Leaders* (Boston: Harvard Business School Press, 2007).

10. Penelope M. Huang, "Gender Bias in Academia: Findings from Focus Groups" (Center for WorkLife Law, UC Hastings College of the Law, San Francisco, 2010), 8, http://worklifelaw.org/pubs/gender-bias -academia.pdf.

Notes to Chapter 1

1. *Price Waterhouse v. Hopkins*, 490 U.S. 228, 236 (1989).

2. Philip Sherwell, "Goldman Sachs Discrimination Case: Court Papers Reveal the Inside Story," *Telegraph*, September 19, 2010, http://www .telegraph.co.uk/finance/newsbysector/banksandfinance/8011140/ Goldman-Sachs-sex-discrimination-case-court-papers-reveal-the -inside-story.html.

3. *Martens v. Smith Barney, Inc.*, 96-cv-3779, S.D.N.Y. (filed May 20, 1996); Susan Antilla, *Tales from the Boom Boom Room* (Princeton, NJ: Bloomberg, 2002), 279.

4. Sheryl Sandberg, "Why We Have Too Few Women Leaders," TED, December 21, 2012, http://www.ted.com/talks/sheryl_sandberg_why_ we_have_too_few_women_leaders.html; Anne-Marie Slaughter, "Why Women Can't Have It All," *Atlantic*, July–August 2012, http:// www.theatlantic.com/magazine/archive/2012/07/ why-women-still-cant-have-it-all/309020/#.

5. Mary Beth Marklein, "College Gender Gap Remains Stable: 57% Women," *USA Today*, January 26, 2010, http://www.usatoday.com/ news/education/2010-01-26-genderequity26_ST_N.htm; Belinda Luscombe, "Workplace Salaries: At Last, Women on Top," *Time*, September 1, 2010, http://www.time.com/time/business/article/ 0,8599,2015274,00.html.

6. Hanna Rosin, "The End of Men," *Atlantic*, July–August 2010, http:// www.theatlantic.com/magazine/archive/2010/07/the-end-of-men/8135/. For a succinct critique, see Stephanie Coontz, "The Myth of Male Decline," *New York Times*, September 29, 2012, http://www.nytimes .com/2012/09/30/opinion/sunday/the-myth-of-male-decline.html? pagewanted=all&_r=0.

7. "Women CEOs of the Fortune 1000," *Catalyst*, November 19, 2012, http://www.catalyst.org/knowledge/women-ceos-fortune-1000.

8. Note that generally, law firms have two tiers of partners: equity partners and salaried partners. Equity partners are part owners of the firm

and are entitled to a proportion of its profits. Many lawyers consider only equity partnership to be "full-fledged" partnership. Barbara M. Flom and Stephanie A. Scharf, *Report of the Sixth Annual National Survey on Retention and Promotion of Women in Law Firms* (New York: National Association of Women Lawyers and the NAWL Foundation, 2011).

9. Claire Cain Miller, "Out of the Loop in Silicon Valley," *New York Times*, April 17, 2010, http://www.nytimes.com/2010/04/18/technology/18women.html?pagewanted=all.

10. Virginia Valian, *Why So Slow? The Advancement of Women* (Cambridge: MIT Press, 1999), 4.

11. Ibid.

12. Shelley J. Correll, Stephen Benard, and In Paik, "Getting a Job: Is There a Motherhood Penalty?," *American Journal of Sociology* 112, no. 5 (2007): 1297–1339.

13. United States Census Bureau, "Profile America: Facts for Features," March 17, 2011, http://www.census.gov/newsroom/releases/archives/facts_for_features_special_editions/cb11-ff07.html.

14. Belle Derks, Naomi Ellemers, Colette van Laar, and Kim de Groot, "Do Sexist Organizational Cultures Create the Queen Bee?," *British Journal of Social Psychology* 50, no. 3 (2011): 519–535; Belle Derks, Naomi Ellemers, Colette van Laar, and Kim de Groot, "Gender Bias Primes Elicit Queen Bee Responses among Senior Policewomen," *Psychological Science* 22 (2011): 1243–1249.

15. Lois P. Frankel, *Nice Girls Don't Get the Corner Office: 101 Unconscious Mistakes Women Make That Sabotage Their Careers* (New York: Warner Books, 2010), 5.

16. Linda Babcock and Sara Laschever, *Women Don't Ask: The High Cost of Avoiding Negotiation—and Strategies for Change* (New York: Bantam Dell, 2007).

17. Ibid., 101.

18. Ibid.

19. Christy Whitman and Rebecca Grado, *Taming Your Alpha Bitch: How to Be Fierce and Feminine (And Get Everything You Want!)* (New York: BenBella Books, 2012), 196.

20. Jean Hollands, *Same Game, Different Rules: How to Get Ahead without Being a Bully Broad, Ice Queen, or "Ms. Understood"* (New York: McGraw Hill, 2002), 65.

21. Eagly and Carli, *Through the Labyrinth*, 6.

22. Harriet Rubin, "Sexism in the Workplace: Sexism," *Portfolio*, March 17, 2008, http://upstart.bizjournals.com/executives/features/2008/03/17/Sexism-in-the-Workplace.html.

23. Amy Tennery, "Scandal in Silicon Valley: Why the Ellen Pao Suit

Isn't Helping Women in Tech," *Time*, June 5, 2012, http://business
.time.com/2012/06/05/scandal-in-silicon-valley-why-the-ellen-pao
-suit-isnt-helping-women-in-tech/; Shira Ovide, "Addressing the
Lack of Women Leading Tech Start-Ups," *Wall Street Journal Blogs*,
August 27, 2010, http://blogs.wsj.com/venturecapital/2010/08/27/
addressing-the-lack-of-women-leading-tech-start-ups/.

24. Emilio J. Castilla and Stephen Benard, "The Paradox of Meritocracy in
Organizations," *Administrative Science Quarterly* 55 (2010): 551.

25. Ibid., 568.

26. Nicole Pelroth and Michael Noer, "The World's Most Powerful People:
The 70 Who Matter," *Forbes*, November 2, 2011, http://www.forbes
.com/powerful-people/.

27. Alastair Lawson, "Sonia Gandhi: Heir to a Dynasty," *BBC News*, April
19, 1999, http://news.bbc.co.uk/2/hi/south_asia/322335.stm.

28. Mika Brzezinski, *Knowing Your Value: Women, Money, and Getting
What You're Worth* (New York: Weinstein Books, 2011).

29. Patricia Linville and Edward E. Jones, "Polarized Appraisals of Out-
Group Members," *Journal of Personality and Social Psychology* 38,
no. 5 (1980): 689–703.

30. Monica Biernat and Diane Kobrynowicz, "Gender- and Race-Based
Standards of Competence: Lower Minimum Standards but Higher
Ability Standards for Devalued Group," *Journal of Personality and
Social Psychology* 72 (1997): 544–557.

31. Judith Warner, "No Ordinary Woman," *New York Times*, October 26,
2008, http://www.nytimes.com/2008/10/26/opinion/26warner-1.html.

32. Project Implicit, Harvard University, accessed July 10, 2012, https://
implicit.harvard.edu/implicit/.

33. Brian Nosek, Mahzarin Banaji, and Anthony Greenwald, "Harvesting
Implicit Group Attitudes and Beliefs from a Demonstration Web Site,"
Group Dynamics: Theory, Research, and Practice 6, no. 1 (2002): 103.

34. John Tierney, "A Shocking Test of Bias," *TierneyLab* (blog), *New
York Times*, November 18, 2008, http://tierneylab.blogs.nytimes.com/
2008/11/18/a-shocking-test-of-bias/; Project Implicit.

35. Project Implicit.

36. B. Keith Payne, Mark B. Stokes, and Melissa A. Burkley, "Why Do
Implicit and Explicit Attitude Tests Diverge? The Role of Structural
Fit," *Journal of Personality and Social Psychology* 94, no. 1 (2008):
16–31.

37. Anthony G. Greenwald, Debbie E. McGhee, and Jordan L. K. Schwartz,
"Measuring Individual Differences in Implicit Cognition: The Implicit
Association Test," *Journal of Personality and Social Psychology* 74,
no. 6 (1995): 1475.

38. Emily Pronin, Daniel Y. Lin, and Lee Ross, "The Bias Blind Spot:

Perceptions of Bias in Self versus Other," *Personality and Social Psychology Bulletin* 28 (2002): 369–381.

39. Ibid., 375–376.

40. Kimberlé Crenshaw, "Mapping the Margins: Intersectionality, Identity Politics, and Violence against Women of Color," *Stanford Law Review* 43, no. 6 (1991): 1241–1299; Ange-Marie Hancock, "When Multiplication Doesn't Equal Quick Addition: Examining Intersectionality as a Research Paradigm," *Perspectives on Politics* 5, no. 1 (2007): 63–79.

BOXES

a. Richard F. Martell, David M. Lane, and Cynthia Emrich, "Male-Female Differences: A Computer Simulation," *American Psychologist* 51 (1996): 157–158.

b. *Wikipedia*, s.v. "Sojourner Truth," accessed February 1, 2013, http://en.wikipedia.org/wiki/Sojourner_Truth.

c. *Wikipedia*, s.v. "George Sand," accessed February 1, 2013, http://en.wikipedia.org/wiki/Georges_Sand.

d. *Wikipedia*, s.v. "Helen Gurley Brown," accessed February 1, 2013, http://en.wikipedia.org/wiki/Helen_Gurley_Brown.

Notes to Chapter 2

1. Peter Glick, "Trait-Based and Sex-Based Discrimination in Occupational Prestige, Occupational Salary, and Hiring," *Sex Roles* 25, nos. 5–6 (1991): 351–378.

2. Alice H. Eagly and Steven J. Karau, "Role Congruity Theory of Prejudice toward Female Leaders," *Psychological Review* 109, no. 3 (2002): 573–598.

3. Barbara F. Reskin, "Rethinking Employment Discrimination and Its Remedies," in *The New Economic Sociology: Developments in an Emerging Field*, ed. Mario F. Guillén, Randall Collins, Paula England, and Marshall Meyer (New York: Russell Sage Foundation, 2002), 218–244.

4. Martha Foschi, "Double Standards for Competence: Theory and Research," *Annual Review of Sociology* 26 (2000): 21–42.

5. Nancy M. Carter and Christine Silva, *The Myth of the Ideal Worker: Does Doing All the Right Things Really Get Women Ahead?* (New York: Catalyst, 2011), 10.

6. Ibid.

7. Michael I. Norton, Joseph A. Vandello, and John M. Darley, "Casuistry and Social Category Bias," *Journal of Personality and Social Psychology* 87, no. 6 (2004): 817–831.

8. Ibid., 820.

9. Ibid., 821.

10. Ibid.

11. Ibid.

12. Ibid., 817.

13. Julie E. Phelan, Corinne A. Moss-Racusin, and Laurie A. Rudman, "Competent yet Out in the Cold," *Psychology of Women Quarterly* 32 (2008): 407.

14. Interview of attorney by Joan C. Williams, March 2005.

15. Interview with National Science Foundation ACE Focus Group participant by Joan C. Williams, January 9, 2007.

16. Reskin, "Rethinking Employment Discrimination and Its Remedies," 225.

17. Raymond S. Nickerson, "Confirmation Bias: A Ubiquitous Phenomenon in Many Guises," *Review of General Psychology* 2, no. 2 (1998): 175–220.

18. Flom and Scharf, *Report of the Sixth Annual National Survey*, 5–6.

19. Madeline E. Heilman and Michelle C. Haynes, "No Credit Where Credit Is Due: Attributional Rationalization of Women's Success in Male-Female Terms," *Journal of Applied Psychology* 90, no. 5 (2005): 905–909.

20. Marilynn B. Brewer, "In-Group Favoritism: The Subtle Side of Intergroup Discrimination," in *Codes of Conduct: Behavioral Research into Business Ethics*, ed. David M. Messick and Ann E. Tenbrunsel (New York: Russell Sage Foundation, 1996), 166.

21. Madeline E. Heilman, "Description and Prescription: How Gender Stereotypes Prevent Women's Ascent up the Organizational Ladder," *Journal of Social Issues* 57 (2001): 662.

22. Frances Trix and Carolyn Psenka, "Exploring the Color of Glass: Letters of Recommendation for Female and Male Medical Faculty," *Discourse and Society* 14 (2003): 191–220.

23. Ibid., 207.

24. Ibid.

25. Ibid.

26. Diana B. Carlin and Kelly L. Winfrey, "Have You Come a Long Way, Baby? Hillary Clinton, Sarah Palin, and Sexism in 2008 Campaign Coverage," *Communication Studies* 60, no. 4 (2009): 328.

27. "Shut Up, Ruth," *Time*, April 11, 1994, http://www.time.com/time/magazine/article/0,9171,980517,00.html; Mallary Jean Tenore, "As Supreme Court Begins New Term, How to Explain Justices' Silences, Interruptions, and 'Aggressive' Questions," *Poynter*, October 3, 2011, http://www.poynter.org/latest-news/top-stories/147856/as-supreme-court-reconvenes-how-to-understand-the-justices-silences-interruptions-and-aggressive-questions/.

28. John A. Bargh and Tanya L. Chartrand, "The Unbearable Automaticity of Being," *American Psychologist* 54, no. 7 (1999): 462–479.

29. Madeline E. Heilman, "Sex Bias in Work Settings: The Lack of Fit Model," *Research in Organizational Behavior* 5 (1983): 269–298.

30. Peter Glick, Korin Wilk, and Michele Perreault, "Images of Occupations: Components of Gender and Status in Occupational Stereotypes," *Sex Roles* 32, nos. 9–10 (1995): 565–582.

31. Ibid., 570.

32. Madeline E. Heilman, Caryn J. Block, and Richard F. Martell, "Sex Stereotypes: Do They Influence Perceptions of Managers?," *Journal of Social Behavior and Personality* 10, no. 4 (1995): 237–252.

33. Project Implicit, https://implicit.harvard.edu/implicit/.

BOXES

a. Professor Ben Barres, e-mail to author Joan C. Williams, December 20, 2012.

b. The strategies in this and subsequent boxes come from Joan's interviews and The New Girls' Network meetings. Which ones will or will not work depends a lot on context, your personality, the personality of the person you are addressing, and the culture of the organization.

c. *The West Wing*, episode 75, directed by John David Coles and written by Aaron Sorkin and Gene Sperling, first broadcast November 27, 2002, NBC.

Notes to Chapter 3

1. Belle Rose Ragins, Bickley Townsend, and Mary Mattis, "Gender Gap in the Executive Suite: CEOs and Female Executives Report on Breaking the Glass Ceiling," *Academy of Management Executive* 12, no. 1 (1998): 29.

2. Burgess and Borgida, "Who Women Are, Who Women Should Be."

3. Madeline E. Heilman, Caryn J. Block, Richard Martell, and Michael Simon, "Has Anything Changed? Current Characterizations of Men, Women and Managers," *Journal of Applied Psychology* 74 (1989): 939.

4. Jill Flynn, Kathryn Heath, and Mary Davis Holt, *Break Your Own Rules: How to Change the Patterns of Thinking That Block Women's Path to Power* (San Francisco: Wiley, 2011).

5. Steven L. Neuberg, "Expectancy-Confirmation Processes in Stereotype-Tinged Social Encounters: The Moderating Role of Social Goals," in *The Psychology of Prejudice: The Ontario Symposium, Volume 7*, ed. Mark P. Zanna and James M. Olson, 103–130 (Hillsdale, NJ: Erlbaum, 1994).

6. Interview with National Science Foundation ACE Focus Group participant by Joan C. Williams, January 9, 2007.

7. MaryAnn Baenninger, "For Women on Campus, Access Doesn't Equal Success," *Chronicle of Higher Education*, October 2, 2011, http://chronicle.com/article/For-Women-on-Campuses-Access/129242/.

8. The statistics we're using on attorney retention come from a 2011 report of the National Association of Women Lawyers (NAWL). The NAWL report compiled data from surveys given to the 200 largest law firms in the country. Only 121 surveys were returned, a 61 percent response rate, and not every firm answered every question. For example, 50 firms answered the question about compensation, meaning that 75 percent of firms didn't answer at all. There's no way to know this for sure, but there's more incentive for those firms with higher numbers of women and male minorities to respond than those with lower numbers. What that means is that the NAWL numbers may significantly overestimate the numbers and pay for women in law firms. We're using them because they're the best numbers we have. But there's a lawyerly lesson here: it's important to look at the fine print. Flom and Scharf, *Report of the Sixth Annual National Survey*, 5, 16.

9. Claude M. Steele, *Whistling Vivaldi: How Stereotypes Affect Us and What We Can Do* (New York: Norton, 2010).

10. Ibid., 111.

11. Ibid., 125.

12. Biernat and Kobrynowicz, "Gender- and Race-Based Standards of Competence."

13. Ragins, Townsend, and Mattis, "Gender Gap in the Executive Suite," 30.

14. Flom and Scharf, *Report of the Sixth Annual National Survey*, 18.

15. Joanna Barsh and Susie Cranston, *How Remarkable Women Lead: The Breakthrough Model for Work and Life* (New York: Crown Business, 2009), 238.

16. Cecilia L. Ridgeway and Shelley J. Correll, "Motherhood as a Status Characteristic," *Journal of Social Issues* 60, no. 4 (2004): 683–700.

Notes to Chapter 4

1. Tina Fey, *Bossypants* (New York: Reagan Arthur, 2011), 211–212.

2. Charlotte Hilton Andersen, "Sarah Palin Bikini Pictures: Fake Photos Hit the Web," *Huffington Post*, September 2, 2008, http://www.huffingtonpost.com/charlotte-hilton-andersen/sarah-palin-bikini-pictur_b_123234.html.

3. Daniel Villareal, "Tim Gunn Thinks Hillary Clinton Has 'Cankles,' Dresses Like She's Confused about Her Gender," *Queerty*, July 27, 2011, http://www.queerty.com/tim-gunn-thinks-hilary-clinton-has-cankles-dresses-like-shes-confused-about-her-gender-20110727/.

4. Scott Wu, "Bill Maher Calls Sarah Palin and Michele Bachmann MILFs," *NowPublic*, April 14, 2010, http://www.nowpublic.com/world/

bill-maher-calls-sarah-palin-and-michele-bachmann-milfs-video
-2605576.html; Tim Herrera, "Tucker Carlson in Trouble for Sarah
Palin MILF Tweet," *AM New York*, March 3, 2011, http://www.amny
.com/urbanite-1.812039/tucker-carlson-in-trouble-for-sarah-palin-milf
-tweet-1.2729060.

5. Andrew J. Bacevich, "How America Conducts Foreign Policy," *Salon*,
April 12, 2011, http://www.salon.com/2011/04/12/barack_obama_iraq_
yemen_libya_wars/.

6. Amy J. C. Cuddy, Susan T. Fiske, and Peter Glick, "The Bias Map:
Behaviors from Intergroup Affect and Stereotypes," *Journal of Personality and Social Psychology* 92, no. 4 (2007): 631–648.

7. "'Sex' refers to the biologically based categories of male and female,
and 'gender' refers to the psychological features frequently associated
with these biological states." Bernd Six and Thomas Eckes, "A Closer
Look at the Complex Structure of Gender Stereotypes," *Sex Roles* 24,
nos. 1–2 (1991): 57, citing Kay Deaux.

8. Judith Butler, "Imitation and Gender Insubordination," in *The Critical
Tradition: Classic Texts and Contemporary Trends*, ed. David H. Rich-
ter (New York: Bedford / St. Martin's, 2007), 1707–1718.

9. Devon W. Carbado and Mitu Gulati, "Working Identity," *Cornell Law
Review* 85, no. 11 (2000): 1265.

10. Fey, *Bossypants*, 216.

11. Carbado and Gulati, "Working Identity."

12. Sharon Meers and Joanna Strober, *Getting to 50/50: How Working Couples Can Have It All by Sharing It All* (New York: Bantam, 2009), 146.

13. Susan T. Fiske, Jun Xu, Amy J. C. Cuddy, and Peter Glick, "(Dis)
respecting versus (Dis)liking: Status and Interdependence Predict
Ambivalent Stereotypes of Competence and Warmth," *Journal of
Social Issues* 55, no. 3 (1999): 476.

14. Peter Glick, Susan T. Fiske, Antonio Mlandinic, José L. Saiz, Dominic
Abrams, Barbara Masser, Bolanle Adetoun, et al., "Beyond Prejudice
as Simple Antipathy: Hostile and Benevolent Sexism across Cultures,"
Journal of Personality and Social Psychology 79, no. 4 (2000): 763–775.

15. Laurie Heatherington, Kimberly A. Daubman, Cynthia Bates, Alicia
Ahn, Heather Brown, and Camille Preston, "Two Investigations of
'Female Modesty' in Achievement Situations," *Sex Roles* 29, nos. 11–12
(1993): 739–754; Laurie A. Rudman, "Self-Promotion as a Risk Factor
for Women: The Costs and Benefits of Counterstereotypical Impression Management," *Journal of Personality and Social Psychology* 74
(1998): 629–645.

16. Linda L. Carli, Suzanne J. LaFleur, and Christopher C. Loeber, "Nonverbal Behavior, Gender, and Influence," *Journal of Personality and
Social Psychology* 68, no. 6 (1995): 1030–1041.

17. Ibid.
18. Dana R. Carney, Amy J. C. Cuddy, and Andy J. Yap, "Power Posing: Brief Nonverbal Displays Affect Neuroendocrine Levels and Risk Tolerance," *Psychological Science* 21, no. 10 (2010): 1363–1368.
19. Ibid., 1364.
20. Amy J. C. Cuddy, "Your Body Language Shapes Who You Are," TED, October 1, 2012, http://www.ted.com/talks/amy_cuddy_your_body_language_shapes_who_you_are.html.
21. Cecilia L. Ridgeway, "Gender, Status, and Leadership," *Journal of Social Issues* 57, no. 4 (2001): 645.
22. Ibid.
23. Ibid.
24. Ibid.
25. Ronald M. Shapiro and Mark A. Jankowski with James Dale, *How to Negotiate So Everyone Wins—Especially You* (New York: Wiley, 2001); Linda Kaplan Thaler and Robin Koval, *The Power of Nice: How to Conquer the Business World with Kindness* (Crows Nest, NSW: Allen and Unwin, 2006); Beverly Engel, *The Nice Girl Syndrome: Stop Being Manipulated and Abused and Start Standing Up for Yourself* (Hoboken, NJ: Wiley, 2008); Frankel, *Nice Girls Don't Get the Corner Office*.
26. Joyce Fletcher, *Disappearing Acts: Gender, Power, and Relational Practice at Work* (Cambridge: MIT Press, 1999); Deborah Prentice and Erica Carranza, "What Women and Men Should Be, Shouldn't Be, Are Allowed to Be, and Don't Have to Be: The Contents of Prescriptive Gender Stereotypes," *Psychology of Women Quarterly* 26 (2002): 269–281; Pamela J. Bettis and Natalie G. Adams, "Nice at Work in the Academy" (unpublished paper).
27. Bettis and Adams, "Nice at Work in the Academy."
28. Mina Cikara and Susan Fiske, "Warmth, Competence, and Ambivalent Sexism: Vertical Assault and Collateral Damage," in *The Glass Ceiling in the 21st Century: Understanding Barriers to Gender Equality*, ed. Manuela Barretto, Michelle K. Ryan and Michael T. Schmitt (Washington, DC: American Psychological Association, 2009), 49–71; Peter Glick and Susan T. Fiske, "The Ambivalence toward Men Inventory: Differentiating Hostile and Benevolent Beliefs about Men," *Psychology of Women Quarterly* 2, no. 3 (1999): 519–536; Rudman, "Self-Promotion as a Risk Factor for Women"; Laurie A. Rudman and Peter Glick, "Feminized Management and Backlash toward Agentic Women," *Journal of Personality and Social Psychology* 77, no. 5 (1999): 1009; Rudman and Glick, "Prescriptive Gender Stereotypes and Backlash toward Agentic Women," *Journal of Social Issues* 57 (2001): 743–762; Laurie A. Rudman and Stephen Kilianski, "Implicit and Explicit Attitudes toward

Female Authority," *Personality and Social Psychology Bulletin* 26 (2000): 1315–1328.

29. Bettis and Adams, "Nice at Work in the Academy."
30. Rudman, "Self-Promotion as a Risk Factor for Women," 642.
31. Madeline E. Heilman and Tyler G. Okimoto, "Why Are Women Penalized for Success at Male Tasks? The Implied Communality Deficit," *Journal of Applied Psychology* 92, no. 1 (2007): 91.
32. Heilman, "Description and Prescription," 668.
33. Madeline E. Heilman, Aaron Wallen, Daniella Fuchs, and Melinda M. Tamkins, "Penalties for Success: Reactions to Women Who Succeed at Male Gender-Typed Tasks," *Journal of Applied Psychology* 89, no. 3 (2004): 426.
34. Ibid.
35. *Hopkins*, 490 U.S. at 234–235.
36. Quoted in Amanda Fortini, "The 'Bitch' and the 'Ditz,'" *New York*, November 16, 2008, http://nymag.com/news/politics/nationalinterest/52184/.
37. Phelan, Moss-Racusin, and Rudman, "Competent yet Out in the Cold," 408–409.
38. Rudman and Glick, "Feminized Management and Backlash," 1009.
39. Duncan Kennedy, "Sexual Abuse, Sexy Dressing and the Eroticization of Domination," *New England Law Review* 26 (1992): 1309–1393.
40. Jennifer L. Berdahl, "The Sexual Harassment of Uppity Women," *Journal of Applied Psychology* 92, no. 2 (2007): 434.
41. Ibid., 426.
42. Jennifer L. Berdahl and Karl Aquino, "Sexual Behavior at Work: Fun or Folly?," *Journal of Applied Psychology* 94, no. 1 (2009): 34–47.
43. John M. Blandford, "The Nexus of Sexual Orientation and Gender in the Determination of Earnings," *Industrial and Labor Relations Review* 56, no. 4 (2003): 624.
44. Cord Jefferson, "The Supply Closet: Almost Half of College-Educated Gays Are Closeted at Work," *Good*, June 21, 2011, http://www.good.is/post/the-supply-closet-almost-half-of-college-educated-gays-are-closeted-at-work/; Blandford, "Nexus of Sexual Orientation and Gender," 624.
45. Nathaniel Miles, *The Double-Glazed Glass Ceiling: Lesbians in the Workplace* (London: Stonewall, 2008), 14.
46. Ibid., 15.
47. Jennifer Saranow Schultz, "Do Lesbians Earn More than Heterosexual Women?," *Bucks* (blog), *New York Times*, December 28, 2010, http://bucks.blogs.nytimes.com/2010/12/28/do-lesbians-earn-more-than-heterosexual-women/; Blandford, "Nexus of Sexual Orientation and Gender," 622–625.

48. Marina Adshade, "What Explains the Lesbian Wage Premium?," *Big Think*, December 13, 2010, http://bigthink.com/dollars-and-sex/what-explains-the-lesbian-wage-premium.

49. Uni Friedman, "Why Do Lesbians Earn More than Straight Women?," *Atlantic Wire*, December 29, 2010, http://www.theatlanticwire.com/business/2010/12/why-do-lesbians-earn-more-than-straight-women/21705/; Blandford, "Nexus of Sexual Orientation and Gender," 625.

50. Doris Weischelbaumer, "Sexual Orientation Discrimination in Hiring," *Labour Economics* 10 (2003): 632.

51. Katharine T. Bartlett, "Only Girls Wear Barrettes: Dress and Appearance Standards, Community Norms, and Workplace Equality," *Michigan Law Review* 92 (1994): 2552.

52. Ibid.

53. Kyrie O'Connor, "The 'Sisterhood of the Traveling Pantsuit,'" *MeMo* (blog), *Houston Chronicle*, August 27, 2008, http://blog.chron.com/memo/2008/08/the-sisterhood-of-the-traveling-pantsuit/.

54. Max Atkinson, "Margaret Thatcher and the Evolution of Charismatic Woman: Part I, Cultural and Vocal Challenges," *Max Atkinson's Blog*, January 3, 2009, http://maxatkinson.blogspot.com/2009/01/margaret-thatcher-and-creation-of.html.

55. Deborah Tannen, *Talking from 9 to 5: Women and Men at Work* (New York: Quill, 1994), 23.

56. Ibid., 36, 47, 153.

57. Cara Hale Alter, "Projecting Credibility and Confidence" (lecture, UC Hastings Leadership Academy for Women, San Francisco, July 22, 2011).

BOXES

a. Cheryl L. Holt and Jon B. Ellis, "Assessing the Current Validity of Bem Sex-Role Inventory," *Sex Roles* 39, nos. 11–12 (1998): 929–941.

Notes to Chapter 5

1. "Clinton Chokes Up, Is Applauded, at Campaign Stop," *CNN*, January 7, 2008, http://articles.cnn.com/2008-01-07/politics/clinton.emotional_1_hillary-clinton-campaign-watch-clinton?_s=PM:POLITICS.

2. Gail Collins, "Hillary's Free Pass," *New York Times*, January 10, 2008, http://www.nytimes.com/2008/01/10/opinion/10collins.html; "Hillary Clinton's Surprise Win," *Economist*, January 9, 2008, http://www.economist.com/node/10492040?zid=311&ah=308cac674cccf554ce65cf926868bbc2.

3. Rupert Cornwell, "Bill and Hillary's Double Trouble: Clinton's 'Two for the Price of One' Pledge Is Returning to Haunt Him, Says Rupert Cornwell," *Independent*, March 9, 1994, http://www.independent.co.uk/

voices/bill-and-hillarys-double-trouble-clintons-two-for-the-price-of
-one-pledge-is-returning-to-haunt-him-says-rupert-cornwell-1427937
.html; Thomas E. Mann and Norman J. Ornstein, "Congress and Health
Care Reform 1993–94," in *Intensive Care: How Congress Shapes
Health Policy*, ed. Julie Rovner (Washington, DC: American Enter-
prise Institute and the Brookings Institute, 1995), 184.

4. Babcock and Laschever, *Women Don't Ask*, 1.
5. Mary E. Wade, "Women and Salary Negotiation: The Costs of Self-
Advocacy," *Psychology of Women Quarterly* 25 (2001): 65–76; Hannah
Riley Bowles, Linda Babcock, and Lei Lai, "Social Incentives for Gender Differences in the Propensity to Initiate Negotiations: Sometimes
It Does Hurt to Ask," *Organizational Behavior and Human Decision
Processes* 103 (2007): 84–103.
6. Bowles, Babcock, and Lai, "Social Incentives for Gender Differences."
7. Ibid.
8. Heilman, "Description and Prescription," 667.
9. Timothy A. Judge, Beth A. Livingston, and Charlice Hurst, "Do Nice
Guys—and Gals—Really Finish Last? The Joint Effects of Sex and
Agreeableness on Income," *Journal of Personality and Social Psychology* 102 (2012): 390–407.
10. Jim Sidanius and Marie Crane, "Job Evaluation and Gender: The Case
of University Faculty," *Journal of Applied Psychology* 19, no. 2 (1989):
174–197.
11. Carli, LaFleur, and Loeber, "Nonverbal Behavior, Gender, and
Influence."
12. Ibid.
13. Ibid., 1040.
14. Prentice and Carranza, "What Women and Men Should Be."
15. Eagly and Carli, *Through the Labyrinth*, 166.
16. Olivia A. O'Neill and Charles A. O'Reilly, "Reducing the Backlash
Effect: Self-Monitoring and Women's Promotions," *Journal of Occupational and Organizational Psychology* 84, no. 4 (2011): 825–832.
17. Ibid.
18. Cecilia L. Ridgeway and Lynn Smith-Lovin, "The Gender System and
Interaction," *Annual Review of Sociology* 25 (1999): 204.
19. Bruce J. Avolio, Jane M. Howell, and John J. Sosik, "A Funny Thing
Happened on the Way to the Bottom Line: Humor as a Moderator of
Leadership Style Effects," *Academy of Management Journal* 42, no. 2
(1999): 219–227; Dawn T. Robinson and Lynn Smith-Lovin, "Getting a
Laugh: Gender, Status, and Humor in Task Discussions," *Social Forces*
80, no. 1 (2001): 123–158.
20. Tannen, *Talking from 9 to 5*, 72.
21. Carrick Mollenkamp, "Sallie Krawcheck on Taking the Fall

—Again," *Marie Claire*, April 17, 2012, http://www.marieclaire.com/career-money/sallie-krawcheck-interview#ixzz1z6qyQIid.

22. Victoria L. Brescoll and Eric Luis Uhlmann, "Can an Angry Woman Get Ahead? Status Conferral, Gender, and Expression of Emotion in the Workplace," *Psychological Science* 19, no. 3 (2008): 268–275.

23. Adam Bryant, "Xerox's New Chief Tries to Define Its Culture," *New York Times*, February 20, 2010, http://www.nytimes.com/2010/02/21/business/21xerox.html?pagewanted=all.

24. Tannen, *Talking from 9 to 5*, 180.

25. Cecilia L. Ridgeway, "Status in Groups: The Importance of Motivation," *American Sociological Review* 47, no. 1 (1982): 76.

26. Gayarti Chakravorty Spivak, "Subaltern Studies: Deconstructing Historiography," in *The Spivak Reader*, ed. Donna Landry and Gerald MacLean (London: Routledge, 1996), 214.

27. Ken Auletta, "A Woman's Place," *New Yorker*, July 11, 2011, http://www.newyorker.com/reporting/2011/07/11/110711fa_fact_auletta.

28. Catharine MacKinnon, *Feminism Unmodified: Discourses on Life and Law* (Cambridge: Harvard University Press, 1987), 16.

BOXES

a. Hannah Riley Bowles, Linda Babcock, and Kathleen L. McGinn, "Constraints and Triggers: Situational Mechanics of Gender in Negotiation," *Journal of Personality and Social Psychology* 89, no. 6 (2005): 951–965.

Notes to Chapter 6

1. Mika Brzezinski, "The 5 Best Work Rules I've Learned," *Cosmopolitan* 254, no. 2 (2013): 120.

2. Zohar Lazar and Drew Magary, "Office Party Survival Guide," *GQ* 83, no. 1 (2013):108.

3. Joan C. Williams and Veta T. Richardson, *New Millennium, Same Glass Ceiling: The Impact of Law Firm Compensation Systems on Women* (San Francisco: Project for Attorney Retention and Minority Corporate Counsel Association, 2010).

4. Bettis and Adams, "Nice at Work in the Academy."

5. Ibid.

6. Ibid.

7. Tannen, *Talking from 9 to 5*, 70.

8. Ibid.

9. Laura J. Kray and Connson C. Locke, "To Flirt or Not to Flirt? Sexual Power at the Bargaining Table," *Negotiation Journal* 24, no. 4 (2008): 488.

10. *Merriam-Webster Online*, s.v. "flirt," accessed January 16, 2013, http://www.merriam-webster.com/dictionary/flirt.

11. Jenna Goudreau, "Flirting Your Way to the Corner Office," *Forbes*, September 3, 2010, http://www.msnbc.msn.com/id/38943620/ns/business-forbes_com/t/flirting-your-way-corner-office/#.T8Pu1L-dMkA.

BOXES

a. Jim Edwards, "Top Female Execs Tell Us Whether It's OK to Burst into Tears at Work," *Business Insider*, April 22, 2013, http://www.businessinsider.com/is-it-ok-to-cry-at-work-2013-4?op=1.

b. Jenna Goudreau, "Crying at Work, a Woman's Burden," *Forbes*, January 11, 2011, http://www.forbes.com/sites/jennagoudreau/2011/01/11/crying-at-work-a-womans-burden-study-men-sex-testosterone-tears-arousal/.

c. University of Miami School of Law, "Soia Mentschikoff," accessed January 22, 2013, http://web-01.law.miami.edu/~robin/soia.php.

d. Herma Hill Kay, "Professor Herma Hill Kay," in *Pioneering Women Lawyers: From Kate Stoneman to the Present*, ed. Patricia E. Salkin (Chicago: American Bar Association, 2008), 113–114.

e. Tiffany Blackstone, "What to Wear to a Summer Job Interview," *Dressed* (blog), *Glamour*, June 30, 2010, http://www.glamour.com/fashion/blogs/slaves-to-fashion/2010/06/what-to-wear-to-a-summer-job-i.html.

f. Staci Zaretsky, "Summer Associates: Please Don't Dress Like Fashion Victims," *Above the Law*, June 5, 2012, http://abovethelaw.com/2012/06/summer-associates-please-dont-dress-like-fashion-victims/.

Notes to Chapter 7

1. Lisa Belkin, "The Opt-Out Revolution," *New York Times Magazine*, October 26, 2003, http://www.nytimes.com/2003/10/26/magazine/26WOMEN.html?pagewanted=all.

2. Ibid.

3. Donna St. George, "Number of Childless American Women in Their 40s Has Risen Sharply since 1970s," *Washington Post*, June 25, 2010, http://www.washingtonpost.com/wp-dyn/content/article/2010/06/25/AR2010062500188.html.

4. About one-third (37 percent) of the women we interviewed did not have children. This is higher than one would otherwise expect. That percentage was driven up by the high percentage of women scientists without children: 78 percent of the New Girls, but only 47 percent of the scientists, were mothers.

5. Correll, Benard, and Paik, "Getting a Job."

6. Belkin, "Opt-Out Revolution."

7. Louise Marie Roth, *Selling Women Short: Gender and Money on Wall Street* (Princeton: Princeton University Press, 2006), 139–140.

8. Ibid., 141.
9. Pamela Stone, *Opting Out? Why Women Really Quit Careers and Head Home* (Berkeley: University of California Press, 2007), 92.
10. Jane Leber Herr and Catherine Wolfram, "Work Environment and 'Opt Out' Rates at Motherhood across High-Education Career Paths" (NBER Working Paper 14717, National Bureau of Economic Research, Cambridge, MA, 2009), 1–63.
11. Joan C. Williams and Cynthia Thomas Calvert, *Solving the Part-Time Puzzle: The Law Firm's Guide to Balanced Hours* (Washington, DC: National Association for Law Placement, 2004); Cynthia Thomas Calvert and Joan C. Williams, *Flex Success: The Lawyer's Guide to Balanced Hours* (San Francisco: Project for Attorney Retention, 2011).
12. Herr and Wolfram, "Work Environment and 'Opt Out' Rates," 37.
13. Stone, *Opting Out*, 120–121.
14. Ibid., 122.
15. Monica Biernat, Faye J. Crosby, and Joan C. Williams, eds., "The Maternal Wall: Research and Policy Perspectives on Discrimination against Mothers," special issue, *Journal of Social Issues* 60, no. 4 (2004); Amy J. C. Cuddy, Susan T. Fiske, and Peter Glick, "When Professionals Become Mothers, Warmth Doesn't Cut the Ice," in ibid., 701–718; Madeline E. Heilman and Tyler G. Okimoto, "Motherhood: A Potential Source of Bias in Employment Decisions," *Journal of Applied Psychology* 93, no. 2 (2008): 189–198; Correll, Benard, and Paik, "Getting a Job."
16. Correll, Benard, and Paik, "Getting a Job," 1330.
17. Joan C. Williams and Stephanie Bornstein, "The Evolution of FReD: Family Responsibilities Discrimination and Developments in the Law of Stereotyping and Implicit Bias," *Hastings Law Journal* 59 (2008): 1327.
18. Cuddy, Fiske, and Glick, "When Professionals Become Mothers."
19. Stephen Benard, In Paik, and Shelley J. Correll, "Cognitive Bias and the Motherhood Penalty," *Hastings Law Journal* 59 (2007): 1365.
20. Ibid.
21. *Frontiero v. Richardson*, 411 U.S. 677, 684 (1973).
22. Deborah L. Rhode, "Myths of Meritocracy," *Fordham Law Review* 65 (1996): 588.
23. Benard, Paik, and Correll, "Cognitive Bias and the Motherhood Penalty," 1385.
24. *Friends*, season 9, episode 11, first broadcast January 9, 2003, NBC.
25. Sarah Fass, "Paid Leave in the States: Critical Support for Low-Wage Workers and Their Families" (brief, National Center for Children in Poverty, Columbia University, New York, March 2009), http://www.nccp.org/publications/pub_864.html.

26. Human Rights Watch, *Failing Its Families: Lack of Paid Leave and Work-Family Supports in the US* (New York: Human Rights Watch, 2011), http://www.hrw.org/sites/default/files/reports/us0211webwcover.pdf.

27. Joan C. Williams, Mary Blair-Loy, and Jennifer L. Berdahl, "Introductory Essay: The Flexibility Stigma," *Journal of Social Issues* 69, no. 2 (2013): 209.

28. Vivia Chen, "Looking into the Equity Box: Women and Partnership Status," *American Lawyer*, September 1, 2010.

29. Williams, Blair-Loy, and Berdahl, "Introductory Essay."

30. Jennifer Glass, "Blessing or Curse? Work-Family Policies and Mother's Wage Growth," *Work and Occupations* 31 (2004): 390.

31. Cynthia Fuchs Epstein, Carroll Seron, Bonnie Oglensky, and Robert Sauté, *The Part-Time Paradox: Time Norms, Professional Life, Family and Gender* (New York: Routledge, 1999), 22.

32. Jason DeParle and Sabrina Tavernise, "For Women under 30, Most Births Occur outside Marriage," *New York Times*, February 17, 2012, http://www.nytimes.com/2012/02/18/us/for-women-under-30-most-births-occur-outside-marriage.html?pagewanted=all.

33. "Realistic & Fair Wages," *MomsRising*, n.d., accessed July 20, 2012, http://www.momsrising.org/issues_and_resources/wages.

34. Arlie Russell Hochschild, "Inside the Clockwork of Male Careers," in *At the Heart of Work and Family: Engaging the Ideas of Arlie Hochschild*, ed. Anita Ilta Garey and Karen V. Hansen (Piscataway: Rutgers University Press, 2011).

35. Madeline Heilman, "Sex Stereotypes and Their Effects in the Workplace: What We Know and Don't Know," *Journal of Social Behavior and Personality* 10, no. 6 (1995): 7.

36. Caroline Gatrell and Elaine Swan, *Gender and Diversity in Management: A Concise Introduction* (London: Sage, 2008), 37.

37. "Cherie Booth Argues for Paternity Leave," *BBC News*, May 16, 2000, http://news.bbc.co.uk/2/hi/uk_news/politics/749613.stm.

38. Adam B. Butler and Amie Skattebo, "What Is Acceptable for Women May Not Be Acceptable for Men: The Effect of Family Conflicts with Work on Job-Performance Ratings," *Journal of Occupational and Organizational Psychology* 77 (2004): 553–564.

39. Rebecca Glauber, "Race and Gender in Families at Work: The Fatherhood Wage Premium," *Gender and Society* 22, no. 1 (2008): 8–30.

40. Correll, Benard, and Paik, "Getting a Job."

41. Beth DeFalco, "NJ Governor Defends His Trip to Florida during Blizzard, Gives State B-Plus for Storm Response," *Star Tribune*, December 31, 2010.

42. Julie Holliday Wayne and Bryanne L. Cordiero, "Who Is a Good

Organizational Citizen? Social Perception of Male and Female Employees Who Use Family Leave," *Sex Roles* 49, nos. 5–6 (2003): 233–246.

43. Butler and Skattebo, "What Is Acceptable for Women May Not Be for Men."

44. Correll, Benard, and Paik, "Getting a Job."

45. Laurie A. Rudman and Kris Mescher, "Penalizing Men Who Request Family Leave: Is Flexibility Stigma a Femininity Stigma?," *Journal of Social Issues* 69, no. 2 (2013): 336.

46. Joseph A. Vandello, Vanessa E. Hettinger, Jennifer K. Bosson, and Jasmine Siddiqi, "When Equal Isn't Really Equal: The Masculine Dilemma of Seeking Work Flexibility," *Journal of Social Issues* 69, no. 2 (2013): 310.

47. Jennifer L. Berdahl and Sue H. Moon, "Workplace Mistreatment of Middle Class Workers Based on Sex, Parenthood, and Caregiving," *Journal of Social Issues* 69, no. 2 (2013): 356.

48. Kristin Choo, "Justice Ginsburg Recalls Bias, Expresses Concerns," *Women's eNews*, November 20, 2000, http://womensenews.org/story/the-courts/001120/justice-ginsburg-recalls-bias-expresses-concerns#.UQiCPR37J8E.

BOXES

a. United Nations, Department of Economic and Social Affairs, *The World's Women 2010, Trends and Statistics*, ST/ESA/STAT/SER.K/19; Angie Mohr, "Maternity Leave Basics: Canada vs. the U.S.," *Globe and Mail*, May 16, 2012, http://www.theglobeandmail.com/report-on-business/careers/career-advice/maternity-leave-basics-canada-vs-the-us/article4197679/; Joan C. Williams and Heather Boushey, *The Three Faces of Work-Family Conflict: The Poor, the Professionals, and the Missing Middle* (San Francisco: Center for American Progress and Center for WorkLife Law, 2010).

b. See generally *Velez v. Novartis Pharms. Corp.*, 4th Am. Compl., available at http://www.sanfordheisler.com/data/public/Amy_Velez_v._Novartis_Pharma_Fourth_Amended_Class_Complaint-63027-1.pdf.

c. *Velez v. Novartis Pharms. Corp.*, 244 F.R.D. 243, 267 (S.D.N.Y. 2007).

d. *Velez*, 4th Am. Compl. at 34–35.

e. *Velez*, 244 F.R.D. at 267.

f. *Velez v. Novartis Pharms. Corp.*, No. 04-9194, 2010 U.S. Dist. LEXIS 125945, *10–11 (S.D.N.Y. Nov. 30, 2010).

g. Ibid. at *13.

h. Margaret Wise Brown, *Goodnight Moon* (New York: Harper, 1947).

i. Maurice Sendak, *Where the Wild Things Are* (New York: HarperCollins, 1963), 1–3.

j. Theodor Seuss Geisel (pseud. Dr. Seuss), *The Cat in the Hat* (Boston: Houghton Mifflin, 1957), 6–8.

k. Lee Speigel, "Rendell: Napolitano Perfect for Homeland Security Because She Has 'No Life,'" *Political Punch* (blog), *ABC News*, December 3, 2008, http://abcnews.go.com/blogs/politics/2008/12/rendell -napolit/.

l. "Young Women Top Unpaid Work List," *BBC News*, February 22, 2008, http://news.bbc.co.uk/2/hi/business/7258390.stm.

m. Martha Minow, e-mail to author Joan C. Williams, January 29, 2013.

n. Julie M. Koivunen, Jeanne W. Rothaupt, and Susan M. Wolfgram, "Gender Dynamics and Role Adjustment during the Transition to Parenthood: Current Perspectives," *Family Journal* 17, no. 4 (2009): 323–328.

o. Ibid.

p. Ibid.

q. Diane Kobrynowicz and Monica Biernat, "Decoding Subjective Evaluations: How Stereotypes Provide Shifting Standards," *Journal of Experimental Social Psychology* 33 (1997): 584.

r. Linda Haas and C. Philip Hwang, "The Impact of Taking Parental Leave on Fathers' Participation in Childcare and Relationships with Children: Lessons from Sweden," *Community, Work & Family* 11, no. 1 (2008): 85–104.

s. Linda Haas, *Equal Parenthood and Social Policy: A Study of Parental Leave in Sweden* (Albany: SUNY Press, 1992), 9–10.

t. Jay Fagan and Marina Barnett, "The Relationship between Maternal Gatekeeping, Paternal Competence, Mothers' Attitudes about the Father Role and Father Involvement," *Journal of Family Issues* 24 (2003): 1020–1034.

u. Richard J. Fletcher, Stephen Matthey, and Christopher G. Marley, "Addressing Depression and Anxiety among New Fathers," *Medical Journal of Australia* 185, no. 8 (2006): 461–463; Robert L. Griswold, *Fatherhood in America: A History* (New York: Basic Books, 1993), 10–33.

Notes to Chapter 8

1. Kobrynowicz and Biernat, "Decoding Subjective Evaluations," 584.

2. Allison Pearson, *I Don't Know How She Does It* (New York: Knopf, 2002), 28.

3. Sara J. Corse, "Pregnant Managers and Their Subordinates: The Effects of Gender Expectations on Hierarchal Relationships," *Journal of Applied Behavioral Science* 26 (1990): 39.

4. American Bar Association Commission on the Status of Women in the Profession, *Visible Invisibility: Women of Color in Law Firms* (Chicago: American Bar Association, 2006), 34.

5. Leslie Morgan Steiner, *Mommy Wars* (New York: Random House, 2006), 15.
6. Meers and Strober, *Getting to 50/50*, 4.
7. Ibid., 64–66.
8. Ibid.
9. Ibid., 65.
10. Sandberg, "Why We Have Too Few Women Leaders." Sandberg further develops this thought, and many others related to the themes discussed in this book, in Sheryl Sandberg, *Lean In: Women, Work, and the Will to Lead* (New York: Knopf, 2013), which came into our hands only a few days before this book went to press.
11. Sandberg, "Why We Have Too Few Women Leaders."
12. Ibid.
13. Ibid.
14. ABA Commission, *Visible Invisibility*, 16.
15. Jonathon Lazear, *The Man Who Mistook His Job for a Life: A Chronic Overachiever Finds the Way Home* (New York: Crown, 2001).
16. Morgan Steiner, *Mommy Wars*, 167.
17. Bill Meers, "Justice Ginsburg's Husband Dies of Cancer Complications, *CNN.com*, June 27, 2010, http://www.cnn.com/2010/CRIME/06/27/scotus.ginsburg.husband/index.html.
18. Lisa Belkin, "When Mom and Dad Share It All," *New York Times Magazine*, June 15, 2008, http://www.nytimes.com/2008/06/15/magazine/15parenting-t.html?pagewanted=3&_r=1.
19. Charlotte J. Patterson, "Families of the Lesbian Baby Boom: Parents' Division of Labor and Children's Adjustment," *Developmental Psychology* 31, no. 1 (1995): 115–123; Megan Fulcher, Erin L. Sutfin, and Charlotte J. Patterson, "Individual Differences in Gender Development: Associations with Parental Sexual Orientation, Attitudes, and Division of Labor," *Sex Roles* 58 (2008): 330–341.
20. Sandberg, "Why We Have Too Few Women Leaders."
21. Meers and Strober, *Getting to 50/50*, 4.
22. Alan Murray, "Pepsi's Indra Nooyi on Balancing Work and Family," *Wall Street Journal*, April 11, 2011, http://live.wsj.com/video/pepsi-indra-nooyi-on-balancing-work-and-family/44313778-BE51-4C1A-9323-8757ED876F78.html#!44313778-BE51-4C1A-9323-8757ED876F78.
23. Ibid.
24. Jean Kimmel, "Child Care, Female Employment, and Economic Growth," *Journal of the Community Development Society* 37, no. 2 (2006): 71–85; Margaret Udansky and Douglas Wolf, "When Child Care Fails: Young Mothers' Experiences with Missed Work and Child Care Problems" (paper presented at the Population Association of America 2006 Annual Meeting Program, Los Angeles, March–April 2006).

25. Sarah M. Allen and Alan J. Hawkins, "Maternal Gatekeeping: Mothers' Beliefs and Behaviors That Inhibit Greater Father Involvement in Family Work," *Journal of Marriage and Family* 61, no. 1 (1999): 199–212.
26. Douglas Stone, Bruce Patton, and Sheila Heen, *Difficult Conversations: How to Discuss What Matters Most* (New York: Penguin Books, 2010), 134.
27. Calvert and Williams, *Flex Success*, 22.
28. Ibid., 38.

BOXES

a. Joshua Coleman, *The Lazy Husband: How to Get Men to Do More Parenting and Housework* (New York: St. Martin's, 2005).
b. 29 U.S.C. § 2601 (2009).

Notes to Chapter 9

1. This quote from Mayer, excerpted from the AOL/PBS series *MAKERS*, does not seem to adequately reflect the Yahoo! CEOs management strategy; in 2013, she doubled paid maternity leave for her employees from 8 weeks to 16 weeks and offered paid paternity leave for 8 weeks. For more information, see Nicholas Carson, "Marissa Mayer Doubles Yahoo's Paid Maternity Leave, Gives Dads Eight Weeks," *Business Insider*, April 30, 2013, http://www.businessinsider .com/marissa-mayer-doubles-the-length-of-yahoos-paid-maternity -leave-gives-new-dads-eight-weeks-off-2013-4.
2. Roger Dobson and Will Iredale, "Office Queen Bees Hold Back Women's Careers," *Sunday Times*, December 31, 2006, available at http://www .women-on-top.nl/wp-content/uploads/office-queen-bees-2-jan-07.pdf.
3. Derks et al., "Do Sexist Organizational Cultures Create the Queen Bee?"; Derks et al., "Gender-Bias Primes Elicit Queen Bee Responses."
4. Robert Krulwich, "The First Woman to Go 'Round the World Did It as a Man," *Krulwich Wonders* (blog), *NPR*, January 24, 2012, http://www .npr.org/blogs/krulwich/2012/01/23/145664873/the-first-woman-to-go -round-the-world-did-it-as-a-man?sc=fb&cc=fp.
5. Carbado and Gulati, "Working Identity," 1300.
6. Partial passing and its discontents: "An employee's use of partial comforting strategies provides employers with a way to avoid confronting their use of stereotypes. In the face of such strategies, employers might tell themselves that, while the stereotypes they hold about outsiders may not (for the moment) apply to the specific outsider employee, the stereotypes are nonetheless valid. The partially passing outsider employee thus becomes the exception to otherwise valid stereotyping rules." Ibid., 1303.

7. Katha Pollitt, "Hers: The Smurfette Principle" *New York Times Magazine*, April 7, 1991, http://www.nytimes.com/1991/04/07/magazine/hers-the-smurfette-principle.html?pagewanted=all&src=pm.
8. Ibid.
9. Rosabeth Moss Kanter, "Some Effects of Proportions on Group Life: Skewed Sex Ratios and Responses to Token Women," *American Journal of Sociology* 85, no. 5 (1977): 965–990; Kanter, *Men and Women of the Corporation* (New York: Basic Books, 1977).
10. Interview with Joan C. Williams, March 2005.
11. Eagly and Karau, "Role Congruity Theory of Prejudice toward Female Leaders."
12. Leonard Karakowsky and J. P. Siegel, "The Effects of Proportional Representation and Gender Orientation of the Task on Emergent Leadership Behavior in Mixed-Gender Groups," *Journal of Applied Psychology* 84, no. 4 (1999): 610–631.
13. Cordelia Fine, *Delusions of Gender: How Our Minds, Society, and Neurosexism Create Difference* (New York: Norton, 2010), 35.
14. Valian, *Why So Slow?*, 310.
15. Paul R. Sackett, Cathy L. Z. DuBois, and Anne Wiggins Noe, "Tokenism in Performance Evaluation: The Effects of Work Group Representation on Male-Female and White-Black Differences in Performance Ratings," *Journal of Applied Psychology* 76, no. 2 (1991): 263–267.
16. Stone, Patton, and Heen, *Difficult Conversations*.
17. Glick et al., "Beyond Prejudice as Simple Antipathy."
18. Elizabeth J. Parks-Stamm, Madeline E. Heilman, and Krystle A. Hearns, "Motivated to Penalize: Women's Strategic Rejection of Successful Women," *Personality and Social Psychology Bulletin* 34 (2008): 237–247.
19. Ibid.
20. Ibid.
21. Virginia W. Cooper, "Homophily or the Queen Bee Syndrome: Female Evaluations of Female Leadership," *Small Group Research* 28 (1997): 483–499.
22. Bettis and Adams, "Nice at Work in the Academy."
23. Margaret Talbot, "The Female Misogynist: The Whole Woman by Germaine Greer," *New Republic* 220, no. 22 (1999): 36.
24. Fine, *Delusions of Gender*, 51–52.
25. Ibid., 52.
26. Derks et al., "Do Sexist Organizational Cultures Create the Queen Bee?"
27. Hanna Rosin, "Why Doesn't Marissa Mayer Care about Sexism?," *XXfactor* (blog), *Slate*, July 16, 2012, http://www.slate.com/blogs/

xx_factor/2012/07/16/new_yahoo_ceo_marissa_mayer_does_she_care_
about_sexism_.html.

28. Jennifer Rindfleish, "Senior Management Women in Australia: Diverse
    Perspectives," *Women in Management Review* 15, no. 4 (2000):
    172–180.

29. Heilman, "Sex Stereotypes and Their Effects in the Workplace," 5.

30. Ibid., 18.

31. Derks et al., "Gender-Bias Primes Elicit Queen Bee Responses."

32. Sharon Mavin, "Queen Bees, Wannabees and Afraid to Bees: No More
    'Best Enemies' for Women in Management?," *British Journal of Man-
    agement* 19, no. 1 (2008): S81.

33. *Ally McBeal*, episode 24, directed by Jonathon Pontell and written by
    David E. Kelley, first broadcast September 14, 1998, Fox.

34. Elayne Rapping, "You've Come Which Way, Baby? The Road That
    Leads from June Cleaver to Ally McBeal Looks a Lot Like a U-Turn,"
    Women's Review of Books 17, nos. 10–11 (2000): 21.

35. Linda Carli, "Gender Issues in Workplace Groups: Effect of Gender and
    Communication Style on Social Influence," in *Gender and Communica-
    tion at Work*, ed. Mary Barrett and Marilyn J. Davidson (Burlington,
    VT: Ashgate, 2006).

36. *Mad Men*, episode 47, directed by Phil Abraham and written by Lisa
    Albert, Janet Leahy, and Matthew Weiner, first broadcast September
    12, 2010, AMC.

37. Felice Batlan, "'If You Become His Second Wife, You Are a Fool': Shift-
    ing Paradigms of the Roles, Perceptions, and Working Conditions of
    Legal Secretaries in Large Law Firms," *Studies in Law, Politics, and
    Society* 52 (2010): 169–210.

38. Ibid., 200.

39. Ibid.

40. Ibid., 202.

41. Ibid., 203.

42. Debra Cassens Weiss, "Not One Legal Secretary Surveyed Preferred
    Working with Women Partners: Prof Offers Reasons Why," *ABA
    Journal*, October 24, 2011, http://www.abajournal.com/news/article/
    not_one_legal_secretary_surveyed_preferred_working_with_women_
    lawyers_prof_/i.

43. Joan C. Williams and Rachel Dempsey, "Hate Your Boss? Ask Your-
    self If Gender Bias Is to Blame," *Huffington Post*, November 28, 2011,
    http://www.huffingtonpost.com/joan-williams/the-bitchy-boss-and-other
    _b_1116937.html.

44. Naomi Ellemers, Henriette van den Heuvel, Dick de Gilder, Anne
    Maass, and Alessandra Bonvini, "The Underrepresentation of Women

in Science: Differential Commitment or the Queen Bees Syndrome?,"
British Journal of Social Psychology 43 (2004): 1–24.

45. Ibid., 11–12 (citing earlier study published in Dutch).
46. Huang, "Gender Bias in Academia," 8.
47. Stephen Benard and Shelley J. Correll, "Normative Discrimination and the Motherhood Penalty," *Gender and Society* 24, no. 5 (2010): 616–646.

BOXES

a. "Top 10 Men Who Were Really Women," *Listverse*, September 4, 2008, http://listverse.com/2008/09/04/top-10-men-who-were-really-women/.
b. Stone, Patton, and Heen, *Difficult Conversations*, 19.

Notes to Chapter 10

1. *Saturday Night Live*, episode 637, first broadcast September 13, 2008, NBC.
2. Lisa Sinclair and Ziva Kunda, "Motivated Stereotyping of Women: She's Fine If She Praised Me but Incompetent If She Criticized Me," *Personality and Social Psychology Bulletin* 26 (2000): 1329–1342.
3. Peter Cantillon and Joan Sargeant, "Teaching Rounds: Giving Feedback in Clinical Settings," *British Medical Journal* 337, no. 7681 (2008): 1292–1294.

Notes to Chapter 11

1. This chapter is adapted from a report given to the National Science Foundation (NSF), for work generously supported by NSF ADVANCE PAID grant no. EHR 1106411.
2. Jodi Kantor, *The Obamas* (New York: Little, Brown, 2012); "Michelle Obama: 'Who Can Write about How I Feel?,'" interview by Gayle King, *CBS This Morning*, January 11, 2012, http://www.cbsnews.com/video/watch/?id=7394714n.
3. Melissa V. Harris-Perry, *Sister Citizen: Shame, Stereotypes, and Black Women in America* (New Haven: Yale University Press, 2011), 289.
4. Ibid.
5. Riché Barnes, "Race, Class, and Marriage: Black Women, Social Mobility, and the Companionate Marriage Ideal" (PhD diss., Emory University, 2009); Joan C. Williams, *Unbending Gender: Why Family and Work Conflict and What to Do about It* (New York: Oxford University Press, 2000).
6. Frances Beal, *Double Jeopardy: To Be Black and Female* (Detroit: Radical Education Project, 1969). One of the most recent contributions to this literature is Gabriella Gutiérrez y Muhs, Yolanda Flores Niemann, Carmen G. González, and Angela P. Harris, eds., *Presumed*

Incompetent: The Intersections of Race and Class for Women in Academia (Boulder: University Press of Colorado, 2012).

7. Isis H. Settles, "Use of an Intersectional Framework to Understand Black Women's Racial and Gender Identities," *Sex Roles* 54 (2006): 589–601.

8. One experimental study (see ibid.) indicates that this sense of isolation is particularly prevalent among black women and is part of their "intersectional identity" as black women. I include it as a racial effect because I also found it among other groups of women-of-color scientists.

9. Marianne Bertrand and Sendhil Mullainathan, "Are Emily and Greg More Employable than Lakisha and Jamal? A Field Experiment on Labor Market Discrimination," *American Economic Review* 94 (2004): 991–1013.

10. Settles, "Use of an Intersectional Framework," 589–601.

11. This is complicated. Settles's study found that did not: "Black women placed equal importance on their race and gender, but the black-woman identity was more important than either the black or the woman identities." However, Settles cites earlier studies that found "a stronger relationship . . . between black and black-woman identity importance than between woman and black-woman identity." Ibid., 598.

12. J. Nicole Shelton and Robert M. Sellers, "Situational Stability and Variability in African-American Racial Identity," *Journal of Black Psychology* 26, no. 1 (2000): 27–50.

13. Ashleigh Shelby Rosette and Robert W. Livingston, "Failure Is Not an Option for Black Women: Effects of Organizational Performance on Leaders with Single versus Dual-Subordinate Identities," *Journal of Experimental Psychology* 48 (2012): 1162–1167.

14. Beal, *Double Jeopardy*.

15. ABA Commission, *Visible Invisibility*, 25.

16. Biernat and Kobrynowicz, "Gender- and Race- Based Standards of Competence," 544–557.

17. Steele, *Whistling Vivaldi*, 104.

18. Adam Galinsky, Erika V. Hall, and Amy J. C. Cuddy, "Gendered Race: Implications for Interracial Dating, Leadership Selection, and Athletic Participation," *Psychological Science* (forthcoming); Phillip Goff, Margaret Thomas, and Matthew Jackson, "Ain't I a Woman? Towards an Intersectional Approach to Person Perception and Group-Based Harms," *Sex Roles* 59, no. 506 (2008): 392–403.

19. Hilary B. Bergsieker, J. Nicole Shelton, and Jennifer A. Richeson, "To Be Liked versus Respected: Divergent Goals in Interracial Interactions," *Journal of Personality and Social Psychology* 99, no. 2 (2010): 248–264.

20. Robert W. Livingston, Ashleigh Shelby Rosette, and Ella F. Washington, "Can an Agentic Black Woman Get Ahead? The Impact of Race and Interpersonal Dominance on Perceptions of Female Leaders," *Psychological Science* 23, no. 4 (2012): 354–358.

21. See also Erika Hall, Katherine Phillips, Laurie Rudman, and Peter Glick, "Double Jeopardy or Greater Latitude: Do Black Women Escape Backlash for Dominance Displays?" (unpublished paper); Kathrynn A. Adams, "Who Has the Final Word? Sex, Race, and Dominance Behavior," *Personality and Social Psychology* 38, no. 1 (1980): 1–8.

22. ABA Commission, *Visible Invisibility*, 26.

23. Robert W. Livingston, "Race, Gender, and the Dynamics of Social Hierarchy Reversal" (lecture, Columbia University's Workshop on Diversity and Inclusion for All, New York, November 30, 2012).

24. ABA Commission, *Visible Invisibility*, xii.

25. Ibid., 72.

26. Ibid., 34.

27. Tannen, *Talking from 9 to 5*, 71.

28. Denise A. Segura, "Chicanas in White-Collar Jobs: 'You Have to Prove Yourself More,'" *Sociological Perspectives* 35, no. 1 (1992): 163.

29. Jody Agius Vallejo, "Latina Spaces: Middle-Class Ethnic Capital and Professional Associations in the Latino Community," *City & Community* 8, no. 2 (2009): 146.

30. Deepali Begati, *Women of Color in U.S. Law Firms: Women of Color in Professional Services Series* (New York: Catalyst, 2009), 45.

31. William Peterson, "Success Story: Japanese-American Style," *New York Times Magazine*, January 9, 1966, 21.

32. Monica H. Lin, Virginia S. Y. Kwan, Anna Cheung, and Susan T. Fiske, "Stereotype Content Model Explains Prejudice for an Envied Outgroup: Scale of Anti–Asian American Stereotypes," *Personality and Social Psychology Bulletin* 31, no. 1 (2005): 43–47; Susan T. Fiske, Amy J. C. Cuddy, Peter Glick, and Jun Xu, "A Model of (Often Mixed) Stereotype Content: Competence and Warmth Respectively Follow from Perceived Status and Competition," *Journal of Personal and Social Psychology* 82, no. 6 (2002): 880.

33. ABA Commission, *Visible Invisibility*, 25.

34. Colin Ho and Jay W. Jackson, "Attitudes toward Asian Americans: Theory and Measurement," *Journal of Applied Social Psychology* 31, no. 8 (2001): 1553–1581.

35. Galinsky and Cuddy, "Overlap between Racial and Gender Stereotype."

36. ABA Commission, *Visible Invisibility*, 10.

37. Ibid.

38. Jennifer L. Berdahl and Ji-A Min, "Prescriptive Stereotypes and Workplace Consequences for East Asians in North American,"

Cultural Diversity and Ethnic Minority Psychology 18, no. 2 (2012): 141–152.

39. Ibid.
40. ABA Commission, *Visible Invisibility*, 11.
41. Ho and Jackson, "Attitudes toward Asian Americans."
42. Benard and Correll, "Normative Discrimination and the Motherhood Penalty."
43. Deepali Begati, *Women of Color in United States Securities Firms* (New York: Catalyst, 2008), 35.
44. Tanya K. Hernandez, "A Critical Race Feminism Empirical Research Project: Sexual Harassment and the Internal Complaints Black Box," *University of California Davis Law Review* 39 (2005–2006): 1235–1304; cf. Lilia M. Cortina, "Assessing Sexual Harassment among Latinas: Development of an Instrument," *Cultural Diversity and Ethnic Minority Psychology* 7, no. 2 (2001): 164–181 (reporting that half of all women, and half of Latinas, experience sexual harassment).
45. Berdahl and Moore, "Workplace Harassment."
46. Martha Chamallas, "Jean Jew's Case: Resisting Sexual Harassment in the Academy," *Yale Journal of Law and Feminism* 6 (1994): 72.
47. Maria L. Ontiveros, "Three Perspectives on Workplace Harassment of Women of Color," *Golden Gate University Law Review* 23 (1993): 818.
48. Ibid.
49. Suni K. Cho, "Converging Stereotypes in Racialized Sexual Harassment: Where the Model Minority Meets Suzie Wong," *Journal of Gender, Race & Justice* 1 (1997): 179, 191, 206.
50. ABA Commission, *Visible Invisibility*, 10.
51. Ontiveros, "Three Perspectives on Workplace Harassment of Women of Color," 820.
52. Ibid., 826.
53. Andrea L. Dennis, "Because I Am Black, Because I Am Woman: Remedying the Sexual Harassment Experience of Black Women," *Annual Survey of American Law*, 1996, 561.
54. Charles B. Adams, "The Impact of Race on Sexual Harassment: The Disturbing Confirmation of Thomas/Hill," *Howard Scroll: The Social Justice Law Review* 1 (1994): 16.
55. Ontiveros, "Three Perspectives on Workplace Harassment of Women of Color," 826.
56. Adams, "Impact of Race on Sexual Harassment," 17.
57. Kimberlé Crenshaw, "Race, Gender, and Sexual Harassment," *Southern California Law Review* 65 (1991–1992): 1472.
58. Settles, "Use of an Intersectional Framework," 598. Settles stresses that this is probably not true of all black women.
59. Ibid., 595.

BOXES

a. "Michele Obama: 'I've Got a Loud Mouth," *Good Morning America*, ABC, May 22, 2007, http://abcnews.go.com/GMA/story?id=3199620.

b. "First Lady Michelle Obama Also Starts Her 2nd Term," Jodi Kantor interviewed by Renee Montagne, *Morning Edition*, NPR, January 21, 2013, http://www.npr.org/2013/01/21/169877161/first-lady-also-starts-her -2nd-term.

c. Jacqueline Jones, *Labor of Love, Labor of Sorrow: Black Women, Work, and the Family from Slavery to the Present* (New York: Basic Books, 1985), 58–60.

d. Susan Saulny, "For Most, Choice of Stay-at-Home Motherhood Is Far from a Luxury," *New York Times*, April 15, 2012, http://www.nytimes .com/2012/04/16/us/politics/ann-romneys-choice-not-typical-of-stay-at -home-mothers.html?_r=0.

e. Emily Kane, "Racial and Ethnic Variations in Gender-Related Atti- tudes," *Annual Review of Sociology* 26 (2000): 426.

f. Eric L. Ray, "Mexican Repatriation and the Possibility for a Federal Cause of Action: A Comparative Analysis of Reparations," *University of Miami Inter-American Law Review* 37, no. 1 (2005): 171–196.

g. Jody Agius Vallejo, "Latina Spaces: Middle-Class Ethnic Capital and Professional Associations in the Latino Community," *City & Commu- nity* 8, no. 2 (2009): 143.

h. Glenn Omatsu, "Liberating Minds, Hearts, and Souls: Forging an Anti- Colonial Framework to Explore the Asian American Experience," in *Social Justice, Peace, and Environmental Education: Transformative Standards*, ed. Julie Andrzejewski, Marta P. Baltodano, and Linda Symcox, 175–192 (New York: Routledge, 2009), 180.

i. Helen Zia, *Asian American Dreams: The Emergence of an American People* (New York: Farrar, Straus and Giroux 2000), 27.

j. Ibid., 43.

k. Peterson, "Success Story," 21; Lin et al., "Stereotype Content Model Explains Prejudice for an Envied Outgroup"; Fiske et al., "Model of (Often Mixed) Stereotype Content," 880.

l. Evan Ramstad, "Are Koreans the Irish of Asia? Here's a Case," *Korea RealTime* (blog), *Wall Street Journal*, October 16, 2012, http://blogs .wsj.com/korearealtime/2012/10/16/are-koreans-the-irish-of-asia-heres-a -case/.

m. Caroline Graham, "'We Have a Stiff Upper Lip—Like You British': Tokyo Residents Show Their True Grit amid Nuclear Chaos," *Daily Mail*, March 20, 2011, http://www.dailymail.co.uk/news/article-1367999/ Japan-nuclear-crisis-We-stiff-upper-lip-like-British-say-Tokyo -residents.html.

n. Asrul Hadi Abdullah Sani, "BTN Taught Me the Chinese Are the Jews of Asia," *Malaysian Insider*, February 27, 2009, http://malaysia -today.net/index.php?option=com_content&view=article&id=28735: btn-taught-me-the-chinese-are-the-jews-of-asia&catid=17:guest -columnists&Itemid=100130.

o. "DGA Report Assesses Director Diversity in Hiring Practices for Episodic TV," *Deadline Hollywood*, September 14, 2011, http://www .deadline.com/2011/09/dga-report-assesses-director-diversity-in-hiring -practices-for-episodic-tv/.

p. Melissa Silverstein, "Only One African American Woman Directed a Top Grossing Film in 2008," *Women and Hollywood* (blog), *IndieWire*, June 7, 2011, http://blogs.indiewire.com/womenandhollywood/only_one_ african_american_woman_directed_a_top_grossing_film_in_2008.

Notes to Chapter 12

1. David A. Matsa and Amalia R. Miller, "Chipping Away at the Glass Ceiling: Gender Spillovers in Corporate Leadership" (RAND Labor and Population Working Paper WR-842, Santa Monica, CA, 2011).

2. Linda A. Bell, "Women-Led Firms and the Gender Gap in Top Executive Jobs" (IZA Discussion Paper 1689, Institute for the Study of Labor, Bonn, Germany, 2005).

3. Karen E. Klein, "How 'Diversity Fatigue' Undermines Business Growth," *Bloomberg Businessweek*, May 14, 2012, http:// www.businessweek.com/articles/2012-05-14/how-diversity-fatigue -undermines-business-growth.

4. Lalith Munasinghe, Alice Henriques, and Tania Reif, "The Gender Gap in Wage Returns on Job Tenure and Experience," *Labour Economics* 15, no. 6 (2008): 1306.

5. IBM, "Biographies: Virginia M. Rometty: Chairman, President and Chief Executive Officer," last updated October 2012, http://www-03 .ibm.com/press/us/en/biography/10069.wss; Stacy Conradt, "6 Interns Who Ended Up Running the Company," *Mental_Floss* (blog), April 6, 2012, http://www.mentalfloss.com/blogs/archives/122551.

6. Carter and Silva, *Myth of the Ideal Worker*, 10.

7. Thomas J. Cooke, Paul Boyle, Kenneth Couch, and Peteke Feijten, "A Longitudinal Analysis of Family Migration and the Gender Gap in Earnings in the United States and Great Britain," *Demography* 46, no. 1 (2009): 147–167.

8. Ibid., 156–158.

9. Glass, "Blessing or Curse?," 383.

10. Audience member at panel during 2012 Annual NAPABA Convention, November 16, 2012.

BOXES

a. Charlotte Werner, Sandrine Devillard, and Sandra Sancier-Sutton, *McKinsey Global Survey Results: Moving Women to the Top* (Paris: McKinsey, 2010).

Notes to Chapter 13

1. John R. Becker-Blease, Susa Elkinawy, and Mark Stater, "The Impact of Gender on Voluntary and Involuntary Executive Departure," *Economic Inquiry* 48, no. 4 (2010): 1102–1118.
2. Eagly and Carli, *Through the Labyrinth*, 56.
3. Katherine Reynolds Lewis, "The Return: A Stay-at-Home Mom Attempts to Go Back to Work after Nearly Two Decades: Can She Revive Her Career?," *Washington Post*, April 4, 2010, http://www .washingtonpost.com/wp-dyn/content/article/2010/03/29/AR201003290 2620.html.
4. Pamela Stone and Meg Lovejoy, "Fast-Track Mothers and the 'Choice' to Stay Home," *Annals of the American Academy of Political and Social Science* 594, no. 1 (2004): 62–83; Monica McGrath, Marla Driscoll, and Mary Gross, "Back in the Game—Returning to Business after a Hiatus: Experiences and Recommendations for Women, Employers, and Universities" (research paper, Wharton Center for Leadership and Change, Philadelphia, 2005), 7, http://knowledge.wharton.upenn.edu/ paper.cfm?paperid=1309.
5. McGrath, Driscoll, and Gross, "Back in the Game," 6.
6. Ibid., 3.
7. Eagly and Carli, *Through the Labyrinth*, 57.
8. Stephen J. Rose and Heidi Hartmann, *Still a Man's Labor Market: The Long-Term Earnings Gap*, report C355 (Washington, DC: Institute for Women's Policy Research, 2004), 10.
9. Mark Sanford Granovetter, "Changing Jobs: Channels of Mobility Information in a Suburban Community" (PhD diss., Harvard University, 1970).
10. Jenny Foss, "Start Your Love Affair with LinkedIn," *Daily Muse*, October 11, 2011, http://www.thedailymuse.com/job-search/start-your -love-affair-with-linkedin/.
11. Chris Rojek, *Frank Sinatra* (Cambridge, MA: Polity, 2004), 119.

BOXES

a. Human Rights Campaign, "An Important Step toward Workplace Equality: An Executive Order on Federal Contractors," n.d., accessed January 4, 2013, http://www.hrc.org/resources/entry/an-important -step-toward-workplace-equality-an-executive-order-on-federal-c.
b. Brzezinski, *Knowing Your Value*, 116, 127.

Notes to Chapter 14
1. Sara Holtz, "Seven Habits of Successful Rainmakers," Remsen Group, n.d., accessed January 12, 2013, http://www.theremsengroup.com/88.

Notes to Chapter 15
1. "Women CEOs," *CNN Money*, 2011, http://money.cnn.com/magazines/fortune/fortune500/2011/womenceos/; Jennifer E. Manning and Calleen J. Shogan, *Women in the United States Congress: 1917–2012* (Washington, DC: Congressional Research Service, 2012), http://www.fas.org/sgp/crs/misc/RL30261.pdf.
2. Arlie Russell Hochschild, "Inside the Clockwork of Male Careers," in *At the Heart of Work and Family: Engaging the Ideas of Arlie Hochschild*, ed. Anita Ilta Garey and Karen V. Hansen (Piscataway: Rutgers University Press, 2011).
3. Williams, *Unbending Gender*, 1–2.
4. Special tabulations of data from the 2011 American Community Survey (U.S. Census Bureau). Alison Gemmill, demography PhD candidate at the University of California, Berkeley, e-mail to author Joan C. Williams, January 23, 2013.
5. United States Census Bureau, "Profile America: Facts for Features."
6. *Bates v. 84 Lumber Co., L.P.*, No. 04:CV-128, 2004 WL 3372691, ¶ 10 (E.D. Ky. 2004) (First Amended Complaint). (Note: This quote appeared in the complaint; the legal opinions do not mention it.)
7. Alexandra Kalev, Frank Dobbin, and Erin Kelly, "Best Practices or Best Guesses? Assessing the Efficacy of Corporate Diversity Policies," *American Sociological Review* 71 (2006): 589–617.
8. Ibid.
9. Bowles, Babcock, and Lai, "Social Incentives for Gender Differences."
10. Andreas Leibbrandt and John A. List, "Do Women Avoid Salary Negotiations? Evidence from a Large Scale Natural Field Experiment" (NBER Working Paper 18511, National Bureau of Economic Research, Cambridge, MA, 2012).

Selected Bibliography

This bibliography is not an exhaustive list of all sources used in the making of this book. Its focus is on the *science* behind the four patterns of bias. Many, but not all, of these sources are experimental social psychology studies.

Adams, Kathrynn A. "Who Has the Final Word? Sex, Race, and Dominance Behavior." *Personality and Social Psychology* 38, no. 1 (1980): 1–8.

Allen, Sarah M., and Alan J. Hawkins. "Maternal Gatekeeping: Mothers' Beliefs and Behaviors That Inhibit Greater Father Involvement in Family Work." *Journal of Marriage and Family* 61, no. 1 (1999): 199–212.

Anderson, Craig, and Brad Bushman. "External Validity of 'Trivial' Experiments: The Case of Laboratory Aggression." *Review of General Psychology* 1, no. 1 (1997): 19–41.

Avolio, Bruce J., Jane M. Howell, and John J. Sosik. "A Funny Thing Happened on the Way to the Bottom Line: Humor as a Moderator of Leadership Style Effects." *Academy of Management Journal* 42, no. 2 (1999): 219–227.

Babcock, Linda, and Sara Laschever. *Women Don't Ask: The High Cost of Avoiding Negotiation—and Strategies for Change*. New York: Bantam Dell, 2007.

Bargh, John A., and Tanya L. Chartrand. "The Unbearable Automaticity of Being." *American Psychologist* 54, no. 7 (1999): 462–479.

Becker-Blease, John R., Susa Elkinawy, and Mark Stater. "The Impact of Gender on Voluntary and Involuntary Executive Departure." *Economic Inquiry* 48, no. 4 (2010): 1102–1118.

Benard, Stephen, and Shelley J. Correll. "Normative Discrimination and the Motherhood Penalty." *Gender and Society* 24, no. 5 (2010): 616–646.

Benard, Stephen, In Paik, and Shelley J. Correll. "Cognitive Bias and the Motherhood Penalty." *Hastings Law Journal* 59 (2007): 1359–1387.

Berdahl, Jennifer L. "The Sexual Harassment of Uppity Women." *Journal of Applied Psychology* 92, no. 2 (2007): 425–437.

Berdahl, Jennifer L., and Karl Aquino. "Sexual Behavior at Work: Fun or Folly?" *Journal of Applied Psychology* 94, no. 1 (2009): 34–47.

Berdahl, Jennifer L., and Ji-A Min. "Prescriptive Stereotypes and Workplace Consequences for East Asians in North American." *Cultural Diversity and Ethnic Minority Psychology* 18, no. 2 (2012): 141–152.

Berdahl, Jennifer L., and Sue H. Moon. "Workplace Mistreatment of Middle Class Workers Based on Sex, Parenthood, and Caregiving." *Journal of Social Issues* 69, no. 2 (2013): 341–366.

Berdahl, Jennifer L., and Celia Moore. "Workplace Harassment: Double Jeopardy for Minority Women." *Journal of Applied Psychology* 91, no. 2 (2006): 426–436.

Bergsieker, Hilary B., J. Nicole Shelton, and Jennifer A. Richeson. "To Be Liked versus Respected: Divergent Goals in Interracial Interactions." *Journal of Personality and Social Psychology* 99, no. 2 (2010): 248–264.

Bertrand, Marianne, and Sendhil Mullainathan. "Are Emily and Greg More Employable than Lakisha and Jamal? A Field Experiment on Labor Market Discrimination." *American Economic Review* 94 (2004): 991–1013.

Bettis, Pamela J., and Natalie G. Adams. "Nice at Work in the Academy." Unpublished paper.

Biernat, Monica, Faye J. Crosby, and Joan C. Williams, eds. "The Maternal Wall: Research and Policy Perspectives on Discrimination against Mothers." Special issue, *Journal of Social Issues* 60, no. 4 (2004).

Biernat, Monica, and Diane Kobrynowicz. "Gender- and Race-Based Standards of Competence: Lower Minimum Standards but Higher Ability Standards for Devalued Group." *Journal of Personality and Social Psychology* 72 (1997): 544–557.

Bowles, Hannah Riley, Linda Babcock, and Lei Lai. "Social Incentives for Gender Differences in the Propensity to Initiate Negotiations: Sometimes It Does Hurt to Ask." *Organizational Behavior and Human Decision Processes* 103 (2007): 84–103.

Brescoll, Victoria L., and Eric Luis Uhlmann. "Can an Angry Woman Get Ahead? Status Conferral, Gender, and Expression of Emotion in the Workplace." *Psychological Science* 19, no. 3 (2008): 268–275.

Brewer, Marilynn B. "In-Group Favoritism: The Subtle Side of Intergroup Discrimination." In *Codes of Conduct: Behavioral Research into Business Ethics*, edited David M. Messick and Ann E. Tenbrunsel, 160–170. New York: Russell Sage Foundation, 1996.

———. "Research Design and Issues of Validity." In *Handbook of Research Methods in Social and Personality Psychology*, edited by H. T. Reis and C. M. Judd. New York: Cambridge University Press, 2000.

Burgess, Diana, and Eugene Borgida. "Who Women Are, Who Women Should Be: Descriptive and Prescriptive Stereotyping in Sex Discrimination." *Psychology, Public Policy, and Law* 5, no. 3 (1999): 665–692.

Butler, Adam B., and Amie Skattebo. "What Is Acceptable for Women May Not Be Acceptable for Men: The Effect of Family Conflicts with Work on Job-Performance Ratings." *Journal of Occupational and Organizational Psychology* 77 (2004): 553–564.

Cantillon, Peter, and Joan Sargeant. "Teaching Rounds: Giving Feedback in Clinical Settings." *British Medical Journal* 337, no. 7681 (2008): 1292–1294.

Carli, Linda L. "Gender Issues in Workplace Groups: Effect of Gender and Communication Style on Social Influence." In *Gender and Communication at Work*, edited by Mary Barrett and Marilyn J. Davidson. Burlington, VT: Ashgate, 2006.

Carli, Linda L., Suzanne J. LaFleur, and Christopher C. Loeber. "Nonverbal Behavior, Gender, and Influence." *Journal of Personality and Social Psychology* 68, no. 6 (1995): 1030–1041.

Carney, Dana R., Amy J. C. Cuddy, and Andy J. Yap. "Power Posing: Brief Nonverbal Displays Affect Neuroendocrine Levels and Risk Tolerance." *Psychological Science* 21, no. 10 (2010): 1363–1368.

Cikara, Mina, and Susan Fiske. "Warmth, Competence, and Ambivalent Sexism: Vertical Assault and Collateral Damage." In *The Glass Ceiling in the 21st Century: Understanding Barriers to Gender Equality*, edited by Manuela Barretto, Michelle K. Ryan, and Michael T. Schmitt. Washington, DC: American Psychological Association, 2009.

Cooke, Thomas J., Paul Boyle, Kenneth Couch, and Peteke Feijten. "A Longitudinal Analysis of Family Migration and the Gender Gap in Earnings in the United States and Great Britain." *Demography* 46, no.1 (2009): 147–167.

Cooper, Virginia W. "Homophily or the Queen Bee Syndrome: Female Evaluations of Female Leadership." *Small Group Research* 28 (1997): 483–499.

Correll, Shelley J., Stephen Benard, and In Paik. "Getting a Job: Is There a Motherhood Penalty?" *American Journal of Sociology* 112, no. 5 (2007): 1297–1339.

Corse, Sara J. "Pregnant Managers and Their Subordinates: The Effects of Gender Expectations on Hierarchal Relationships." *Journal of Applied Behavioral Science* 26 (1990): 25–47.

Cuddy, Amy J. C., Susan T. Fiske, and Peter Glick. "The Bias Map: Behaviors from Intergroup Affect and Stereotypes." *Journal of Personality and Social Psychology* 92, no. 4 (2007): 631–648.

———. "When Professionals Become Mothers, Warmth Doesn't Cut the Ice." In "The Maternal Wall: Research and Policy Perspectives on

Discrimination against Mothers," edited by Monica Biernat, Faye J. Crosby, and Joan C. Williams, special issue, *Journal of Social Issues* 60, no. 4 (2004): 701–718.

Derks, Belle, Naomi Ellemers, Colette van Laar, and Kim de Groot. "Do Sexist Organizational Cultures Create the Queen Bee?" *British Journal of Social Psychology* 50, no. 3 (2011): 519–535.

———. "Gender Bias Primes Elicit Queen Bee Responses among Senior Policewomen." *Psychological Science* 22 (2011): 1243–1249.

Eagly, Alice H., and Linda L. Carli. *Through the Labyrinth: The Truth about How Women Become Leaders*. Boston: Harvard Business School Press, 2007.

Eagly, Alice H., and Steven J. Karau. "Role Congruity Theory of Prejudice toward Female Leaders." *Psychological Review* 109, no. 3 (2002): 573–598.

Ellemers, Naomi, Henriette van den Heuvel, Dick de Gilder, Anne Maass, and Alessandra Bonvini. "The Underrepresentation of Women in Science: Differential Commitment or the Queen Bees Syndrome?" *British Journal of Social Psychology* 43 (2004): 1–24.

Fine, Cordelia. *Delusions of Gender: How Our Minds, Society, and Neurosexism Create Difference*. New York: Norton, 2010.

Fiske, Susan T., Amy J. C. Cuddy, Peter Glick, and Jun Xu. "A Model of (Often Mixed) Stereotype Content: Competence and Warmth Respectively Follow from Perceived Status and Competition." *Journal of Personal and Social Psychology* 82, no. 6 (2002): 878–902.

Fiske, Susan T., Jun Xu, Amy J. C. Cuddy, and Peter Glick. "(Dis)respecting versus (Dis)liking: Status and Interdependence Predict Ambivalent Stereotypes of Competence and Warmth." *Journal of Social Issues* 55, no. 3 (1999): 473–489.

Foschi, Martha. "Double Standards for Competence: Theory and Research." *Annual Review of Sociology* 26 (2000): 21–42.

Fulcher, Megan, Erin L. Sutfin, and Charlotte J. Patterson. "Individual Differences in Gender Development: Associations with Parental Sexual Orientation, Attitudes, and Division of Labor." *Sex Roles* 58 (2008): 330–341.

Galinsky, Adam, and Amy J. C. Cuddy. "The Overlap between Racial and Gender Stereotypes: Towards an Understanding of the Gender Composition of Interracial Marriages." Unpublished paper.

Glick, Peter. "Trait-Based and Sex-Based Discrimination in Occupational Prestige, Occupational Salary, and Hiring." *Sex Roles* 25, nos. 5–6 (1991): 351–378.

Glick, Peter, and Susan T. Fiske. "The Ambivalence toward Men Inventory: Differentiating Hostile and Benevolent Beliefs about Men." *Psychology of Women Quarterly* 2, no. 3 (1999): 519–536.

Glick, Peter, Susan T. Fiske, A. Mlandinic, José L. Saiz, Dominic Abrams,

Barbara Masser, Bolanle Adetoun, et al. "Beyond Prejudice as Simple Antipathy: Hostile and Benevolent Sexism across Cultures." *Journal of Personality and Social Psychology* 79, no. 4 (2000): 763–775.

Glick, Peter, Korin Wilk, and Michele Perreault. "Images of Occupations: Components of Gender and Status in Occupational Stereotypes." *Sex Roles* 32, nos. 9–10 (1995): 565–582.

Goff, Phillip, Margaret Thomas, and Matthew Jackson. "Ain't I a Woman? Towards an Intersectional Approach to Person Perception and Group-Based Harms." *Sex Roles* 59, no. 506 (2008): 392–403.

Greenwald, Anthony G., Debbie E. McGhee, and Jordan L. K. Schwartz. "Measuring Individual Differences in Implicit Cognition: The Implicit Association Test." *Journal of Personality and Social Psychology* 74, no. 6 (1995): 1464–1480.

Hall, Erika, Katherine Phillips, Laurie Rudman, and Peter Glick. "Double Jeopardy or Greater Latitude: Do Black Women Escape Backlash for Dominance Displays?" Unpublished paper.

Harris-Perry, Melissa V. *Sister Citizen: Shame, Stereotypes, and Black Women in America*. New Haven: Yale University Press, 2011.

Heatherington, Laurie, Kimberly A. Daubman, Cynthia Bates, Alicia Ahn, Heather Brown, and Camille Preston. "Two Investigations of 'Female Modesty' in Achievement Situations." *Sex Roles* 29, nos. 11–12 (1993): 739–754.

Heilman, Madeline E. "Description and Prescription: How Gender Stereotypes Prevent Women's Ascent up the Organizational Ladder." *Journal of Social Issues* 57 (2001): 657–674.

———. "Sex Bias in Work Settings: The Lack of Fit Model." *Research in Organizational Behavior* 5 (1983): 269–298.

———. "Sex Stereotypes and Their Effects in the Workplace: What We Know and Don't Know." *Journal of Social Behavior and Personality* 10, no. 6 (1995): 3–26.

Heilman, Madeline E., Caryn J. Block, and Richard F. Martell. "Sex Stereotypes: Do They Influence Perceptions of Managers?" *Journal of Social Behavior and Personality* 10, no. 4 (1995): 237–252.

Heilman, Madeline E., Caryn J. Block, Richard F. Martell, and Michael Simon. "Has Anything Changed? Current Characterizations of Men, Women and Managers." *Journal of Applied Psychology* 74 (1989): 935–942.

Heilman, Madeline E., and Michelle C. Haynes. "No Credit Where Credit Is Due: Attributional Rationalization of Women's Success in Male-Female Terms." *Journal of Applied Psychology* 90, no. 5 (2005): 905–909.

Heilman, Madeline E., and Tyler G. Okimoto. "Motherhood: A Potential Source of Bias in Employment Decisions." *Journal of Applied Psychology* 93, no. 2 (2008): 189–198.

Heilman, Madeline E., and Tyler G. Okimoto. "Why Are Women Penalized for Success at Male Tasks? The Implied Communality Deficit." *Journal of Applied Psychology* 92, no. 1 (2007): 81–92.

Heilman, Madeline E., Aaron Wallen, Daniella Fuchs, and Melinda M. Tamkins. "Penalties for Success: Reactions to Women Who Succeed at Male Gender-Typed Tasks." *Journal of Applied Psychology* 89, no. 3 (2004): 416–427.

Ho, Colin, and Jay W. Jackson. "Attitudes toward Asian Americans: Theory and Measurement." *Journal of Applied Social Psychology* 31, no. 8 (2001): 1553–1581.

Judge, Timothy A., Beth A. Livingston, and Charlice Hurst. "Do Nice Guys —and Gals—Really Finish Last? The Joint Effects of Sex and Agreeableness on Income." *Journal of Personality and Social Psychology* 102 (2012): 390–407.

Karakowsky, Leonard, and J. P. Siegel. "The Effects of Proportional Representation and Gender Orientation of the Task on Emergent Leadership Behavior in Mixed-Gender Groups." *Journal of Applied Psychology* 84, no. 4 (1999): 610–631.

Kobrynowicz, Diane, and Monica Biernat. "Decoding Subjective Evaluations: How Stereotypes Provide Shifting Standards." *Journal of Experimental Social Psychology* 33 (1997): 579–601.

Kray, Laura J., and Connson C. Locke. "To Flirt or Not to Flirt? Sexual Power at the Bargaining Table." *Negotiation Journal* 24, no. 4 (2008): 483–493.

Leibbrandt, Andreas, and John A. List, "Do Women Avoid Salary Negotiations? Evidence from a Large Scale Natural Field Experiment." NBER Working Paper 18511, National Bureau of Economic Research, Cambridge, MA, 2012.

Lin, Monica H., Virginia S. Y. Kwan, Anna Cheung, and Susan T. Fiske. "Stereotype Content Model Explains Prejudice for an Envied Outgroup: Scale of Anti–Asian American Stereotypes." *Personality and Social Psychology Bulletin* 31, no. 1 (2005): 43–47.

Linville, Patricia, and Edward E. Jones. "Polarized Appraisals of Out-Group Members." *Journal of Personality and Social Psychology* 38, no. 5 (1980): 689–703.

Livingston, Robert W., Ashleigh Shelby Rosette, and Ella F. Washington. "Can an Agentic Black Woman Get Ahead? The Impact of Race and Interpersonal Dominance on Perceptions of Female Leaders." *Psychological Science* 23, no. 4 (2012): 354–358.

Mavin, Sharon. "Queen Bees, Wannabees and Afraid to Bees: No More 'Best Enemies' for Women in Management?" *British Journal of Management* 19, no. 1 (2008): S75–S84.

Neuberg, Steven L. "Expectancy-Confirmation Processes in Stereotype-Tinged Social Encounters: The Moderating Role of Social Goals." In *The Psychology of Prejudice: The Ontario Symposium, Volume 7*, edited by Mark P. Zanna and James M. Olson, 103–130. Hillsdale, NJ: Erlbaum, 1994.

Nickerson, Raymond S. "Confirmation Bias: A Ubiquitous Phenomenon in Many Guises." *Review of General Psychology* 2, no. 2 (1998): 175–220.

Norton, Michael I., Joseph A. Vandello, and John M. Darley. "Casuistry and Social Category Bias." *Journal of Personality and Social Psychology* 87, no. 6 (2004): 817–831.

Nosek, Brian, Mahzarin Banaji, and Anthony Greenwald. "Harvesting Implicit Group Attitudes and Beliefs from a Demonstration Web Site." *Group Dynamics: Theory, Research, and Practice* 6, no. 1 (2002): 101–115.

O'Neill, Olivia A., and Charles A. O'Reilly. "Reducing the Backlash Effect: Self-Monitoring and Women's Promotions." *Journal of Occupational and Organizational Psychology* 84, no. 4 (2011): 825–832.

Payne, B. Keith, Mark B. Stokes, and Melissa A. Burkley. "Why Do Implicit and Explicit Attitude Tests Diverge? The Role of Structural Fit." *Journal of Personality and Social Psychology* 94, no. 1 (2008): 16–31.

Phelan, Julie E., Corinne A. Moss-Racusin, and Laurie A. Rudman. "Competent yet Out in the Cold." *Psychology of Women Quarterly* 32 (2008): 406–413.

Prentice, Deborah, and Erica Carranza. "What Women and Men Should Be, Shouldn't Be, Are Allowed to Be, and Don't Have to Be: The Contents of Prescriptive Gender Stereotypes." *Psychology of Women Quarterly* 26 (2002): 269–281.

Pronin, Emily, Daniel Y. Lin, and Lee Ross. "The Bias Blind Spot: Perceptions of Bias in Self versus Other." *Personality and Social Psychology Bulletin* 28 (2002): 369–381.

Ridgeway, Cecilia L. "Gender, Status, and Leadership." *Journal of Social Issues* 57, no. 4 (2001): 637–655.

———. "Status in Groups: The Importance of Motivation." *American Sociological Review* 47, no. 1 (1982): 76–88.

Ridgeway, Cecilia L., and Shelley J. Correll. "Motherhood as a Status Characteristic." *Journal of Social Issues* 60, no. 4 (2004): 683–700.

Ridgeway, Cecilia L., and Lynn Smith-Lovin. "The Gender System and Interaction." *Annual Review of Sociology* 25 (1999): 191–216.

Robinson, Dawn T., and Lynn Smith-Lovin. "Getting a Laugh: Gender, Status, and Humor in Task Discussions." *Social Forces* 80, no. 1 (2001): 123–158.

Rosette, Ashleigh Shelby, and Robert W. Livingston. "Failure Is Not an

Option for Black Women: Effects of Organizational Performance on Leaders with Single versus Dual-Subordinate Identities." *Journal of Experimental Psychology* 48 (2012): 1162–1167.

Rudman, Laurie A. "Self-Promotion as a Risk Factor for Women: The Costs and Benefits of Counterstereotypical Impression Management." *Journal of Personality and Social Psychology* 74 (1998): 629–645.

Rudman, Laurie A., and Peter Glick. "Feminized Management and Backlash toward Agentic Women." *Journal of Personality and Social Psychology* 77, no. 5 (1999): 1004–1010.

———. "Prescriptive Gender Stereotypes and Backlash toward Agentic Women." *Journal of Social Issues* 57 (2001): 743–762.

Rudman, Laurie A., and Stephen Kilianski. "Implicit and Explicit Attitudes toward Female Authority." *Personality and Social Psychology Bulletin* 26 (2000): 1315–1328.

Rudman, Laurie A., and Kris Mescher. "Penalizing Men Who Request Family Leave: Is Flexibility Stigma a Femininity Stigma?" *Journal of Social Issues* 69, no. 2 (2013): 322–341.

Sackett, Paul R., Cathy L. Z. DuBois, and Anne Wiggins Noe. "Tokenism in Performance Evaluation: The Effects of Work Group Representation on Male-Female and White-Black Differences in Performance Ratings." *Journal of Applied Psychology* 76, no. 2 (1991): 263–267.

Settles, Isis H. "Use of an Intersectional Framework to Understand Black Women's Racial and Gender Identities." *Sex Roles* 54 (2006): 589–601.

Shelton, J. Nicole, and Robert M. Sellers. "Situational Stability and Variability in African-American Racial Identity." *Journal of Black Psychology* 26, no. 1 (2000): 27–50.

Sidanius, Jim, and Marie Crane. "Job Evaluation and Gender: The Case of University Faculty." *Journal of Applied Psychology* 19, no. 2 (1989): 174–197.

Sinclair, Lisa, and Ziva Kunda. "Motivated Stereotyping of Women: She's Fine If She Praised Me but Incompetent If She Criticized Me." *Personality and Social Psychology Bulletin* 26 (2000): 1329–1342.

Six, Bernd, and Thomas Eckes. "A Closer Look at the Complex Structure of Gender Stereotypes." *Sex Roles* 24, nos.1–2 (1991): 57–71.

Steele, Claude M. *Whistling Vivaldi: How Stereotypes Affect Us and What We Can Do*. New York: Norton, 2010.

Trix, Frances, and Carolyn Psenka. "Exploring the Color of Glass: Letters of Recommendation for Female and Male Medical Faculty." *Discourse and Society* 14 (2003): 191–220.

Valian, Virginia. *Why So Slow? The Advancement of Women*. Cambridge: MIT Press, 1999.

Vandello, Joseph A., Vanessa E. Hettinger, Jennifer K. Bosson, and Jasmine Siddiqi. "When Equal Isn't Really Equal: The Masculine Dilemma of Seeking Work Flexibility." *Journal of Social Issues* 69, no. 2 (2013): 303–322.

Wade, Mary E. "Women and Salary Negotiation: The Costs of Self-Advocacy." *Psychology of Women Quarterly* 25 (2001): 65–76.

Wayne, Julie Holliday, and Bryanne L. Cordiero. "Who Is a Good Organizational Citizen? Social Perception of Male and Female Employees Who Use Family Leave." *Sex Roles* 49, nos. 5–6 (2003): 233–246.

Index

Page numbers followed by a "b" indicate boxes.

About the Authors

Joan C. Williams is Distinguished Professor of Law and Founding Director of the Center for WorkLife Law at the University of California Hastings College of the Law. She is the author of eleven books, including *White Working Class: Overcoming Class Cluelessness in America* and the prize-winning *Unbending Gender: Why Family and Work Conflict and What to Do about It*.

Rachel Dempsey is a writer and attorney. Her writing has appeared in publications including the *Huffington Post* and *Psychology Today*. She lives in Oakland, California, with her partner and two cats.